INTO THAT HEAVEN OF FREEDOM

The impact of apartheid on an Indian family's diasporic history

Mohamed M. Keshavjee

Foreword by Ahmed Kathrada

MAWENZI
HOUSE

We acknowledge the support of the Canada Council for the Arts for our publishing program. We also acknowledge support from the Government of Ontario through the Ontario Arts Council.

ONTARIO ARTS COUNCIL
CONSEIL DES ARTS DE L'ONTARIO
an Ontario government agency
un organisme du gouvernement de l'Ontario

Canada Council for the Arts
Conseil des arts du Canada

Cover design by Minaz Nanji and Mohammed Adra

Cover image: Street scene from "Marabastad - a Fountain of Life"' City of Tshwane, Central District Management, Region 3

Library and Archives Canada Cataloguing in Publication

Keshavjee, Mohamed M., author

Into that heaven of freedom / Mohamed M. Keshavjee.

Issued in print and electronic formats.

ISBN 978-1-927494-63-9 (bound).–ISBN 978-1-927494-27-1 (paperback).
ISBN 978-1-927494-64-6 (html)

1. Keshavjee, Mohamed M. 2. Keshavjee family. 3. Ismailites–South Africa–Biography. 4. South Africa–Biography. I. Title.

BP195.I82.A25 2015 297.8'22092268 C2015-905126-6
C2015-905127-4

Printed and bound in Canada by Coach House Printing

Mawenzi House Publishers Ltd.
39 Woburn Avenue (B)
Toronto, Ontario M5M 1K5
Canada
www.mawenzihouse.com

Dedicated to:

My mother, Koolsam, for instilling the necessary hope in us,
My father, Nazaraly, for teaching us not to hate,
My wife, Amina, for sustained encouragement,
My 11 siblings, for all the fun of growing up together,
And all those millions—South Africans and others—who gave their lives to the cause of freedom for the people of South Africa.

Where the Mind Is Without Fear

Where the mind is without fear and the head is held high
Where knowledge is free
Where the world has not been broken up into fragments
By narrow domestic walls
Where words come out from the depth of truth
Where tireless striving stretches its arms towards perfection
Where the clear stream of reason has not lost its way
Into the dreary desert sand of dead habit
Where the mind is led forward by thee
Into ever-widening thought and action
Into that heaven of freedom, my Father, let my country awake.

RABINDRANATH TAGORE, *Gitanjali*

Contents

Acknowledgements

THIS NARRATIVE IS BASED ON MY OWN EXPERIENCES AND memories. In the process of writing this book I have interviewed many people and what I relate from these conversations is my interpretation, and as with all interpretations, it has its own perspective. The interest and liveliness of our accounts of our lives comes from the necessary myopia of our individual vision, which is not all-encompassing or comprehensive. I have written this account of my life in order to make sense of it, to come to terms with my own demons and limitations. Others will have their own versions of the life and world I outline here, and that adds to the interest of its narrative. We all narrate, and our narrations will always differ from each other and thus sometimes be complementary and at others at variance; all of this makes for interesting reading, reflection, and debate. If I have started a conversation amongst my readers about their own antecedents and their personal recollections, I shall be happy. I would then have written a memoir and I may have helped to jog the memories of my readers. We become a family of story tellers and thus make some sense of and celebrate our respective lives.

I owe gratitude to many people who have helped me in this journey of discovery and self-discovery. These include the people I have interviewed, many of whom have since passed away. My thanks also go to: my wife Amina, who worked diligently on the formulation of the first draft and helped me put my initial thoughts together, ably assisted by Saida Hasham who did the typing; Mila Velshi, Saida and Yasmin Hasham, Zulfiqar Meghani, Hafiz Samnani and Isabelle Cirot for typing all subsequent drafts, Deanne and Habib Jamal for their generosity and for making their home available to me, where part of this book was written; Barkat Fazal for his continued encouragement; Karim Rawjee and Vafiahmed and

Fatima Rawjee for their hospitality in South Africa; Mariam Bagas and Juki Motani for their help in Pretoria; the late Mohamedhussein J Rajani and his wife Rashida of Bombay for arranging all my visits to Gujarat; Guli Keshavjee, Gulshan Sultanali Guiga, Sakina Keshavjee, Koolsam M Keshavjee, Khanum Keshavjee, Kasu Chandani, and Rajabaly Nanji for help in compiling the Family Tree; Mo Keshavjee for so efficiently and creatively designing the family tree: Sadru Khoja (Dolfie) for providing me all the necessary contacts over the many years; Laura Lourens and Sasa Subban for their generous help in obtaining information on the cover photograph; City of Tshwane Central District Management for usage of the photograph; Murad Velshi for being my contact with the larger family globally and being in constant touch with them with regard to this book; the late Karim Janmohamed for helping me gain valuable insights into the African Asian diasporic situation; Raficq Abdulla for reading and commenting on my draft chapters; Ameer and Rashida Keshavjee for being always available to check family facts and guidance on how to understand them with wisdom; Zahur Ramji for photo editing and permission for use of his photograph of President Nyerere and President Mandela; Minaz Nanji and Mohammed Adra for ongoing assistance on graphics; Yusuf Keshavjee, Karim Mohamedali (Mamdoo) Keshavjee, Anish and Nazir Akbarali, and Anwar Hajee for post-publication logistical help in Toronto, Nairobi and Johannesburg; and Nurjehan Aziz and MG Vassanji of Mawenzi House, my publisher, who were always ready to balance my wishes as an author with their publishing requirements.

Last, but not least, I am deeply indebted to Amin Kassam for his invaluable editorial help in shaping what was largely an unmanageable corpus into a readable text. In this, his knowledge of African affairs gained as group managing editor of a leading Kenyan newspaper company in the 1970s, coupled with his journalistic experience in India and Europe, provided me with an added lens through which to view my own diasporic existence. Without him, this work would have been daunting.

Should any person have been inadvertently left out in this endeavour, my sincere thanks are due to them, with apologies for the oversight.

While all the above have played an important role in this endeavour, I take full and exclusive responsibility for what is in this book and they are in no way responsible for any of its shortcomings.

Foreword

THE MODERN HISTORY OF SOUTH AFRICA IS ONE OF THE struggle for a birthright by the majority of its people. Apartheid, meaning "apartness," took its toll on the lives of millions. Through a network of unjust laws, the principles of Calvinism were used in a distorted manner by a White minority to justify the worst forms of racial oppression, whereby a large majority of non-Whites were classified, and then categorized, for differential treatment solely on the basis of the colour of their skin. South Africa's racial laws during the period of apartheid violated every clause of the Universal Declaration of Human Rights, making the country, in the words of former President Nelson Mandela, "a skunk of the world."

The year 1948 was an important watershed in the country's chequered history. The first all-Afrikaner administration came to power, mainly on the promise to solve the country's racial problems according to the traditional policy of *baaskaap* (White ascendancy). A series of measures were undertaken to fulfil this promise. For example, legislation was enacted to forbid Africans from entering cities and towns for the purpose of seeking work unless they had a special permit, euphemistically termed a pass. The government hid the racial character of laws with euphemisms.

Two such laws were the Mixed Marriages Act, which forbade marriages between Whites and non-Whites, and the Immorality Amendment Act, which banned intimate relationships between people of different races. The Population Registration Act classified the entire population by racial groups and officials used "scientific" methods such as running a comb or a pencil through a person's hair to determine the degree of curliness, which would determine whether he or she should fall into a "Coloured" or "Black" category. The Group Areas Act, one of the cornerstones of apartheid, forcibly uprooted 3.5 million people from their settled homes and threw them into racial locations, while the Bantu Education Act effectively limited African aspirations so that, in the words of one of apartheid's pioneering architects, Dr Hendrik Verwoerd, the African would aspire for no place in the European society "above the levels of certain forms of labour"—truly an education geared towards servitude. Cinemas, libraries, parks, beaches, swimming pools, hospitals, ambulances, schools, elevators, restaurants, hotels, public toilets, post offices and transport and sports facilities, were all segregated. Not all of these existed in the Black areas, and those that did were of grossly inferior quality. Even to speak about this inequitable situation was tantamount to treason. Under the Suppression of Communism Act, the minister of justice could ban anyone suspected of being a "communist," without trial or legal representation.

It is against this general backdrop that the author of this work gives us a picture of life in an urban location situated a mile from Pretoria's Union Buildings, which produced its own voices of resistance—people such as Rhemtulla Velshi Keshavjee, with whom I attended the World Youth festival in Berlin in 1951; Ismail Mahomed, who, through his persistent battle against the Group Areas Act, became its greatest living authority; and democratic South Africa's first non-White Chief Justice, just before his early death in 2001; and Mrs Thayanayagee Pillay, who throughout the infamous Treason Trial of 1956 provided all the accused, including Mr Mandela and myself, with food and refreshment.

These were not the only people who fought for "freedom." Lack of freedom leads to poverty. In the words of Nader Fergamy, a leading Egyptian sociologist and economist and the principal author of the *Arab Human Development Report*, "a person who is not free is poor. A woman who is not empowered is poor, and a person who has no access to knowledge is poor." There were some, who as the author clearly shows, contributed to freedom by building schools, rehabilitating the indigent, feeding the hungry in the townships, or, like Dr Dolly Keshavjee, caring for the sick. Some provided the indigenous people with opportunities. One such person was Habib Keshavjee, who opened his cinema to rising Black artists, providing singers and actresses such as Miriam Makeba and Dolly Rathebe the opportunity to express their talent on stage. When Canada Lee and Sidney Poitier came to South Africa to film *Cry, the Beloved Country*, Habib Keshavjee gave them a platform to voice their indignation at what they saw being meted out to their fellow non-Whites. There were others, like Dr Ronnie Pillay and Ahmed Dockrat, who worked with moderate groups allied to Churches, businessmen and professionals who through dialogue tried to bring about a peaceful transition to a democratic South Africa. They worked under the Council for Human Rights, headed by Father Nye, but that brought them under constant police surveillance, and in many cases harassment, leading to the refusal of a passport to travel overseas. However, despite all these odds, they did what they felt was required of them.

The author's narrative begins in Bombay in 1978, which leads him to a series of flashbacks through which we see the emigration of his family from Gujarat in western India to Pretoria, the capital of the Boer republic of the Transvaal in the 1890s. We see the relentless struggle for economic survival against numerous odds, and the building of a basic infrastructure to create enough resources to ensure the survival of future generations. It is here that we encounter his family's contact with Mohandas Karamchand Gandhi, whose teachings had an abiding influence on them, as on many other South Africans. His vignettes of the "location," or Marabastad as it was called, are evocative of the life of non-Whites in urban South Africa. From the smell of a curry ball shop, to the figure of the night watchman in the cold wintry night, to the description of the inhuman pass raids with white policemen wielding their sjamboks on the backs of defenceless African workers, to the beautiful crooning of Coloured singers huddled behind a cart, the voices of South Africa speak eloquently to us. In this segregated setting, we encounter many individuals—ordinary human beings—and the author is also able to discern the lone voices of those few Whites who, in their own little way, were able to contribute to human betterment and in the process transform their own lives.

He takes us through the "wind of change" that was blowing at gale force across Africa in the 1960s, and then the life encountered by his extended family in colonial Kenya, where they were closely associated with the African nationalists. It is towards the end of this period that he himself reasserts his human dignity, on the eve of Kenya's independence, and makes Kenya his home. However, he encounters problems which were unfortunately to continue in some parts of Africa.

In a normal situation, anyone who has experienced racial discrimination would be bitter and himself become a bigot, but in the case of the author it comes out clearly that he saw the problem in its larger human and sociopolitical context. He and his family help an African family to escape the murderous regime of the tyrant Idi Amin Dada in 1972. At the time of the Ugandan expulsion of Asians, as a lawyer practising in Kenya, he helps African clients to acquire their own homes and represents poor clients without remuneration whenever they need legal help.

While the author is mindful of the predicament of Asian communities in some African countries, of which he is a keen student, he is not oblivious to the plight of the African people. His narrative shows the contribution made by ordinary people of all races to human betterment and cautions against a simplistic approach to racial stereotyping, which he regards as neither true to the very spirit which informed the struggle against racism nor constructive towards a genuinely nonracial society which is the need of Africa today.

Through his worldwide travels, the author is well placed to describe the Indian diaspora. His own search for a homeland required him to qualify as a lawyer three times on three continents. He witnessed different types of discrimination, in some cases institutionalized discrimination in the form of professional limitations. Yet in each case he successfully overcame those and excelled and continued to provide services to the indigent as a defence lawyer in Kenya, helping asylum seekers in England, and as a lawyer helping immigrants in Canada. His story, in microcosm, reflects the narrative of every Indian family in Africa, with all its hopes and aspirations, as well as its shortcomings and limitations. His work is unmistakably a labour of love. Through years of travel, travail, observation, and experience he brings new insights into issues born out of a human struggle for a better tomorrow, presented with humour and irony, without losing the sense of proportion, compassion, care, and understanding which are so critical to interracial understanding today.

It is my earnest hope that more families in South Africa will put their rich experiences of the apartheid years, whether in South Africa or elsewhere, on paper. It is only then that we will be able to discover what unites us all in this rainbow nation today and set aside the colour of our skins that divided us so inexorably in the South Africa of the past.

AHMED KATHRADA, Johannesburg, 2015

Prologue

AS THE FLIGHT FROM TORONTO MADE ITS FINAL DESCENT TO Bombay's Santa Cruz airport in the early hours of a March morning in 1978, my wife Amina and I could see a small segment of the city's slum, a torn and decrepit carpet of huddled structures spread out below us. That tight, untidy conglomeration of shanties and ramshackle huts crammed with a multitude of people was my first glimpse of poverty in India. The residents were preparing to face another day and hundreds of braziers were smouldering, producing slender columns of smoke that rose dreamily into the morning sky as if to lick the sleek belly of our aircraft in a gesture of welcome.

As soon as we exited the plane, we were met by a warm, humid breeze, the caressing aftermath of the night's monsoon rain. It was thickened by an odour, a mixture of spices, sewage and human perspiration, the confounding product of the overcrowded city.

The airport was stifling inside, its oily heat barely dispersed by a few old fans creaking arthritically, doing nothing more than displacing the stale, overripe air from one part of the hall to another without respite. The walls were a drab, functional glossy cream and the blue-painted cement floor was cracked in some places and in need of repair. A thin, solitary woman, wearing a dark green, greasy sari, dipped a mop into a bucket of dirty water and splashed it on the floor in a forlorn effort to wash away the accretion of dirt stuck to it. The immigration officers, in badly fitting khaki uniforms, wore an early-morning look of half-sleep thickened by the heat and humidity. A servant appeared, walking towards the officers with appropriate obsequiousness, carrying a small metal rack holding about a dozen glasses of hot milky tea which he placed on the counter before each officer.

I made my way to the nearest immigration counter—not without a sense of anxiety—where I encountered the stare of a middle-aged officer wearing a Gandhi cap. A rigid pencil moustache gave him the suggestion of a military look. He peered at me from behind a grille of grimy metal bars which did not quite extend all the way across the front of the counter. For a moment I felt a little confused. It was déjà vu. I had seen such an immigration counter in South Africa as a child and could faintly recall the smell and the insidiously threatening air. I had to adjust to presenting myself to a person in authority who was not White but an Indian like me, who had the power either to let me into his country or to deny me entry. It was a strange, disorienting feeling. How could this brown man, who could have been a relative of mine, have such power? The colour of his skin was not right. He was on the wrong side of the counter.

As I took out my leaf-green passport, which did not have an Indian visa in it, and handed it to the officer, I said a prayer under my breath that he would grant me entry. The thought of being a pariah just because of the colour of my passport, or the colour of my skin, my race, my faith, my age, my height, my size, my ideology or my profession, was demeaning. It effaced my individuality as a human being. All these characteristics had at one time or another been held against me. There had to be some place on earth where having a brown or black skin was not a crime.

The officer slowly flipped through the pages of the passport, embossed with the South African plant, the protea, occasionally looking up at me, pursing his lips, and then back at the pages. It seemed to take ages. I felt both vulnerable and guilty for no apparent reason. I had come to India on a whim and could recall the voices of many friends in Canada telling me, "Go ahead, they may let you in," and others warning me, "They hate green South African passport holders." I had been told that at one time there had even been signs in Indian public buildings reading, "No South Africans or dogs."

At last the immigration official reached the final page of my passport. He then looked at me and, moving his head from side to side in the customary Indian manner, which anywhere else would have been a sign of negation, said in a gentle singsong voice, "You are welcome in our country, sir. You can stay as long as you wish. But I am so sorry, sir, I cannot stamp your passport. You see, sir, our government does not recognise the passport of your country. I am so sorry, but that is the situation. It is nothing against you personally. Sir, you are welcome in India. I will even give you a separate piece of paper with a stamp on it and nobody will bother you. These are our government rules regarding your country. We have to respect them. I hope you will understand."

I did understand, with a sense of great relief. I was flattered by his addressing me as "sir" so many times. I had never heard such a welcome anywhere else in all my travels across three continents. I was being accepted in the place where my ancestors had been born and raised, which was therefore also part of my own history.

I crossed the threshold into India proper, into the airport's great hall that led to the street outside. I was full of anticipation but did not know what to expect. In South Africa, the country of my birth, I had known who I was not; here in India, the country of my ancestors, I did not know who I was. It was the start of a journey of self-recognition but also of a telling distance.

Chapter 1

Incredible Bombay

IN THE HALL, WE WERE GREETED BY OUR HOSTS, JAFFER Lillani—in his early fifties, well-dressed, portly, round-faced, with sleeked-down hair—and Farida Patel, a tall and stately social worker from a well-to-do middle class background. As we stepped outside the airport building, a gaggle of taxi drivers and porters rushed up to us, clamorously offering their services. Our hosts told them, "*Theek hai, kootch baat nahii hai*" ("It's okay, we'll manage"). However, some of the more desperate younger men continued to follow us doggedly, hoping to earn something by symbolically adding their muscle power to Jafferbhai's by touching the trolley loaded with our luggage as he pushed it.

As new arrivals to the city, Amina and I found their gestures of help intrusive, but later we realized that they had been desperate pleas for succour in a world that had no use for them. Each person tried to touch the trolley at least once, as if it was a holy relic, so that his claim to a tip could be vindicated. Having no loose Indian rupees to give them, I felt distressed and uncomfortable. To add to the confusion, the trolley's front wheel kept getting jammed, and we progressed towards Jafferbhai's car with uncertain movements that made us hostage to the tight group of people around us.

Amina and I tried not to stare at the many men, women and children sleeping on the pavement and the beggars gesticulating as they asked passers-by for alms. They seemed not to have eaten for days. We felt ashamed and yet disgusted, our distaste increasing our guilt. How could anyone even start to change this situation of poverty and despair? Noticing our distress, Jafferbhai and Farida tried to reassure us, telling us that such sights were normal in Bombay—which only made things worse.

Unlike us, they were aware of the professionalisation of much of the begging in Bombay, to be captured years later by Madhur Bhandarkar's movie *Traffic Signal*, which revolved around the flourishing "poverty industry" at traffic lights in the city, run by gangsters, politicians and policemen.

We made our way slowly through the multitude and finally reached Jafferbhai's car. Our luggage was quickly stowed in the boot and we drove off. As we left the airport, we merged into a stream of cars and lorries spewing out choking exhaust fumes and creating a cacophony of noise with their hooters and klaxons as they sped down the road. On the pavements beside the road, legions of pedestrians formed and re-formed whirlpools of busy movement, along with food vendors, unauthorised money changers and parking boys, all jostling for morsels of Bombay's enormous wealth. A fleet of monotonously similar yellow and black Fiat taxis, their meters sticking out like snorkels on the driver's side, were parked next to the pavement, ready to ferry people to the south of the city, perhaps even to the plush hotels overlooking the sea on the fashionable Marine Drive, which had been renowned during British colonial rule as "the Queen's necklace."

Bombay was stupefying. The sounds and sights, not to mention the smells, were disorientating and somewhat terrifying to untried travellers such as Amina and I. The very air was drenched with poverty. We were in the midst of a Malthusian mass of seething humanity, a vision of purgatory that turned our sense of order upside down. The city was a reminder of a medieval past as well as a presage of an ugly Darwinian future when an overpopulated world runs out of resources and totters on the verge of universal anarchy.

As we drove south, we passed through the seamless flow between public and private domains that typifies the Bombay street scene. It was as if we were peering through the walls of houses into kitchens and sleeping quarters. The pavements were open bedrooms, with some of the sleepers resting their skeletal and apparently sick bodies on the criss-crossed ropes of charpoys. Next to those wooden bedsteads were women sitting on the ground, frying puris. We saw a barber shaving a customer next to a handcart on which a gnarled old man sat stitching hessian bags. When we stopped at a traffic light, a woman sitting on the ground on the other side of the road was picking lice from a little girl's hair with intense, myopic concentration. Nearby, a long-haired sadhu in a flowing yellow robe, his face surmounting an equally long and greasy beard streaked with grey, sat next to a small roadside shrine housing three idols in a niche. He appeared to be in deep meditation despite the fumes, heat, and incessant noise. A few feet from him, a mobile paanwallah, with his masalas arranged around him in small containers, was folding betel leaves around a spoonful of various ingredients into tasty triangles for his clients, his fingers moving with slow elegance.

At another traffic light, we saw an emaciated woman wearing a grimy green sari, with a little child on her hip. Mucus was running from her nose, which had a small brass ring hanging from it. Accompanied by a little girl without an arm, she came to the car and knocked on the window, begging for alms. Our hosts told us that the girl's arm had probably been amputated in order to evoke compassion from passersby. Instead of easing our discomfort, that information emphasized our personal alienation from the reality that confronted us. Just behind the woman was an old man in a *lungi*, the normally white loincloth grey with dust and dirt. Apparently blind, he was led by a young boy who also tried to attract our attention by tapping on the car window.

Garish signs advertised wares and services in English and Devanagari scripts, and giant billboards displayed paintings of suave, moustachioed, macho film stars and starry-eyed dancing girls, announcing the latest Hindi movie, promising a brief respite from everyday reality to the harassed masses, an alternative holographic reality that was as enticing as the depictions of the gods of the Hindu pantheon.

Every bit of space was taken up by someone or some family. The people who lived and worked in the streets, powerless against the elite that regarded them as an unfortunate oversight in the great scheme of things, seemed to have developed a protective sense of solitude that gave them a fig leaf of individuality, setting them apart from the impervious strangers amongst whom they struggled to make ends meet as they fought daily hunger and insecurity. I felt an air of incipient violence just under the surface of that busy scene, the violence of crowds, the toxic restlessness of a mob in the making. Perhaps it was only the paranoic reaction of freshly arrived visitors to that extraordinary city.

We made our way to Dharavi, one of the biggest slums in the world. It was a place of dull, half-acknowledged despair that stank of spices, kerosene, excrement, and sewage, which gathered in beetle-black pools of oily liquid. The stench entered the car even though the windows had been rolled up. We found later that the residents of Dharavi barely subsisted, with some working for a pittance in unregulated businesses, curing leather—work considered fit only for the "untouchable" caste. Some scavenged in other areas of the city for waste thrown out by the rich, which they took back to their slum to sort into stacks of useful scraps.

Further on, we passed palm trees leaning against a hard blue sky and worn-out fields interspersed with concrete apartment blocks amid derelict, mildewed intervals of exhausted space beaten down by the humidity of summer and monsoon rains, begrimed by the mass of people who occupied them. Suddenly, the scene changed and we saw a huge stretch of waste ground on which stood an immense conglomeration of mud huts covered with a combination of rush matting, filthy rags, beaten-out tin cans and dusty cataracts of dry plastic. That urban hellhole was packed with people and animals, each restricted to a minute space. Our hosts told us that that swollen sore of shanties was deemed by some people to be reasonable housing.

As our journey through the city continued, newer suburbs came into view and I realized that Bombay could be very deceptive, that the city also had a modish side. As we drew closer to the centre, we passed various clubs for the rich and cricket pitches, tokens of the British Empire taken up with enthusiasm by post-colonial Indians. We entered the beautiful built-up environment around the sea with its palatial mansions surrounded by palm trees and hotels. We had left louring purgatory for a paradise insulated from the suffering. On the horizon was Nariman Point, with the Indian Express Building rising from it, making a statement of wealth and modernity.

Our hosts gave us a running commentary on the various buildings and sights before finally depositing us at the pleasant, three-star Natraj Hotel on Marine Drive. Attractive girls in their mid-twenties, dressed in brightly coloured silk saris, welcomed us in sing-song accents. We were allocated an air-conditioned room and asked whether we wanted to be "DNDed." I wondered if that was some kind of fumigation that newcomers to India had to undergo after the harrowing experience we had just had, and was relieved to discover that the acronym DND only meant "Do not disturb." The next morning we went to the luxurious Oberoi Hotel, which had a swimming pool on the mezzanine floor. A group of tourists were tanning themselves in the thick monsoonal sunlight. From that level, we could pick out the skyline of the section of Bombay across the Back Bay as well as the busy pavements below. From the perspective of that swimming pool, we were witnesses to the widening chasm between the rich in their thousands and the poor in their millions, the First and Third worlds jostling uneasily against each other.

♦

Amina and I were paying for our trip with the money we had saved by foregoing the traditional wedding banquet after our marriage in Toronto. For Amina, it was a working trip; she was going to evaluate the management of the tuberculosis programme at the Prince Aly Khan Hospital in one of the suburbs of Bombay, as well as investigate the extent of tuberculosis in some of the slum areas. So while I felt guilty and was soaked with repugnance over the suffering of the poor in the city, Amina was there as a physician who wanted to help alleviate some of that suffering.

Jogeshwari East was our first port of call. The living conditions in the slum were appalling; the people there had clearly endured long-term deprivation, starvation, and malnutrition. Amina's conversations with the inhabitants revolved around living conditions, nutrition, availability of life-sustaining drugs and the persistence of drug-resistant strains of the tuberculosis bacillus. It was harsh reality, a million miles away from the preoccupations of the rich.

I used my new Voigtlander camera to good effect. The slum provided a stark setting for capturing Third World realities, something that had sparked my interest at Queen's University in Kingston, Canada, where I had been an interviewer for the Canadian University Service Overseas, an organisation which recruited Canadian graduates to work in Third World countries. While walking around the slum, I came across a garbage heap with a mangy dog scavenging in it. Nearby was a boy defecating in the open. I wanted to capture the scene, but I also wanted to be discreet, to maintain a modicum of privacy for the boy, so I decided to take the photograph from behind him. However, just before I could click the shutter, he finished and got up. A group of urchins who had been following me noticed that I had not been able to take the picture and shouted "*Besi ja, taro photoparaai che!*" ("Sit down, your photograph is being taken!"). The boy immediately and gracefully reassumed a squatting position, aligning his anatomy to his outpouring.

While I found the incident comical, it also made me reflect on the cultural nature of modesty and shame. Indians have different notions of shame that many of us find strange, but then non-Westernized Indians, for their part, also find such concepts in rich Western societies odd. The norms that we regard as natural are but the product of history, the results of centuries of development of social manners and obligations as well as of life in societies where the population density is low enough to make privacy possible.

By that evening, I came to the realization that the chaos and human drama that Bombay was unfolding was too much to absorb in a single short visit despite my Indian origins. It was just too much! I felt I needed space! I had to get away for a while! Therefore, I decided to visit the part of Gujarat from which my family had originated. While Amina had no objection, she reminded me that "this is the reality, this is what happens in India and other poor countries. This is also what causes disease and is one of the reasons why I am in this country, to help people to actually set up programmes to cure tuberculosis or to prevent the disease."

It is difficult to improve health without good sanitation. According to UN estimates, 55% of the Indian population still defecate out of doors—a practice born out of necessity in a country where the development of public amenities has failed to keep pace with economic and demographic growth. Writer and historian Malise Ruthven perceives the country's sanitation problem as being "emblematic of India's failure, as an emerging economic giant, to include most of its population in its achievements." A former government minister, Mani Shankar Ayar, warns that "we're seeing a failure to bring 900 million people inside the system of entitlements."

Many organizations are helping the Indian government to change this situation. Among them is the Aga Khan Development Network (AKDN), which brings together a number of development agencies, institutions, and programmers that work primarily in the poorest parts of Africa and Asia. The Aga Khan Foundation (AKF), an agency of the AKDN which commissioned Amina's visit to India in 1978, has also, in partnership with other NGOs and agencies, rehabilitated one of Delhi's poorest quarters, situated in the Nizamuddin area of the city. The projects include organized collection and disposal of refuse, and provision of public toilets which are then managed by the local community, with users being charged a small fee to meet cleaning and supervision costs. Lack of toilet facilities, particularly for females, is one of the reasons cited for low female attendance in schools. A school in Nizamuddin has been given a comprehensive makeover funded by the AKF in collaboration with one of India's oldest charities, the Sir Ratan Tata Trust. Since the introduction of this scheme, female dropout rates have declined dramatically in Delhi as well as in Gujarat where a similar programme has been initiated. In addition, the AKF and its partners have enabled the construction of proper accommodation for squatters.

I flew on an Indian Airlines flight to Rajkot, the nearest town to my ancestral village of Chotila. My ancestors had set out almost a century previously from Gujarat in the Kathiawar peninsula to make new lives for themselves in the uncertain and dark edge of Africa. Kathiawar is a rugged part of India that suffered from droughts and famines in the nineteenth century, but it is also the birthplace of three leaders who fought relentlessly for India's political independence from the British—Mahatma Gandhi, Sardar Vallabhbhai Patel, and Mohamedali Jinnah. As I neared Rajkot, I did not realize that I was about to enter a new phase of my association with India—something that was going to engage my interest for the next thirty-five years of my life.

Chapter 2

Chotila: Dates and Ghee

THE BOEING 737 CARRYING ME DESCENDED LIKE A GREAT BIRD of prey from the skies and landed at Rajkot airport at 8 AM on 11 March 1978. Even though I have flown hundreds of thousands of miles over four decades, I never cease to marvel at how such a monster of a machine, a silver leviathan, can take to the air and rise to heights no bird can attain. I find it both a beautiful and fearsome experience.

As the plane taxied along the runway, I was filled with excitement and impatient anticipation, a vague but pervasive feeling of returning to something important but as yet nameless. I peered eagerly out of the porthole. The dry and dun landscape was as parched as the grasslands of Africa during the dry season. The airport had only one small, white, innocuous building, no different from those in colonial Africa.

As I alighted, I stared back at the glinting liveried tail of the jet, which rose imperiously towards the sky as if lording it over the impoverished Gujarat landscape. For a moment the scene seemed incongruous, an ancient pastoral setting in which sat that modern jet, in the middle of nowhere. The drabness of the airport building contrasted against vivid dots of colour—parrot green, crimson, deep purple, edged with gold—on the saris of women working in a field nearby. Their slow graceful movements reminded me of exotic birds. I could hear people around me speaking Gujarati, which for me meant history, my own history, now grounded in a place rather than only in an exilic memory. I felt a sense of homecoming. Less than forty kilometres away, in an unmarked grave, lay the remains of the man whose name I shared with almost a thousand extended family members who now lived across the face of the earth on six continents. I wanted to get to Chotila as quickly as possible.

After picking up my suitcase, I found the nearest working telephone to ring Dinker Joshi, the only contact I had, who had been at school with my brother Ameer in South Africa. Dinker sounded pleased to hear from me and told me how to get to Chotila. No sooner had I put down the receiver than a small, sharp-featured man suddenly popped into the dark hall, emerging like a fish from the river of light outside. "I am Ramnik," he said. "Do you want to go to Chotila? I can take you there in my taxi." He had obviously been listening to my conversation. I girded myself to haggle over the price, but in his typically Gujarati way he disarmed me. "Don't worry, you can give me whatever you feel like. I will take you there. I will also wait for you," he told me. I felt embarrassed to have been ready to bargain for as low a price as possible and felt obliged to pay him a reasonable fee for the trip. We settled on 96 rupees, with which he seemed to be content.

Ramnik was in his early twenties. He was a smoker, a packet of *biri*s peeking out of the pocket of his short-sleeved white shirt. Like all taxi drivers in the state, he spoke good idiomatic Gujarati and was well informed about local matters. To anything I asked, he responded, "*Jem tamne fave te pramane hoon karish*" ("I'll happily do what you want") or "*Kai wandho nahi*" ("No problem") or "*Kai viadhi na karo, hoon badhu sambarilays*" ("Don't worry, I'll take care of everything"). He was the personification of the Gujarati attribute of placing a good reputation before money.

His dark eyes flashing proudly, Ramnik handed me his business card. It was in the name of "Jethalal Joshi," but "Ramnik" had been stamped in glaring red ink in all four corners, making it clear that he was his own boss. His car, a sturdy Indian-made black Ambassador, was a veritable workhorse, an old, well-used vehicle which made me feel comfortable as soon as I settled myself in the leather front seat. The car had decals on the windscreen promoting places, products, and people from all over the world.

Once we started driving towards our destination, Ramnik asked where I was from. "Toronto," I said. "Do you know a Rhemtullabhai, whose father was taught by Mahatma Gandhi?" he inquired. "He is my cousin," I replied, "and in fact he mentioned you to me." Ramnik was chuffed; not only was the world reflected on the windscreen of his car, but he was also talked about in far-off lands. I was now his ward, a precious find to be taken care of. He stopped at his favourite paan stall and shouted through the car window, "*Ey Nathoo, beh mitha laav*" ("Hey, Nathoo, bring me two sweet ones"). The stall owner grabbed two betel leaves, pasted them rapidly with paan masalas and added grated betel nut and pieces of sweet coconut. He then folded the leaves around that concoction and proudly gave the result to Ramnik.

Ramnik also ordered a packet of Indian *biri*s, lit one and inserted it in his mouth so that it dangled from one side. He switched on his car radio and revved his engine. The radio blared out an Asha Bhosle song from the movie *Mere Sanam*. The song, with its horse-and-cart clip-clop beat, provided an appropriate backdrop for the bumpy road journey to Chotila. Ramnik very obviously wanted to make my visit to Chotila an enjoyable experience.

"You will like it there, but they may ask you to stay overnight. And quite often, they expect a donation," he informed me in a low voice as if he was sharing a confidence. However, my worry was not so much the impending donation as the facilities I would be offered for an overnight sojourn. "I will tell them that you have other engagements," Ramnik assured me. "Don't worry, I'll be with you all the time."

We drove across a landscape shattered by the sun and battered by millennia of human cultivation, an exhausted, skeletal place, dry and unforgiving. There were a few stunted trees bent like crones, a straggle of palms, a solitary acacia here and there. Sometimes we saw a banyan tree. The fields, for the most part, were covered with sparse, anaemic crops. In some, irrigation pumps sucked water out from below the ground and the land erupted into rebellious colour with the bright yellow of mustard plants or the green of young wheat. The road, supposedly a national highway, was barely metalled. It was a busy scene, with lines of camels striding along in slow motion, impervious to the harsh countryside; cows, representing the divine on earth, ignoring their owners and other road users as they ambled on; and hump-backed oxen with tough brown hides, like battered leather-bound books, lumbering through the dust and haze. From time to time we passed scrawny horses laboriously pulling overloaded rickety carts in a distracted and haphazard way.

Our journey through the meagre landscape had a certain absent-minded quality to it. We kept almost colliding with meandering animals and their keepers as we negotiated our way. There was timelessness in that countryside of extremes, where people and animals lived daily with the prospect of imminent death which we, coming from a rich and developed world, avoided facing by hiding ourselves in the busy distractions of our modern lives. These people lived in the slow lane. And then there was our old car, a reminder of the new, thrusting, industrial modern world of machinery and speed and Faustian ambition, which would take apart that ageless and pastoral scene with an intrusive arrogance.

Groups of women walked with slow, swaying movements in dignified lines by the side of the road. They were dressed in highly coloured saris of vermilion, turquoise, indigo, aquamarine, all draped in the same way yet all individual and distinct. Some wore wide red skirts dimpled with tiny mirrors which flashed with pinpoints of light in the sun. Some carried large unwieldy bunches of twigs, others had copper or earthenware jugs perched on their shoulders; and yet others balanced pregnant sacks of grain on their heads.

"Does it ever rain here?" I asked Ramnik. "During the monsoon the earth is like a carpet, all sorts of green, very nice, very good," he replied.

After about forty kilometres, Ramnik came to a halt in front of a small wood-and-iron shop. A low, single-storey building with a big double-door and corrugated iron frontage, it was similar to the Indian ones I had known as a child in Africa. It had bars across its big windows, presumably to deter burglars. "Here we are," Ramnik said, "this is Chotila." The other buildings on the street were drab double-storey ones, with shops on the ground floor and living quarters on the upper one. I decided to walk around in order to get a sense of the village. I wanted to settle my feeling of bewildered homecoming, to locate the ghostly ancestors who seemed to be waiting for my arrival. They haunted the hot sunny street and tumble-down houses.

The primary landmark, in the centre of Chotila, was the Gulabchand Tower with a stained clock face at the top. The village was surprisingly busy. Cows, buffaloes, goats, emaciated dogs with lolling tongues, stringy cats, shepherds, vendors, bicycles, and pushcarts, a conglomeration of things, creatures, and people jostled each other in the single street. The market was alive with traders and customers. Vendors with their produce—jaggery, sesame seeds, nuts, dates, turmeric, cayenne pepper, coriander, cardamom, cinnamon sticks and green peppers—piled up chin-high by the side of the street were calling out their wares with alarming ferocity. I noticed that the jaggery was peppered with flies. Pushcart bells tinkled and cows wandered around at a leisurely pace with a supercilious air as though they were the proprietors of the village. People shouting to each other added to the cacophony.

I picked my way gingerly through the streets and arrived at the shop of one of the village elders, Mohan Ebrahim Bhoga, the oldest man in Chotila. He looked the quintessential Gujarati elder, wise and gentle and commanding respect. There was nothing brutish about him; if anything, he exuded a rather feminine quality of gentleness, and above all of *adab* (respect) towards guests. He honoured me by putting on his white turban as I entered the shop. Ramnik introduced me with ambassadorial dignity as if solemnly announcing a prince: "He is from the Keshavjee family of Africa and Canada."

The old man, sitting cross-legged on a mattress on the floor, gestured with a lazy but imperious wave of a bony hand to his son, Habib, to make way for me and beckoned me to sit opposite him. I greeted him with the deference due to an elder, like a diplomat from a strange land paying a visit to a local dignitary. He asked Habib to bring some dates and ghee, which was a staple food of the local people. I stifled a sense of apprehensiveness, which I hoped my host had not noticed.

"How is Hassan?" he asked. Hassan was a friend of his who had visited Chotila a few years earlier.

"Hassan is no longer alive," I responded.

"Oh dear," he said, "So he has passed away. He was not an old man."

"He died in Nairobi six years ago," I informed him.

"You know, he was born here and was Naran Keshavjee's son," he told me with the gravitas appropriate to my report of Hassan's demise.

The dates and ghee arrived. The old man dipped a date into the ghee, patted it into a smooth mouthful and handed it to me. "*Khaa, beta*" ("Eat, my dear boy"), he said.

The glutinous coating of raw ghee made me slightly nauseous and I tried to decline the delicacy politely, but he persisted. "Chotila produces the world's finest ghee," he said proudly. "Najrali Anandjee was the pioneer of this product. His ghee went as far as Africa in the 1890s. You must have heard of him. They are known as the Gillanis. They are a big clan. Their sons left the village to settle in Tanganyika."

How could I have the temerity to refuse that special product of Chotila, no matter how my taste buds might react to it? No sooner had I downed the first date than Mohanbhai was ready with another. He also asked Habib to bring me water from the well. When the water arrived, in a traditional metal vessel, I eyed it with some disquiet but could not refuse it. "This is from the *sakario kuvo* [sweet well]. Your ancestor Keshavjeebapa had the well dug for the village," he said, raising his eyebrows as a sign of respect for my ancestor. "We have all drunk from this well for decades. You must try the water. It is really sweet."

Although he was an elder and therefore behaved with proper decorum, it was clear to me that Mohanbhai regarded me as a distinguished visitor from a rich and foreign land and was both proud and happy to meet me. He asked me, "How are your properties? Are you receiving your rents?" "We haven't asked for rent for eighty-four years," I replied, adding ruefully, "What would they pay now and how on earth could we really ask for rent?" "You should ask," he said firmly. "It is your right and these people are doing well. You have allowed them to fall into the habit of not paying. You should not let that continue. You should go for what is yours." He was adamant; he wanted to protect my rights and thus protect the order and mercantile health of the village.

"Manjeebhai, your grandfather, had three stands." I knew from my parents that a stand was what older people in Gujarat called a small plot of land on which a shop was constructed. "The tenants are doing well. They are sitting on something that does not belong to them. Hassanaly [his other son] will take you to meet them. He will also show you the properties that belonged to your granduncles Velshibapoo, Jivanbapoo and Naranbapoo." He commanded Hassanaly to take me to Manjeebhai's properties. "*Muktoma*" ("Don't let them get away with it") he exhorted me.

After that rather formal meeting ended, Hassanaly took me to a shop owned by Manjeebhai. I was followed by a crowd who eyed my camera with lively curiosity and yearning. At the shop, which I photographed from different angles with the adopted expertise of a would-be surveyor, I unwittingly gave the impression that I was going to put it up for sale. A small group of people emerged from nearby houses and placed themselves in front of the shop, staring at me with awe and not a little resentment. Somehow, they had got wind of the fact that someone from Canada had descended on the village and that the shop they were occupying belonged in part to him.

Three men stood in front of the others to receive me. One was short, slightly built, and in his early fifties, with a gaunt face and white stubble on his chin. He was accompanied by an older man with a flash of white hair and beard, who appeared to be the father. The third seemed to be his younger brother. To curry favour with me, the men insisted that I have dinner with them that night, promising me the finest delicacies prepared with pure Chotila ghee. That invitation was followed by importunate entreaties to stay the night at their home.

As if on cue, Ramnik suddenly appeared out of nowhere like the ghost in *Hamlet*. "Keshavjeebhai is a lawyer," he said with a certain superciliousness. "He has come from Canada and has to be in Rajkot this evening. He has to meet some very important business associates. He cannot keep them waiting." The mention of my profession only reinforced their resolve to treat me with the obsequious hospitality that they felt was necessary to protect their interests. "You have to stay," they pleaded. "This is the first time ever that you have come to visit us. You must honour us. How can you leave so soon? Please be our guest." But Ramnik was adamant—his charge needed protection and he was resolute about providing it.

From Manjeebhai's property, we went to the jamatkhana (place of Ismaili gathering), an ornate two-storey building with a carved wooden balcony at the centre of the village. It had been constructed in 1923 by Velshibapoo, who had returned from South Africa in order to build it, with the approval of the Imam, on land owned jointly by him and Manjeebhai. In the compact jamatkhana courtyard, we met Samaratma, daughter of Mohanbhai's brother Alibhai Bhoga, who was caretaker of the building. Samaratma looked very much like a Gujarati matriarch, with a gap between her blouse and *gagro*, leaving a strip of ample midriff exposed like a large bow window. A big bunch of keys was attached to her sari on one hip. Her face was fig-brown, and straggly curls of hair, dyed ginger, peeked out from beneath her head covering. Her radiant smile gave her a surprising youthfulness.

She regaled us with legends about her ancestors and told us that she had helped with the construction of the jamatkhana by carrying bricks on her head to the site. Her sister had also helped and had left Chotila later to make her home in Penang, Malaysia, where she had married one Gulamhussein Jamal Bhaloo. Samaratma reminisced about Velshibapoo, who had overseen the construction in the 1920s: "He really mobilised all of us and made us work like ants," she recalled. Velshibapoo had also persuaded others, including his wife Jabubai's nephews, who later emigrated to Burma, to get involved in the construction.

Samaratma had a few cows in the courtyard and cautioned me not to go too close to them. She showed me a water pump which Velshibapoo had installed in the courtyard. She told me that many years later he had asked for a water sample to be sent to South Africa to be analysed for mineral deficiencies. Samaratma could remember long-ago events but not their exact dates. To her, everything had just happened "the other day." However, her stories helped me to connect with the people from my childhood—identical weather-beaten faces, the same way of talking, the same Gujarati nuances and gestures with a touch of benign sarcasm, the same powerful matriarch who knows everyone. And above all, the same encompassing warmth and sense of adab towards guests.

On my return to Mohanbhai's shop, I realized that he resembled my maternal grandfather, Kanjee Kassam Panchaan (Bapa), with whom I had spent some memorable years during my childhood in South Africa. It was under his cool black metal bed at 181 Grand Street in Pretoria's Asiatic Bazaar that I had sought refuge from my irate parents and eldest brother Rex when playing truant from school. And it was under his bed that I had first smelled the scent of a kidney mango, a box of which he always kept for his two favourite grandsons, Ami (Ameer) and Maman. Maman was the way people from Gujarat pronounced my name.

Like Bapa's pronunciation of my name, time had generally stood still in Chotila, in spite of the arrival of the electricity grid, availability of clean water from the Keshavjee well, and the road to Rajkot being metalled. The people were still the same, following the same tried and tested customs, marrying and dying in the same place, working at the same things, living out their unsung lives in their little wood-and-iron shops in the same way.

I asked Hassanaly to take me to the cemetery where all the village ancestors were buried. The gate was locked and we looked for the caretaker but could not find him. Walking around, we came across a middle-aged man dressed in peasant clothing, a Maulvi Saheb with a long unkempt beard, who suggested that we climb over the low gate. We did so and found ourselves in the part of the cemetery where members of the Kapadia family were interred. A famous member of the family today is the Indian film star Dimple. "All the Khojas have been buried here for the last 200 years," Hassanaly informed me ("Khoja" is what the Gujarati Ismailis have been known as for centuries), pointing to a dusty corner of the cemetery where spiky shrubs grew on a few grave mounds, which bizarrely reminded me of a punk hairstyle.

I stood there and offered prayers for the souls of all the deceased. As I did so, my mind went back to the nineteenth century, when many Indians had been scattered like leaves in a storm, ending up in distant and foreign lands. I wondered what imperatives had led them to leave behind everything that was so near and dear to them, to make a new life in strange and often inhospitable countries thousands of miles away. Why had Mother India "expelled" them so mercilessly and let them become victims in the major colonial games of that time in which she was just a spectator? I explored this issue later and found that the reasons for the migration lay in the political and environmental conditions that prevailed in the nineteenth century in the Kathiawar peninsula. Those conditions are described in the next chapter.

Chapter 3

Kathiawar in the Nineteenth Century

THE KATHIAWAR PENINSULA, A PART OF THE STATE OF Gujarat, lies in the northwest corner of India, jutting out like a clenched fist into the Arabian Sea. The peninsula has a multitude of cities and villages, whose names in many cases have been taken as surnames by the people who originated from there. The religious and cultural mix of this busy and densely populated region reflects much of what is found in the rest of India. One encounters Hindus, who are subdivided into castes, various Muslim communities, and Parsis.

In the nineteenth century, a combination of drought and massive economic disruptions brought about by British colonization made life a nightmare for the inhabitants of the peninsula. When Britain conquered the area, nepotism and corruption were rife under princely rule and the subjects were bled pitilessly, but the British allowed that to continue. They also implemented a free-market policy, letting food merchants charge as high a price as they wanted. The situation was made worse by the imposition of a land tax. Those who were unable to pay that tax, or were late in paying it, had their land confiscated. The victims were left with no choice but to borrow money at exorbitant rates of interest from usurers. When those loans could not be repaid, civil courts introduced by the British handed over their land to the loan sharks, who then hoarded harvests to drive up food prices, thus exacerbating the inflationary spiral.

Throughout India, British imperialism leached the land and its people of their wealth and traditional crafts, which were brutally and efficiently displaced by new manufacturing techniques being developed in Britain as part of the monumental changes brought about by the agricultural and industrial revolutions. Not only was the manufacturing capacity of

India destroyed, but India was also forced to import goods from Britain. Arguably, without the colonial wrecking of the Indian economy, the effects of natural disasters on people's lives would have been much less during the nineteenth century.

The series of droughts that afflicted Kathiawar left much of the population not only unable to feed themselves and their families, but also without fodder for their farm animals. Money needed to combat famine through relief and job-creation programmes was diverted to other uses such as financing the British military campaigns in Afghanistan. During the first half of the nineteenth century there were seven famines, which resulted in about 1.5 million deaths. The last quarter of the century witnessed twenty-four famines, leading to about 28.5 million deaths. People in other parts of India also suffered starvation.

The inhabitants of Kathiawar created new wisdoms to sum up their appalling predicament; one said that it would be much better to go to Africa and die there when death called, than to remain in India and die prematurely because there was no food. Migration was the only choice for hundreds of thousands of Indians, and from 1830 to 1870, between one and two million workers from all over India migrated to new countries. That trend continued well into the early twentieth century. Some of the migrants ended up in East and South Africa. Most of the migrants to South Africa were tied by contracts to individual farmers and treated as de facto slaves. Some later migrants, termed passenger Indians because they paid their own fares from India, were allowed to be petty traders but restricted to areas specifically allocated to them.

As has happened throughout human history, villains were quick to take advantage of those desperate to migrate. The experiences of a group of migrants who travelled from Madras to Durban in South Africa in two old, rusting steamers—*SS Truro* and *SS Belvedere*—in November 1860 were typical. The stinking steamers, infested with cockroaches and rats, were hellholes for the passengers. Some were raped by the drunken and brutal crew, others were beaten, and yet others died of disease and malnutrition during the voyage of several weeks. The exhausted men, women, and children, who had been conned by smooth-talking and unscrupulous recruiters for the South African White farmers with visions of a new and more promising destiny in Africa, disembarked in Durban full of hopes that were soon to be dashed. What the passengers did not know was that the treatment meted out to them would one day sow the seeds of the dismantlement of the British empire.

The Indian labourers, referred to as "coolies" by the White colonialists of Natal province, were abused and exploited by their employers, who treated them as commodities although slavery had been formally abolished throughout the British Empire in 1833. Their so-called labour contracts were in fact a form of vassalage, turning them into indentured labourers working for a pittance for five years. The White sugarcane planters needed them because the Zulu tribesmen of the province shunned labour on White-owned farms. The labourers died of dysentery, cholera, malaria, and snakebite. Forced to live in primitive conditions in unhealthy hovels without basic facilities, they were not given any medical care. If workers absconded to another farm, hoping that they would be treated more humanely there, they would be returned and flogged for their "desertion."

Some people in India were encouraged by news of success from their kin who had gone to South Africa as passenger Indians later. For instance, in 1893, in a village called Makda, not far from Chotila, a young Memon trader, Cassam Noormohamed, received such news from his brother-in-law, who had just opened a small shop in Transvaal province. Cassam was excited and decided to migrate to Africa as well.

Cassam was managing to survive as a timber dealer, transporting wood to Bamanbore and Chotila, where there was a small Memon community. He sold the wood to the village merchants and in turn bought cotton and produce from them, which he then sold on to other villages. He had a friend in Chotila, Jivan, the eldest son of Keshavjee Ramji, my great grandfather, who was one of the elders of the village. Cassam would frequently stay overnight at Jivan's home and they would spend hours discussing the terrible situation in India.

The following conversation is a composite of several between Cassam and Jivan. It, and the information about the two men, are based on family narratives handed down over the generations.

"What future do we have in these villages, where even our livestock has to be abandoned for want of water and food?" Cassam asked his friend one day. "You are relatively fortunate. You have your brothers, some wealth and your own agricultural land. Today, the *rabaars* and *barwaads* (peasant farmers) grow cotton and bring it to you and you are able to clean it, husk it, bale it and send it to Bombay for export. But will this last? The land in Gujarat is becoming fragmented, people are unemployed, starvation is all about us. And what is more, our overlords, the Rajwansi, have imposed all sorts of taxes on us. They are impoverishing us and devastating our country. They can only humble India by humbling us, its sons and daughters. Let us go and earn an income overseas. Can you imagine what respect we will command when we come back one day successful and wealthy?"

"What is the alternative?" asked Jivan. "Where can we really go?"

"Africa," responded Cassam, "there are riches to be won there." To bolster his suggestion, he added, "There are Gujarati Muslims in Pitoria and Jonsburg. They have made money, big money. A few even own steamers. Some of them send money back to their villages to help them. I have family there, they'll look after both of us. We may have to struggle a bit, but imagine what the rewards will be! We can come back to our villages here in India with lots of money and walk tall."

Cassam was passionate and eloquent and Jivan was persuaded, but he wondered how to raise the matter with his parents. Mithima, his mother, would die at the very suggestion of his departure. He was the eldest in a family of six children. His father was growing old and was in debt. Jivan was his principal support. It was he who went to Gondal and Rajkot to purchase goods and who organized the family finances through the system of *hoondi* (verbal promises) with which goods were purchased. Moreover, he had a wife, Ladoobai, who was from Gondal, and a young son, Madhoobhai. If he left, he would be upsetting age-old traditions and the delicate system of family obligations that helped them to survive and maintain a sense of meaning in their lives. How would the family ever manage if he tore up his roots and renounced his obligations?

Cassam realized Jivan's problem and offered to speak to his parents on his behalf. "I will explain the situation to them. They will understand. Even my parents were reluctant to let me go at first, but today they have begun to see the wisdom of it.

In the last decades of the nineteenth century, life in Chotila was not easy for Jivan's father, Keshavjee Ramji Murji, known in our family as Keshavjeebapa, but it was relatively comfortable when compared with the dire poverty of many other villagers. He owned some farmland and property and had a few shops, but those earned him an income that was just enough to feed and clothe his family.

In a society where children represented continuity and stability, he was the proud father of four sons and two daughters. Of the sons, Jivan, the eldest, was in overall charge of the family business. Naran, the second son, used a bullock cart to run a small transport business. Velshi, third in line, was the family bookkeeper, and Manjee, the youngest, ran a small grocery shop in the village. The family's living expenses came out of a common kitty overseen by Keshavjeebapa, Jivan and Velshi. Of the daughters, Santok, who lived in Gondal, was married to Kanjee, the only son of Kassam Panchaan, and Manek was married to Hirji Nanji Jutha. Keshavjeebapa also arranged the marriages of Jivan to Ladoobai, daughter of Varin Panchaan (Kassam Panchaan's brother), who was Kanjee's cousin, and of Naran to Prembai, Kanjee's sister.

Manek, famously known in the clan as Manekfaiba, was a successful marriage broker. Legend had it that she could get anybody married off to the fairest Gujarati damsel purely on the basis of a photograph. All the young family members as well as many other eligible village girls and boys found suitable partners through her. After her brother Jivan had established himself in South Africa, and on his advice, she sent her only son Valjee there to be taught the principles of business and become a trader.

In addition to the small village shops in which the family sold daily necessities such as millet flour, spices, rice, mung beans and ghee, Keshavjeebapa had a few warehouses (godowns) for storing the three prized products that he sold—wool, grain and cotton. He purchased the wool from peasant farmers, agreeing on the price a year in advance and then giving them a loan to tide them over. That arrangement, which was in conformity with the rules of the Sharia on licit financial transactions, was also used for the sale and purchase of cotton. When the wool was delivered, Keshavjeebapa, other family members, and some village hands loaded it onto bullock carts and transported it to the warehouses for cleaning, carding, and dispatch to other middlemen, who in turn exported it via Bombay to London. Two of the prominent middlemen who were involved in the trade at that time were Nanji Premji Badlawalla and Mohan Bhoora.

Businesses were generally run with a capital of about 5,000 rupees, which was a largish sum in the village at that time. All of Keshavjeebapa's businesses and their turnover would not have exceeded 25,000 rupees in value. Like many others in the village, Keshavjeebapa was known as a khetiwari, a farmer eking out a living from the soil. Agriculture was regarded as a perennial and respected calling, as reflected in the Gujarati proverb, *Utam kheti, madhya vehpaar, khaneet nokri*, meaning that of farming, business, and salaried employment, farming is the best way to earn an income; business is next best, but one should never work for someone else. The subtext here is that anyone who works for someone else will always be a menial. There is also a deeper cultural belief that *baraka* (grace) only comes to one who has his/her own basket (business) into which God can place bounty.

The village and its inhabitants, though humble, played an important role in the economy of the taluka. The Anandjee brothers, Najrali and Mohan, sons of Mohamed Anandjee, were known as the ghee kings of Chotila. A part of Chotila was named Mamanpara after them, and it continues to be called that today. They amassed their wealth by bartering village products with peasant farmers from the surrounding countryside, who made small amounts of ghee from butter, which they brought to Chotila in little clay pots. The Anandjees collected the ghee and poured it into four-gallon tins. Each day, 200 tins of ghee were transported to Bombay for export to Africa and other parts of the British Empire. Among the other village families were Alibhai Bhoga, the Jiwabhais, and the Chagan Lalji family, known as the Kapadias because they traded in cloth.

Keshavjeebapa was not only involved in business, he was also a de facto social worker long before that term came into existence. In the 1850s, he had a well dug on the outskirts of Chotila. In 1988, because demographic growth had made the well water insufficient for the villagers' needs, our family from across Canada, Kenya, and the US upgraded it. Keshavjeebapa was also a *vaid* (practitioner of the ancient Indian healing system of Ayurveda) prescribing herbal medicines to the poor. Life was generally pleasant and peaceful for him, but during the famine of the last quarter of the nineteenth century, he found himself in a debilitating and inextricable cycle of debt, which caused him deep anguish. In a small, closely knit society like Chotila, to be in debt and unable to repay the money was a social calamity worse than leprosy. Humiliated, he vowed to walk barefoot on the scorching Gujarat earth until his creditors were fully paid off. When his son Velshi heard of that, he prevailed upon him to break his vow, promising that he, Velshi, would pay off all the creditors over time. As it transpired, Velshi was only able to redeem his pledge after migrating to South Africa, where he did well. In 1923 he returned to India, tracked down all the creditors, or the children of those who were no longer alive, and paid them the amounts owed by his father.

Despite these difficulties, life in the villages of Kathiawar did have some happier aspects. There was a strong communal spirit among the villagers, which was especially evident in various rites of passage—birth, marriage, and death—when the villagers gathered to celebrate or mourn. That spirit showed particularly during inter-village weddings, when a *jaan*—the wedding party of a bridegroom from another village—arrived in Chotila, playing musical instruments as they came, and stayed for several days. Usually the bridegroom would be paraded in the village on a white horse, and he would be followed by the rest of the wedding party to the accompaniment of shenai music performed by village musicians. The visitors would bring local delicacies from across Gujarat. Chotila's high-quality ghee was the foundation of Surat's delicious sweetmeats, particularly its *suthar faini*. Thaan was famous for another sweetmeat, *pendas* and Gondal for its *marcha* – chillies. During marriage celebrations people exchanged such delicacies and everybody ate communally out of big trays known as *thaalas*.

Keshavjeebapa could not see any future for his sons in India. He kept thinking of the farmans of the Ismaili Imam of the time, Sir Sultan Mahomed Shah Aga Khan, advising his followers to leave Kathiawar and seek a new, more rewarding future elsewhere, particularly in Africa. It was against this backdrop that Cassam turned up at the Keshavjee home to plead Jivan's case. "I have some family members in South Africa. They are doing very well out there. They will help us. Jivan and I can work and save a lot of money," Cassam assured Jivan's parents. "We will send you money from there. In fact, people have done extremely well and have been sending money back to their villages, and their families are beginning to feel the difference. Many people have gone from Ranavav, Porbander, and Kutiana; some from Jamnagar and Junagadh. One of them now even owns a shipping line. Please let Jivan come with me, I will look after him," he entreated.

Jivan's mother, Mithima, was distraught. "Oh my Jivan, if you go away, when will I ever see you again?" she cried. "I will be dead and gone. Africa is so far, it is across the ocean. You might as well consider this my funeral. With you gone, what will I do?"

However, Keshavjeebapa saw merit in Cassam's proposal. "Let him go," he counselled his wife. "He represents the new generation. If we tie him down, we will be limiting the destiny of our children, and their children, and their children." He then added bitterly, "We have no hope in Gujarat. Look at me, I am like a dead man because I can't pay my debts. My honour has been tainted. Let's be courageous and let him go. Allah will take care of him."

"Mother," beseeched Jivan, "I need your blessing. Let me go and I will work hard to bring out the rest of the family. I will call for you and you will be able to come and join me in a new life."

"Oh my Jivan, how will I ever live without you? I will be dead by that time," sobbed Mithima, but deep in her heart she knew she had to allow her eldest son to leave the family home, perhaps forever.

Keshavjeebapa looked at his son with sadness and pride and granted permission on behalf of both himself and his wife: "Go, my son, go in the name of God. Look for new pastures. Life, after all, is a search for better conditions."

Jivan and Cassam then started planning their journey, first to the nearest main railway junction, Thaan, in a hired bullock cart (the family cart being needed for business), then by train to Bombay where they would board a ship. On the evening of the appointed day in 1894, all the villagers gathered to wish them "Godspeed." In accordance with Gujarati custom, Mithima placed a coconut under one of the cart's big wheels; the cracking of the coconut would augur a trouble-free journey and success in their lives.

The two friends carried their belongings, basically cotton dhotis, some woollen frock coats, and linen, as well as some spices, in a wooden trunk with a crude ill-fitting padlock. After the trunk had been placed in the cart, Jivan bent down and touched his parents' feet as a mark of filial respect and devotion. Keshavjeebapa placed his hand on Jivan's shoulder and intoned, "May God be with you. May you enjoy health and prosperity," almost as if he was saying a prayer. Then he said to Cassam, "Work together. Help each other with honesty and unity. The future belongs to you. Our life is in the past. You will need to open a new door for future generations. Go with courage and hope. Go in the name of God." Sensing that he might never see his parents again, Jivan tried to hide his tears.

Then Cassam and Jivan climbed into the back of the cart, which was covered with a tarpaulin to shield passengers from the elements, and sat down on a rough bench that had been padded with straw and overlaid with a soft mat for comfort. They waved goodbye as the cart driver urged the bullock through the main street out of Chotila. Night had fallen. There was no moon and the only light came from the swaying oil lamp under the tarpaulin, which threw a weak, flickering, golden glow onto the dusty track as the cart trundled on at a steady walking pace. The journey to Thaan would take several hours.

After about an hour, Jivan opened a box of food that his mother had given him. It was typical Gujarati fare for travellers and she had cooked enough to sustain him and his friend till Bombay as well as delicacies to eat on the boat. He took out a metal container with *farfras*—savouries made with *channa* dough—in it, which he dipped into the salted, fried chillies she had packed for them. For a sweet, she had given them freshly fried *jalebis*. After they had eaten, they sat side by side with their shoulders propping each other up. The slow, swaying movements of the cart, the monotonous groaning of the big wheels, and the gently tinkling bells on the bullock induced a sleepy reverie.

They arrived at the Thaan railway station late that night and joined the throng of other travellers, some with only bundles of clothing and a *tiffin* (a multi-tiered food container) tucked under an arm, waiting for the train to Bombay, known colloquially as the Bapoogadi for the slow speeds at which it travelled. Those who were migrating were surrounded by bemused relatives and bustling friends who had come to bid them farewell. No sooner had the train pulled in, emitting clouds of steam and hissing as it stopped in the small station, than Jivan and Cassam jumped into a third-class carriage and secured a space for themselves.

It was way past midnight, and the compartment was crowded and ripe with the odour of warm bodies and stale tobacco smoke. Despite the lateness of the hour, everyone seemed eager to talk. The laughter and jovial banter made the narrow compartment seem like a bazaar. Everyone wanted to know where their fellow travellers had come from, where they were going and why they were travelling. The loquacity left no room for private reflection.

Many of the passengers were on their way to Africa, to places with exotic names such as Mombasa, Dar es Salaam, Zanzibar, Mauritius and Madagascar. Others were going to Penang in Malaya and to Fiji in the Pacific. Some were going to East Africa to join the crews constructing the Kenya-Uganda railway line, others were hoping to start new lives as petty shopkeepers and small businessmen. All these excited and apprehensive men—for only men were migrating—came from Kathiawar. As the night drew on, the passengers became quiet and some of them dozed off.

As dawn broke, the train arrived at the Bombay Central Station. Cassam's friends had told him of a *musafarkhana* (travellers' hostel) that provided basic food and lodging for only a few rupees. They hailed a rickshaw and were taken to it. After depositing their belongings with the caretaker, they had enough time to get to the Mackenzie shipping agents to buy their deck class tickets to South Africa. Then they explored some parts of central Bombay, an exciting and frightening experience for villagers who had never been in a great, bustling and not entirely friendly city where the mass of people were strangers to each other.

A rickshaw took them around at a swaying, leisurely pace. Bombay was already the leading metropolis of colonial India, the largest city east of Suez, with a reputation for style, business, entertainment, and marvellous diversity. Its streets and squares, and the alleyways with their peculiar smells combining spices, sewage, human and animal odours, were—literally—breathtaking, noisy, fetid and humid. They seemed to be on the verge of chaos.

Presiding over the press and sweat of humanity were the majestic colonial buildings built by the British, which filled Cassam and Jivan with wonder. They visited the large parks, with emerald swards of grass tended by squads of gardeners, and marvelled at fine-looking trees—some squat and fat palms swaying with the breeze, others with high elegant branches—that were totally different from the ones that barely survived in their village.

Jivan and Cassam called on many friends who had left their villages for a new life in the city. They could see how their friends had changed, becoming more worldly-wise. However, their friends cautioned, the city was not a paradise. There were more opportunities to earn a living, but there was also more competition, less friendliness, and people were always on their guard.

After the courtesy calls were over, Cassam and Jivan visited the Apollo Bunder area, fronting the Arabian Sea, where the ships docked against the backdrop of the ancient Elephanta caves. A flotilla of rusting, run-down passenger ships were being prepared there to take India's human cargo across the world's oceans to other British colonies that needed their labour and ingenuity. The ships, looking like dark, ghostly apparitions in the soft haze of sea mist, were berthed at the Ballard Pier, Princess Docks and Yellowgate Docks. Cassam and Jivan could barely make out their outlines.

Jivan and Cassam caught a glimpse of the beautiful villas of British sahibs overlooking the sea, mansions with lovely white-painted wooden verandas behind high palm trees. They could only gaze wistfully at those palaces of the rich, knowing that they were excluded from them. South Africa was their only hope of making better lives for themselves.

Chapter 4

Racism in South Africa in the Late Nineteenth Century

JIVAN AND CASSAM LEFT THEIR RESPECTIVE VILLAGES THIRTY-four years after the two steamers arrived in South Africa with the first consignment of indentured Indian migrants. South Africa was a racist society in the late nineteenth century, with two White groups—the Boers (known as Afrikaners) and the British—struggling for supremacy. Both sides were fighting for hegemony but were equally committed to suppressing all non-Whites.

The British needed labourers in Natal because the local people refused to work on their plantations, so the Natal government negotiated for migrant workers with the British colonial government of India. This resulted in the first consignment of indentured labourers on the *SS Truro* on 16 November 1860, an event suffused with irony, as their plight led in less than a century to the beginnings of the dismantlement of the empire. Slavery had been banned in the British Empire, but the indentured labourers were paid a pittance, fed minimum rations, housed in hovels, received no medical care, and were flogged mercilessly at the slightest excuse.

A new wave of immigration emerged during the next decade, with some Indians paying their own way to South Africa to become shopkeepers there. Gandhi wrote about a trader in Mauritius, Sheth Abubaker Amad, who decided to migrate to South Africa after hearing that one of his relatives had gone from India to Natal as a petty trader and had done very well for himself. At that time, the focus of the English settlers was more on making big profits through the indentureship system, so Sheth Amad, who had persuaded an Englishman to join him in his commercial venture, was able to open a shop without any opposition. Soon news of his prosperity reached Porbander in India, with the result that other Indians, including Bohras from Surat and Hindu accountants from Gujarat, decided to follow suit, either to work in such enterprises or to set up their own small businesses.

My family were among the Indians who paid their own passage to South Africa in order to go into business there. These Gujarati-speaking "passenger" Indians, mainly Muslims, were later joined by some Urdu-speaking Muslims and a few Marathi-speaking Kokanee Muslims. At first, the traders set up businesses in Durban, but later they moved into the interior, opening small shops on the way.

The Indians made an immense economic contribution to the development of Natal. An editorial in the *Natal Mercury* in early 1865 observed that sugar exports had risen from £26,000 in 1863 to £100,000 in 1864 because of the use of Indian labour. In 1901, the Protector of Indian Immigrants warned that if Indian labour were withdrawn, the "country would at once be simply paralysed." In 1903, Sir Liege Hulett, the former prime minister of Natal, publicly acknowledged that Durban had been built through Indian commercial enterprise.

After their contracts expired, some indentured labourers managed to obtain jobs as domestic servants, railway and council workers, and coal miners in northern Natal. Many took up vegetable farming. In the early part of the twentieth century, the working conditions of Indians changed to those of regular wage labourers, who still lived in dire poverty but were free to change employers.

The entrepreneurial skills and hard work of Indian traders enabled them to make deep inroads into a market which till then had been monopolized by European shopkeepers, which created antagonism towards them from as early as 1884-85. As the number of European shops closing down in Natal because of the competition increased, the government passed laws and regulations to curtail the rights of Indians. Over time, similar legislation was passed in other parts of South Africa.

The total Indian population in Natal at that time (1890) was approximately 80,000, with smaller numbers settled in the Boer republics of the Transvaal and the Orange Free State and the British colony of the Cape. In Natal, some White plantation owners campaigned for indentured labourers to be forced to return to India after their contracts expired. A second group advocated the imposition of a heavy annual capitation tax on labourers who did not re-indenture themselves on the expiry of their first period of five years. Both groups had the same object in mind, namely to make it impossible for ex-indentured labourers to live as free people in Natal under any circumstances. The agitation reached such serious proportions that the government of Natal appointed a commission to look into the matter. The evidence recorded by the commission showed that the demands were unfair and that the presence of the former indentured labourers was of economic benefit to the entire population.

Nevertheless, the government of Natal laid the demands of the anti-Indian groups before the colonial government of India. Effectively, the government of India was being asked to accept proposals that would have reduced indentured labourers to perpetual slavery, thereby sullying the reputation of the British as colonial rulers, so it rejected the demands. Natal was a crown colony, with the Colonial Office being fully responsible for its government, so Natal could not look for help in that quarter either. For this and similar reasons, a movement was started to change the status of Natal to that of a dominion, so that it would still be a part of the British Empire but self-governing. After this status was granted in 1893, the Colonial Office had no problem accepting the demands.

The government of Natal then proposed imposition of an annual poll tax of £25—more than four years' income—on every Indian whose indentureship contract had expired. With the help of Indian traders in Natal, the labourers protested to the imperial government and the government of India. Lord Elgin, the governor-general of India, declared the amount excessive but ultimately accepted a poll tax of three pounds, equivalent to nearly six months' earnings of an indentured labourer. The tax was levied not only on the labourer, but also on his wife, daughters aged 13 years and above and sons aged 16 years and above. Most labourers had a wife and children, so the annual poll tax per family was at least £12, an excessive sum in those days.

Free Indians were also targeted after some of them registered as voters. A bill disenfranchizing all Asians who were not already on the electoral roll was introduced in the Legislative Assembly in 1894 and, despite an Indian petition with 400 signatures, was enacted into law. A memorandum bearing ten thousand signatures was then sent to Lord Ripon, Secretary of State for the Colonies, who disallowed the legislation because it amounted to a legally sanctioned colour bar. The Natal government subsequently introduced another bill that removed the racial distinction but still used ambiguous phrasing to disqualify Indians indirectly. The Indians protested against that as well, but without success.

The European population of Natal at that time was 40,000. The number of Zulus was 400,000. In addition, there were 60,000 indentured, 10,000 ex-indentured and 10,000 free Indians. The Whites, therefore, had a phobia about being overwhelmed by hordes of Indians if they were permitted to immigrate freely. This led to the enactment of two more laws that appeared to be non-discriminatory but in practice imposed severe restrictions on Indian trade and Indian immigration into the province. The first Act prohibited anyone from trading without a licence, but in practice Europeans found it easy to obtain one while Indians faced endless difficulties, often requiring the services of a lawyer, which many could not afford. The second Act limited immigration into the colony to those who were able to pass the education test in a *European* language.

In other parts of South Africa, prejudice against Indians had begun to grow even before 1880. In the Boer republic of Transvaal, they were regarded as inferior beings. The first Indian to arrive in the Transvaal was the earlier-mentioned Abubaker Amad, who purchased land in one of Pretoria town's principal streets in 1881 and opened a shop there. As others followed his example, the European traders started to become worried and began an anti-Indian campaign in the newspapers. Petitions were submitted to the Volksraad, the Afrikaner parliament, calling for the Indians to be expelled and their businesses closed down. Among other things, the petitions accused the Indian population of being disease-ridden sexual predators.

The racist campaign led to a bill denying Indians land ownership rights. Prominent members of the Indian community sent a delegation to President Paul Kruger to protest against the bill, but Kruger did not even allow them to enter his house and they had to stand in the courtyard. After listening to them for a while, he told them, "You are the descendants of Ishmael and therefore, from your very birth, born to slave for the descendants of Esau.

As the descendants of Esau, we cannot admit you to rights placing you on an equal footing with ourselves. You must rest content with what rights we grant to you."

The anti-Indian bill was passed in 1885. It forced every Indian trader to register at a cost of £25 and stated that no Indian could own land or enjoy citizenship rights. After the Indians protested, the British government officially objected to the law as being in contravention of a treaty between the Boers and the British, which, among other things, secured the rights of British subjects. However, the Boers responded that the British government had previously given its consent, express or implied, to that law.

The matter was then referred to arbitration and in 1886 the law was amended in accordance with the arbitral award, reducing the registration fee to three pounds and allowing Indians to own fixed property in such locations, wards, and streets as were specifically set apart for their residence by the Transvaal government. The statute considered Indians a health hazard, and all those selected locations were in insalubrious and unwanted places at a safe distance from the towns where Whites lived and worked. They had no water supply and other public utilities. To make matters worse, the Afrikaner government did not respect the amended law and continued to withhold the right of Indians to purchase freehold land even in the designated locations.

Indians also met with hostility in the Orange Free State, with the Volksraad passing a law barring them from owning fixed property, carrying on any mercantile or farming business or enjoying any franchise rights. Indian traders were expelled from the province with nominal compensation. Only those that received special permission were allowed to settle as labourers or hotel waiters. As a result, when the Anglo-Boer war broke out, the only Indians in the Orange Free State were a few waiters.

Indians in the Cape Colony fared somewhat better for a long time, with the White population generally accepting them as temporary labourers and placing no restrictions in the trading sector and on the purchase of land. However, there were limits on their immigration and their children were not permitted to attend public schools or receive other public services. The reason for the fewer restrictions was that there was a fair proportion of Malays, migrants from present-day Indonesia and Malaysia, some of whom had arrived in the seventeenth century as slaves of the Dutch colonizers. They were viewed by the more liberal Dutch in the colony as part of their own population, and so paid-up, or at least affiliated, members of the human race.

The Malays were Muslims and soon started interacting with their Indian coreligionists. In due course, there was some intermarriage. Fluent in Dutch and its South African variant Afrikaans, the Malays had largely adopted many of the habits and manners of the Afrikaner colonists. Many had Dutch blood in their veins. Some had gone for higher education to England; one example was Doctor Abdul Rahman of Cape Town, who became a member of the old colonial legislature, only to lose the position after the creation of the Union of South Africa. In addition, the Malay settlement was the oldest of the migrant ones and the chief centre of culture in that part of the country, which produced, according to Gandhi, "sober, gentlemanly and large-hearted Europeans." Nevertheless, the poison of racial bigotry did eventually begin to seep into the Cape and two anti-Indian laws were passed, one virtually stopping all immigration of free Indians into the colony and the other affecting trade licences.

By 1894, the year in which my granduncle Jivan arrived in the country, the door to immigration was firmly closing in most of South Africa. In the Transvaal, ironically, the only restriction on immigration was the registration fee of three pounds, so when Natal and the Cape Colony closed their ports to Indians, newly arrived immigrants were able to enter the Transvaal through Delgoa Bay in what is today known as Mozambique, which was then a Portuguese colony.

Some thirteen statutes curtailing the Indians' right of entry into South Africa, their free movement in the country, and their right to trade freely had been passed by the turn of the nineteenth century, mainly in Natal, Transvaal, and the Orange Free State.

It was against this background that a young Gujarati lawyer named Mohandas Karamchand Gandhi arrived in 1893. He was in South Africa to represent the interests of Dada Abdulla, a Gujarati Memon trader in Durban, who was suing a distant cousin, Sheth Tyeb Haji Khanmohamed, over failure to fulfil the terms of a promissory note for some £40,000, a large sum even by today's standards. Abdulla had already retained White

South African lawyers but also wanted the services of a person who could offer advice from an Indian standpoint. Since a lawyer from India would not be allowed to practise there, that person would also attend to the office correspondence, which was largely in English. In addition to helping to prepare the case, he could act as a liaison between Abdulla and his White lawyers. For his services, Gandhi received a first class return passage by steamer to South Africa, a fee of 100 guineas and all his living expenses whilst he was in the country. Gandhi had agreed to accept the assignment for a year.

Gandhi arrived in Durban on 23 May, dressed impeccably in a white shirt, black tie, black frockcoat, striped trousers, a black turban, and black patent leather shoes. Little did he know then what lay in store for him, and for the world at large, in his long struggle towards self-realization. His first brush with a South African magistrate came a few days after his arrival, when Abdulla took him to the Durban court to observe the proceedings. The English magistrate asked him to remove his turban, but Gandhi refused to do so and left the court. After the *Natal Advertiser* reported the confrontation, Gandhi wrote to the paper explaining that, "as it is a mark of respect amongst Europeans to take off their hats, in like manner it is in Indians to retain one's headdress."

Abdulla's case had been filed in Pretoria because Khanmohamed was a trader there, and he asked Gandhi to go there to discuss the case with his lawyers. Gandhi bought a first class train ticket for the first part of the journey, but at Maritzburg, the capital of Natal, a fellow passenger complained to the authorities about having to share the compartment with a dark-skinned person and two railway officials ordered Gandhi to leave the train. Since his bags were in the custody of the train master, Gandhi found himself shivering without an overcoat in a cold dark waiting room at an altitude of 2000 feet. The next morning he continued to Charlestown, on the border with Transvaal, in another train.

The next stage of the journey, from Charlestown to Johannesburg, was by coach. Even though there was space inside, the coach leader insisted that Gandhi should sit on the coachbox with him. When the coach arrived at Pardekop, the coach leader decided to sit next to the driver and have a smoke and ordered Gandhi to sit on a dirty sackcloth on the footboard.

When Gandhi wanted to sit inside since there was still space there, the coach leader started beating him. Gandhi still refused to move and the coach leader gave up, but he threatened to retaliate when the coach reached Standerton. Luckily, Abdulla had made arrangements for someone to meet Gandhi at Standerton, who ensured his safe continuation of the journey to Johannesburg in another, larger, coach. For that part of the trip, he sat inside and there was no bullying.

In Johannesburg, Gandhi met Abdulla's agent, one Abdul Gani, to whom he related his experiences. Gani told him that conditions in the Transvaal were far worse and that he would have to travel to Pretoria by third class. Regardless of that forewarning, Gandhi purchased a first class ticket and boarded the train. At Germiston, a railway guard ordered him to go to a third class compartment but an Englishman, the only other passenger in the compartment, intervened, telling the guard, "I do not mind in the least his travelling with me."

It was evening when the train reached Pretoria and Gandhi, nervous that he would be rebuffed, hesitated to ask the stationmaster whether there were any hotels where he could spend the night. By chance he met an African American who told him that his employer, an American named Johnston, ran a hotel nearby and that he had no colour prejudice. Johnston allowed Gandhi to stay at the hotel on condition that he had his meals in his bedroom in order to avoid conflict with the White guests in the public dining room. Gandhi agreed, but Johnston, feeling uncomfortable about the arrangement, raised the matter with the other guests and they agreed that Gandhi could join them in the dining room.

The following morning, Gandhi met AW Baker, an attorney with the legal firm acting for Abdulla, who was able to arrange accommodation for him with a family at 35 shillings a week. Within a week of his arrival in Pretoria, Gandhi arranged a meeting with the Indian community leaders through Khanmohamed, who was as influential in the Transvaal as Abdulla was in Natal. The community was made up mainly of Muslims, largely Memons, who were trading in the insalubrious Marabastad location a mile from Pretoria town, which had been created under the Law of 1885 to segregate non-Whites. In addition, a very small group of Indians were trading in the downtown area, among them a Memon businessman named Mohamed Hajee Joosub, from Ranavav in Gujarat. Gandhi was carrying a letter of introduction to him from his father and met him at his home. As a result of that meeting, Joosub provided him with accommodation and board in the kitchen behind his shop.

At the get-together with the community leaders, Gandhi dwelt on the need to be truthful in business and emphasized that the need was even greater in a foreign country, because "the conduct of a few Indians was a measure of the millions of their countrymen." Gandhi also spoke about the necessity of cultivating good sanitary habits and appealed to the community to dispense with all distinction between Hindus, Muslims and Christians. He suggested the formation of an association to make representations to the authorities about the hardships Indians faced and agreed to help them in that endeavour.

During his stay in Pretoria, Gandhi unwittingly walked on a footpath banned to Indians and a policeman pushed and kicked him off the pavement onto the street. This happened outside Kruger's house in Struben Street, not far from Marabastad. A Quaker friend of Gandhi's, Michael Coates, witnessed the incident and urged him to press charges against the policeman, but Gandhi refused to do so on the grounds that he did not feel it appropriate to seek redress in court for grievances that were personal to him. Coates reprimanded the policeman, who apologized to Gandhi, but Gandhi felt that was unnecessary, "as I had already forgiven him." His quixotic and obstinate allegiance to justice for others seemed to have already taken root by that time.

Gandhi realized that "to look after the firm's case and to take up the question of Indian grievances at the same time would be to ruin both." Therefore he decided to collect as much background information on the conditions of the Indians in South Africa as possible, but not to take any action on their plight until he was able to give the issue his fullest attention.

Knowing from the outset that the adversarial process was both time consuming and expensive, and realizing that only the lawyers would profit from litigation, Gandhi wanted to bring about a compromise between Abdulla and Khanmohamed. He had a very junior position among the lawyers working on the case, but because of his untiring endeavours to mitigate the inequalities and injustices suffered by the Indian community, he had become well known and respected. He had also established a good rapport with his client, Abdulla, as well as with the defendant, Khanmohamed, and persuaded the two men and the senior lawyers to move the case from litigation to arbitration. A few days later, the arbitrator handed down a decision that Khanmohamed should pay £37,000 and all court costs, to the delight of Abdulla. Khanmohamed was threatened with bankruptcy, so Gandhi persuaded Abdulla to accept payment in instalments.

I find it fascinating that the culture that Gandhi portrayed was reflected almost a hundred years later in the person of Nelson Mandela. Both were imprisoned in Johannesburg Fort, though at different times, in the twentieth century. On the eve of South Africa's transition from apartheid to multiparty democracy the country faced the dreadful possibility of a bloodbath, and Mandela, who later became the country's first democratically elected president, was able to draw on Gandhi's philosophy as well as on the African concept of *ubuntu*. According to Archbishop Desmond Tutu, in *No Future Without Forgiveness*, "A person with *ubuntu* is open and available to others … for he or she has a proper self-assurance that comes from knowing that he or she belongs in a greater whole and is diminished when others are humiliated or diminished when others are tortured or oppressed or treated as if they were less than who they are."

With the conclusion of the case, Gandhi's South African stay was coming to an end. At a farewell function given in his honour, he was told that the Natal Legislative Assembly was debating the Franchise Amendment Bill to disenfranchise the Indian community. He warned the Indians that it was the beginning of a much greater danger to their existence and they requested him to stay and help them to fight the Bill. They offered to pay him for his services, but after reflection he refused to be financed through public money. He said he would help them whilst earning his keep by providing legal services. A group of business people agreed to give him a retainer for that purpose and Gandhi immediately started preparing all the necessary petitions against enactment of the Bill.

Despite the petitions, the Bill was enacted into law, and Gandhi then sent a petition with ten thousand signatures to Secretary of State for the Colonies, Lord Ripon. These signatures represented almost the entire population of free Indians in Natal colony. Gandhi also wrote to Dadabhai

Naoroji, the grand old man of India who was then an MP in the British parliament, apprising him of the plight of South African Indians. In the same year, 1894, he founded the Natal Indian Congress, which is one of the oldest political parties in Africa, and became its first honorary secretary. He was also admitted as an advocate of the Supreme Court of Natal.

This part of Gandhi's life and work is important to this narrative for several reasons. Firstly, it provides a good backdrop to the situation in the country in the year that my own forebears arrived. It also creates the necessary background against which immigration was taking place. Secondly, many South African families have had connections with Gandhi to varying degrees. Some marched with him, others spent time in prison with him, yet others sacrificed enormously for the cause that he advocated. My granduncle Velshi, who offered him hospitality when he visited Marabastad, sent his son Rajabali to study at his boarding school on Tolstoy Farm near Johannesburg in 1912. Our family absorbed some solid values through Gandhi's influence on my granduncle and his son Rajabali.

Thirdly, and more importantly, Gandhi's activities show the determination and tenacity of the man against all odds. It must have been deeply demeaning for a man of his education and background to be physically beaten in a country so far from his home. Nonetheless, he stayed on and championed the cause at a time when material gains could easily have prompted him to take the line of least resistance and ignore the harsh realities of the society in which the non-Whites lived in South Africa, which were to continue well into the twentieth century. Additionally, the children and grandchildren of some of the individuals associated with him, such as AM Kachalia and Thambi Naidoo, played a major role in the twentieth-century struggle against apartheid, and some of them had a close connection with Marabastad and members of our family. Others, such as Nana Sita, a veteran champion of nonviolence, originally from Marabastad, spent time working with Gandhi when he lived for a while on Vermeulen Street in Pretoria town with a Hindu bookkeeper named Vyas.

Much has been written of Gandhi's activities in Durban, and a long time later about his work in Johannesburg, but very little or nothing has been written about his one-year stay in Pretoria. Few people know that, following his cremation, some of his ashes were scattered in the Apies

River in the Apies River in Marabastad, which he had often frequented during his stay in Pretoria. I shall refer later to more of his work in the Transvaal, which was the crucible in which he became the Mahatma-in-the-making and as such South Africa's greatest gift to India.

Chapter 5

Voyage to a New Future

AT THE TIME WHEN GANDHI WAS TRYING TO PREVENT THE enactment of the Franchise Amendment Bill in South Africa, Jivan and Cassam were about to begin their voyage. This was in 1894. After a few days in Bombay, they made their way to the Ballard Pier and boarded a huge passenger liner with a black hull and two great yellow funnels. Their fellow deck passengers were hundreds of *loonghi*-clad turbaned workers and peasants, as well as a large number of women and children who were going to join husbands who had emigrated. Jivan and Cassam went down to the deck class and secured a small space where they could place their trunk and bedding. The ship was crammed and many of the deck passengers would have to sleep in close and fetid proximity to cows, horses, and sheep that had also been taken on board.

Overcrowding was an endemic problem on ships that carried migrant labour to the outposts of the British Empire in the nineteenth century. Despite repeated complaints, neither the shipping companies nor the colonial government of India paid any attention to the welfare of the passengers. As early as 1839, Lord Brougham, referring to the rate of mortality among Indian labourers on boats bound for British Guyana, remarked, ". . . mortality and massacre of the voyage far exceeded the African [slave trade] middle passage itself."

Jivan and Cassam had decided to enter South Africa through Port Elizabeth because they had been told that the officials there were more sympathetic to non-White newcomers. On disembarking from the ship at that port, they were met by some friends of Cassam's Pretoria relatives, who took them to an Indian area called Malabar and offered them a place to stay. The friends provided them with basic necessities. Within a week, they were loaned a few shillings and taught how to conduct a small street vending business, known as a ferry business, despite their minimal and broken English. All they needed to do was obtain a pushcart in which they would place produce such as egg plants, okra (picturesquely termed "ladyfingers"), green chillies, and mangoes and then sell them house to house in the White neighbourhoods. They would also vend soap, trinkets, combs, mirrors, and other small items to households of all races.

Each morning, the two budding merchants awoke before dawn and went to the Indian market to do manual work for which they were paid in vegetables and fruit. They then worked the streets in the suburbs with their cart. When they rang a door bell they would hear children shout to their parents, "Mummy! Sami the coolie is here! Do we want anything today?" Sometimes, unfriendly Whites would roughly warn them off or set their slavering dogs on them.

In the evenings, Jivan and Cassam would prepare and eat chapatis and rice with a curry of cabbage, okra, eggplant, potatoes, or spinach. Their aim was to travel to Pretoria, which was booming because of the gold rush that had begun in 1886. Cassam's relatives in Pretoria had offered to put them up once they arrived there. However, first they had to save enough money to travel to Pretoria and to open a small shop there and so become their own masters. The Transvaal had imposed a registration fee of £25 on Indian traders, which represented over a year's work for the two men. Even after the fee was reduced to £3, it was still a big sum for them.

After some months in Port Elizabeth, Jivan and Cassam had enough money to pay for their journey north to Pretoria and to pay the registration fee there. In Pretoria they made their way to Prinsloo Street, where a few Gujarati Muslim traders, members of the Memon community, lived. They had settled there since the 1880s and their current de facto leaders were Abubaker Amad, Mohamed Hajee Joosub, Cassim Adam, Ahamed Khamisa and NM Ebrahim. There was an unwritten code among the Indians in the town that anyone of Indian origin could live amongst them without cost for three months, after which they would be given about five pounds with which to start their own business. The gift acted both as an incentive and as a bond that tied the members of the community more closely to each other.

Jivan and Cassam received some help from their fellow Muslims, among them Ahamed Khamisa and Cassim Adam who had some experience of immigration rules and knew Europeans who were able to help with obtaining permits. The Indian traders entrusted Jivan with some goods on credit, which he supplemented by purchasing additional consumer items before working the suburbs of Pretoria. He sold food and household items to Afrikaner households and itinerant African workers, mainly mineworkers passing through the town. In 1896, he took a lease on a small shop at 112 Prinsloo Street and started his own small retail business which he named KJ Keshavjee and Company. The "K" denoted "Khoja," his ethnic background, distinguishing him from Memons and Kokanee Muslims.

Jivan was instrumental in establishing the first Khoja Ismaili settlement in southern Africa. Having gained a foothold in business, he was at last in a position to arrange for his wife, children, and relatives to join him. He also invited his parents to move to South Africa as he had promised, but Keshavjee Ramji declined because of his age. He enjoyed great respect and standing in his village and had no appetite for moving and starting life all over again. Mithima, on the other hand, found the prospect of going to a new land exciting, but she was only able to do so after the end of the Anglo-Boer War and Keshavjee Ramji's death in 1901. She found South Africa too strange; the food did not suit her and she was unable to obtain the Chotila ghee that she loved. Moreover, she missed the company of her daughter Manek and son Naran. Therefore, after a few months, she decided to return to India and was escorted back by her son Velshi and son-in-law Kanjee.

As more Indians arrived and settled in Pretoria, White residents began to complain and, between 1892 and 1893, the authorities moved the migrants (except those who had owned or rented property in designated areas in the town centre before 1889) to the new location called Marabastad, later known as the Asiatic Bazaar. In 1896, Jivan took possession of a small room at the corner of Boom and Jerusalem Streets. In India he had gone regularly to jamatkhana, and at the earliest opportunity he established the first jamatkhana in Marabastad. He was appointed the first *mukhi*, or chief functionary, by the Imam Sir Sultan Mahomed Shah Aga Khan III. In the course of time, he became known as the elder of the Keshavjee family and was admired and respected by everyone back in Chotila. People started referring to him as Jivanbapoo (father Jivan). In 1898, Jivanbapoo invited Nanji Amarsi Hooda of Limbdi in Gujarat to come to Pretoria to teach religion to the children, making him the first teacher of religious education in the Pretoria Ismaili community. Jivanbapoo paid the passage cost from India.

Jivan was tall, his handsome face graced by a full black beard. He had high cheek bones and deep-set-brown eyes which danced and sparkled with intelligence and determination. When he smiled, his whole face beamed. He had charisma and exuded authority as a family elder. Even when he was a young man in India, people had looked up to him as an elder and saviour. Whenever he went out in Pretoria, he wore a long black frock coat over a white collarless shirt with a gold stud at the neckline. A black matching *kofia*, an Indian cap, added to his dignity. He had probably chosen that apparel because it lent gravitas to his already prepossessing appearance. He was known to many of the Whites in Pretoria town, who frequented his shop for bargain-price groceries and daily household items. As the first Ismaili to settle in Pretoria, he provided encouragement and assistance to the growing community.

The only other Ismaili known to be living in South Africa at that time, who came after Jivanbapoo, was an advocate named Rahim Karim Khan. His forebears were Iranians. RK Khan, as he was known, had qualified as a barrister at Lincoln's Inn, London, where he had studied on a scholarship provided by the Aga Khan. He was a member of the Supreme Court of Judicature in England and an advocate of the Supreme Court of South Africa. In time, Khan became a close associate of Gandhi, and for five years he was the secretary of the Natal Indian Congress, which Gandhi had established in 1894. He was a good lawyer and devoted his life to his profession. Politics, in which he played a prominent role, also became a passion. He settled in Durban, which had a larger and more established Indian community, so his life experiences were quite different from those of Jivanbapoo in the Transvaal. At the time of his death in October 1932, he left an estate worth £45,000 to a trust for the uplift of poor Indians in Natal, and the money was used to set up the RK Khan Hospital and a string of dispensaries, also named after him, which were linked to the hospital. Jivanbapoo and RK Khan's paths did not cross in the 1890s, it being difficult for Indians living in one part of South Africa to travel to another region of the country. Nevertheless, they did establish limited contact towards the middle of the first decade of the twentieth century. In the 1920s, Jivanbapoo's nephews Goolam and Habib Keshavjee worked with him in the South African Indian Congress, which he often chaired and of which they were members.

As KJ Keshavjee and Company began to prosper, Jivanbapoo asked his father in Chotila to send his younger brother Velshi to join him. Velshi arrived in South Africa in 1897 and over time became known in the family as Velshibapoo. The two men decided to expand the business by opening a small grocery shop in Marabastad, about a mile from the original one.

Velshi was then about twenty-seven years old and had experience in village trading in India. He was not as tall as Jivanbapoo but had the same high cheek bones in an imposing face surmounted by a kofia. In contrast to his brother's ample beard, he sported a fine goatee. Dressed in Gujarati clothing, usually a loose cotton shirt over pyjama-type cotton trousers, he wore sandals even in winter. Velshi was the studious brother and had a good understanding of history and current world events. Unusually for Indians of that time, he kept a diary in which he recorded what he experienced each day. He was an astute businessman and helped Jivanbapoo by recording the daily transactions of the company.

Among the Indian businessmen in Pretoria that Velshi counted as friends were AM Kachalia and Cassim Adam, and he also befriended a Gujarati Hindu bookkeeper known as JP Vyas. It was through Vyas that he came to know of Gandhi, with whom he later became friends. As time went on, Velshi became the informal ambassador of the Keshavjee family to the wider community in South Africa and Eastern Africa.

In 1898, Jivanbapoo and Velshibapoo decided to lease plots, known as ervens, in the Bloed Street area. Soon after that, the Anglo-Boer War of 1899-1902 broke out and British subjects had to leave the Transvaal or face internment by the Boers. Velshibapoo returned to India while Jivanbapoo is said to have gone to Mozambique, where an Ismaili community was beginning to set down roots and where he knew people who could help him to set up a business. While the war was still going on, news arrived that Keshavjeebapa had died in Chotila.

The war was a trying period for my granduncles, and for many other Indians who were British citizens living in the Transvaal, creating uncertainty about their future. Its ramifications for race relations in South Africa continue to this day. The war followed the discovery of gold and diamonds in Boer territories and subsequent attempts by the British to seize control of the Transvaal. The pretext used by the British was the Boer mistreatment of immigrants. During the war, 26,000 Boer women and chidren died in British concentration camps, which left deep scars among the Afrikaners.

The British won the war and in 1910 established the Union of South Africa, comprising the Cape, Natal, Orange River Colony, and the Transvaal. The Union had the status of a dominion of the British Empire and was a constitutional monarchy with a governor-general representing the British monarch. The territories of the Union were allowed to maintain their existing racial laws, and various governments progressively whittled away whatever rights the non-White population had been allowed till then.

When the war came to an end in 1901, Jivanbapoo and Velshibapoo returned to South Africa and resumed their business on Prinsloo Street. For reasons that are not clear, while returning from India, Velshibapoo jumped off the ship near Portuguese East Africa and swam the short distance in shark-infested waters to the shore of Delgoa Bay. It is possible that he made the voyage to Africa before the Anglo-Boer War ended and felt that if the Afrikaners won the war, he would have a better chance of re-entering the Transvaal as a resident of the Portuguese colony than as a British subject. By jumping off the boat at Delgoa Bay and disappearing into the jungle, he was able to make his way to Lourenço Marques and register himself as a resident there. He also registered his two sons Allibhai and Rajabali, who were still with his wife in India, as residents. Thus, if he needed to settle in Portuguese East Africa he could be reunited with his wife and sons with little difficulty.

There is another story in the Keshavjee family, about Mohamed Bawa, who went to South Africa on the same ship as Velshi Keshavjee, most likely after the Anglo-Boer War. So friendly did he and his wife become with Velshibapoo and his wife Jabubai that they agreed that, if the Bawas had daughters, they would get them married to Velshi's two sons, Allibhai and Rajabali, who were still babies then. The story goes that there was a misunderstanding over Mohamed's disembarkation permit and he and his wife had to return to India. Eventually, they ended up in Kismayu, British Somaliland, where Mohamed Bawa started a transport business and bought a farm on which he cultivated mangoes, becoming a well-known business figure in the area. He and his wife had four daughters and a son. In 1917, when the eldest daughter Amrath came of age, Mohamed invited Velshibapoo to travel to Kismayu with Allibhai, who was then around nineteen years old, so that the young couple could meet. Allibhai and Amrath got on well and they were married. In 1923, Rajabali, in his early twenties, married the other daughter, Jena, and returned with her to South Africa.

Once Velshibapoo had arrived in Marabastad, he and Jivanbapoo acquired further erven and secured the help of Coloured builders to construct small shops roofed with sheets of corrugated iron. Those humble buildings, on Bloed Street, also contained the family's living quarters. KJ Keshavjee and Company expanded over the years from Prinsloo Street in the downtown area to Bloed Street in Marabastad, with a line of retail shops all facing the Coloured location. Bloed Street was the designated boundary of the Asiatic Bazaar. In some cases the plots extended northwards to Grand Street, thus creating the basis for future expansion. All those properties were held on 21-year leases.

Jivanbapoo's son Madhavjee had remained in India with my grandfather, Manjee Keshavjee. Velshibapoo's and Jivanbapoo's cousins and nephews in Chotila and Gondal had heard that their relatives were thriving in Africa and were all keen to migrate there. Once the Keshavjee retail business was growing steadily, Jivanbapoo and Velshibapoo were in a position to give their family members jobs. New rules were being put in place that would effectively ban Indians from entering South Africa, so the brothers kept an eye on which ports were still partly open and advised their relatives accordingly. Jivanbapoo warned his family members in Chotila to leave as soon as possible but advised his brother Naran to remain in India for a while. The other brother, Manjee, was told to travel to South Africa with Madhavjee, Jivanbapoo's eldest son. After Velshibapoo, the next people to arrive were my mother's maternal grandparents, Nanji Amarsi Hooda and his wife Galal (mentioned earlier).

Jivanbapoo also counselled his cousins Chagan Jiwa and Nimji Anandjee, his nephew Valjee Hirji and his sister Santok's husband Kanjee to migrate quickly. After migrating, Chagan Jiwa started a shop and eating house in Eastlynne, a little away from Pretoria. Related to Jivanbapoo on his father's side and able to rattle off the family genealogy from memory, he often reminded his cousin that their connection went back seven generations. To cope with the restrictions, some migrants even travelled without papers. One old man succeeded in bringing a male family member through the Portuguese border, disguised as his daughter, late at night, when the immigration officials were tired and less vigilant. His "daughter" pretended to be asleep, so the official waved them through without scrutiny.

Jivanbapoo's nephew Ebrahim remained in India after his father, Kanjee Kassam, migrated. A few years later Kanjee Kassam returned to escort his family to South Africa and was devastated to find that his wife Santok, who was Jeevanbapoo's sister, and both his parents had died while he was at sea. Naranbapoo then looked after Ebrahim while Kanjee Kassam returned to Pretoria to establish himself. Later, Naranbapoo, when he left for South Africa, took Ebrahim with him. Kanjee Kassam and Ebrahim then started KK Khoja and Company, selling paraffin in tins. Over the years, the enterprise became highly successful and in the late 1920s Kanjee Kassam was in a position to help finance the Royal Kinema Bioscope then being constructed by the Manjee Keshavjees.

My grandfather Manjee Keshavjee had arrived in South Africa in 1901 with Madhavjee, Jivanbapoo's son, and they worked as waiters in Durban for some time while waiting for permits to enter the Transvaal. On his arrival in Pretoria, Manjee began working in the Prinsloo Street shop, which had a mainly Dutch and African clientele and was doing well. Soon, Manjeebapoo asked his wife Noorbai in Chotila to join him with their infant daughter Sakina, who was then about eighteen months old.

The three Keshavjee brothers, after a few years in the partnership, started to disagree on business matters, an unfortunate family development which led to the dissolution of the partnership. The elder brother, Jivan, took the Prinsloo Street shop and one corner in Bloed Street whilst Velshi took other premises in Bloed Street and set up his shop at the corner of Grand and Sixth Streets. Jivanbapoo changed his shop name from KJ Keshavjee and Company to Keshavjee Ltd. Velshi traded as V Keshavjee and Sons. Manjee took over the building at the corner of Bloed and Jerusalem Streets in Marabastad, but, tragically, his premises were damaged by a fire and he had to close the shop. He moved to Prinsloo Street in 1912 and opened a shop, M Keshavjee and Company, in close proximity to Keshavjee Ltd. Manjee's enterprise lasted well into the 1970s. Meanwhile, the various relatives whom Jivanbapoo had sponsored to migrate to South Africa began to look for opportunities for themselves. With small loans from friends and the little capital they had saved, they began to consider setting up their own little corner shops in various parts of Marabastad and beyond. Most of these businesses incorporated "Khoja" in their name.

"Khoja" was an ethnic marker. Many Gujarati Ismailis (known as Khojas in their homeland) who entered South Africa in the early part of the twentieth century and who were not directly related to Jivanbapoo took on the name "Khoja" as a surname, trading name, or both. This may have been for practical reasons, as some of them were immigrationally sponsored by him. Others may have found the name conducive to setting up new businesses as he had by then established himself as a successful businessman and was using the initial K (for Khoja) in the trading name. The name originates from the Persian word *khwaja*, which eventually became distorted over the centuries to Khoja in India, and conveys the sense of honourable person or master. These families established themselves in commercial activities ranging from providing translation services in the Supreme Court in Johannesburg and running wholesale and retail shops in various parts of the Transvaal, to manufacturing candles, producing mango pickles, and growing hops.*

These families and others in the Cape worked hard, prospered and established their reputations as good businessmen in their respective fields. They brought up younger generations who were keen to serve the community and those around them under the community's social governance framework that the Imam had given them. Under that enabling framework, enterprising individuals such as Habib Velshi Keshavjee, Goolam Manjee Keshavjee, Sherbanoo Velshi Keshavjee and Roshankhanoo Manjee Keshavjee were able to introduce modern concepts of education and health care in the 1940s under the aegis of the Aga Khan Provincial Council, that helped to provide the Ismaili community with the necessary bulwarks to withstand the difficulties that apartheid would pose for the next fifty years.

Jivanbapoo was not the only Ismaili to migrate to South Africa on his own initiative. For example, as mentioned in the note, the Hajee Ramjee family came on their own and started a retail business in Northern Transvaal in 1915. Hajee Ramjee's four brothers settled in Madagascar. According to their family narrative, the brothers were travelling from India to Africa when their ship was damaged by a storm and ended up near Madagascar, where they disembarked and established themselves. One brother, Hajee Ramjee ended up in South Africa while the others remained in Madagascar. Most of the family is now based in France, Madagascar, and Canada.

Another prominent family, that of Kanji Vally, originated from Diu and Daman in Goa. They opened a shop specializing in crockery and kitchenware in the Diagonal Street area of Johannesburg in 1902, trading as Kanji Vally and Company, with a branch office in Bombay. Rahemtullah Kanji Vally and his cousin, Ebrahim Virji Vally, became well known in the Johannesburg area, with the latter becoming a respected businessman producing candles in the early 1930s. The Sarif Janmohamed family of Jamnagar set up grocery and fancy goods stores as well as some cinemas in Stellenbosch and Paarl in the Cape in the 1930s. The Karsan family established a grocery business in Uitenhage, Port Elizabeth, as early as the 1930s and remained there well into the twenty-first century.

Cassim Ali, also from the Gujarat, came into the country on his own and developed a thriving business, and in due course became an important landowner with some prize property in a good European area in Pretoria West. Nanji Amarsi Hooda stayed for a while in South Africa but returned to India in the mid 1920s.

The Keshavjees and most other Ismailis in Pretoria were related to each other in Gujarat through intermarriage over many generations. In Gujarat, the clan name, or *atak*, is based on the name of a common ancestor or even a common physical location from which a group originates. This was a common practice amongst Muslims even in the early years of Islam, and it was the basis of Prophet Muhammad's (pbuh) lineage. The clan atak of the Keshavjees is Dharani, which signifies their origin from the common ancestor Dhara. Thus, the lineage of the first Keshavjee in the clan was Keshavjee Ramji Murji Kanji Chayya Jutha Dhara. Most of the Ismailis in South Africa who are not Keshavjees belong to the Gillani clan. Mithima, Keshavjeebapa's wife, was a Gillani, as were many other women that the Keshavjees married in India. Some of the women, for example my maternal and paternal grandmothers, were from the Hooda clan. The Kanji Nanji Amarsi family are Hoodas. We have relatives in Sri Lanka, the Saboor Chatoor family, who are also Hoodas. They settled in Ceylon in the early part of the twentieth century and established themselves as leading spice traders. A large part of the Chotila Gillani family, particularly the family of Najrali Anandjee, the ghee king of Chotila, ended up in Tanganyika. Their descendants are settled in many parts of the world today and call themselves Gillani. Jivanbapoo's eldest grandson, Noormohamed, married Amrath, the granddaughter of Najrali Anandjee, with the help of Manekfaiba. The marriage lasted a lifetime and the couple had thirteen children who started new lives and settled across three continents.

♦

After moving his business to Prinsloo Street, around 1912, Manjeebapoo supplemented his stock with fancy goods that catered to the taste of the White clientele in downtown Pretoria. Though there were more sophisticated European retail stores in the area, Indian shops were more popular with both Whites and Africans, because Whites received credit facilities and Africans could find all types of household goods in an Indian shop that an itinerant population might require for their daily needs.

After the dissolution of the Keshavjee partnership, Manjeebapoo kept very much to himself and went about his business without fuss or show. His main aim was to build up M Keshavjee and Company as a leading wholesale business in the Pretoria area. He had a good friendship with a number of Memon traders in the Prinsloo Street area who respected his honesty. Among his close friends were two leading businessmen, Essa Hassim and Tarmohamed Peermohamed, the latter known famously as TPM of Carolina, a trading district in the Transvaal. Another well-known businessman, Noormohamed Ayob, was also a valued associate.

Manjeebapoo had been in his early twenties when he first arrived in the country. He was now a thin man of medium height with a straight nose and high forehead. He was not of very fair complexion and sported a small moustache that was neatly trimmed. He normally wore a white cotton shirt which he had sewn himself. On top of the shirt he wore a dark brown, collarless wool coat, and a black kofia on his head rounded off the ensemble, giving him a stylish air. One of the abiding aims of his life was to build a permanent jamatkhana on Boom Street. In 1916 he was appointed the mukhi of the Pretoria jamatkhana, with Nimji Anandjee as the kamadia. (As explained earlier, the mukhi is the chief functionary of a jamatkhana; the kamadia is akin to his deputy.)

Every Sunday, Manjeebapoo would climb with his sons Ismail and Goolam into his creaking cart drawn by a mule and slowly ride down Boom Street east, all the way to Prinsloo Street in downtown Pretoria. When they arrived at his shop, he would place a little mat on the middle of the concrete floor and upend two small wooden boxes for the boys to sit on. He would then explain to them the rudiments of the family business with meticulous care so that they would understand the need to have an expansive business vision whilst retaining accuracy in the running details. He would explain to them how they could gain optimum advantage by buying and selling the right goods at the right time. They were given the secrets of business accounting at the end of each day's trading and he impressed upon them the importance of banking the day's income as soon as practicable. They also learnt about which people to approach, and how to do so, if there was a cash shortfall. However, he emphasized, they should avoid putting themselves in such a position. Manjeebapoo was a stern father but also a loving one, and every Sunday he would reward his sons for their diligence and attentiveness by preparing fried sardines, one of their favourite meals, which they would eat together at the shop.

Initially both the boys attended the Good Shepherd School, but later transferred to a Coloured school in Marabastad, which was run by a

Methodist missionary named Miss Ferguson, who was accompanied by her sister Miss Emily and their niece Miss Tarlton. They taught the boys spartan discipline and inculcated good values in them. Miss Ferguson taught them hymns and the Bible—which Manjeebapoo did not mind since Islam considers Jesus to have been a prophet and it would be good for the boys to get a good moral education. The Ismaili religious education was imparted to the boys by my maternal grandmother, Kanjee Kassam's wife Mongi Nanji Hooda, a daughter of Nanji Amarsi Hooda, who was invited by Jivanbapoo to South Africa for this purpose.

Like other Indians of his generation, Manjeebapoo did not have a professional career in mind for his sons. School was for learning basic numeracy and it was trade that would be their lifeblood, their means of survival. He insisted that they spend some hours in the shop each day to learn the basics of the trade. He taught the elder son, Ismail, how to run the business while the second son, Goolam, who was better with figures, practised bookkeeping and was in charge of updating the cash book at the end of each day. That was in keeping with good Gujarati business traditions, and at a time when businesses were small family enterprises struggling to survive, each family often trained one son to handle the cash.

Manjeebapoo's wife, Noorbai Tarbhai Jamal, who was part of the Hooda clan as noted earlier, was originally from Tithwa in Gujarat. Her family were originally Ismailis and later followed the Shia Ithna Ashari tariqah (persuasion) of Islam and emigrated to Africa, settling initially in Lamu, Kenya, where her father Tarbhai Jamal worked as a small trader. In due course, his sons Rajabaly and Kassim emigrated to Kampala, Uganda, where they became leading businessmen. Noorbai had a few brothers and sisters, one of whom lived in Bombay. Today the Hooda extended family numbers over a thousand individuals who are spread out across the world but are based mainly in Dubai, Toronto and London.

Naranbapoo, the second-eldest brother of the Keshavjee clan, continued to live in Chotila while his siblings migrated. He was a mukhi of the Chotila Jamatkhana in 1908. He had a small transport business consisting of a few bullock carts. His father had died in 1901 and he was looking after his aged mother Mithima and his sister Manek. He had the ascetic appearance of a hermit and lived a simple life, organizing his activities with clockwork regularity. Twice a week, he would accompany Manek, who was partly blind, to do the household laundry at the Bogavo river, which runs through Chotila. He dressed very simply in homespun khadi cloth, and like a Sufi mendicant he wore a heavy blanket around his shoulders when he meditated early each morning.

Manjeebapoo realized that it would be difficult for the unworldly Naranbapoo to start a business in a new country, so he invited him to migrate with the assurance that all his family's living expenses in South Africa would be paid by M Keshavjee and Company. Naranbapoo migrated in 1912, accompanied by his wife Prembhabu and twin sons Hassan and Noormohamed and daughters Rahemat and Khatija. His eldest daughter, Poori, had already been married to Sacoor Alibhai from Keshod in Gujarat, who had set up a small shop in Inhambane, Portuguese East Africa, to sell household goods to settlers and Africans in the southern part of the colony.

Naranbapoo became an important father figure in the business. Manjeebapoo's business began to thrive in the years after the First World War. As menioned earlier, he had built a good relationship with members of the business community, largely the Memons, who had a high degree of trust in him. They bought from him and sold to him and assisted him when he required any help. The firm became one of the important retail outlets on Prinsloo Street and Manjeebapoo then expanded into wholesale business and started importing goods directly from England, with Stephen Fraser of the UK as his shippers. He even imported cloth directly from Britain. With the help of the Standard Bank he established a good international credit rating and became a respected name in local trading circles. The goods he imported doubled in value as a result of the war. He was the only Indian wholesaler dealing in groceries in the Pretoria area at that time.

In late 1916, Manjeebapoo decided to trade in hides purchased from farmers and hunters in the area. On 11 March 1917, while he was at the shop in Prinsloo Street, he complained of flu-like symptoms. That was followed by headaches, nausea and vomiting, and Naranbapoo immediately summoned an ambulance and informed Jivanbapoo. Manjeebapoo was placed on a stretcher as neighbours gathered around the shop. Waving to them, he noticed the young daughter of a Jewish neighbour named Bosmonlik and told Naranbapoo in Gujarati, "Please, when you come back from the hospital send this little girl a box of chocolates from the shop." He also took a handful of sovereigns and distributed them to all the children who had gathered around, as a sort of valediction.

Jivanbapoo instructed Manjeebapoo's eldest son Ismail to accompany him in the ambulance while Goolam took care of the shop. They rode to the hospital in the makeshift ambulance, which was essentially a wooden box on wheels drawn by two mules. On the way, Manjeebapoo gave Jivanbapoo instructions on what to do while he was in hospital. With a nostalgic sigh, he lamented that he had never bought his children any good things in life and asked Jivanbapoo to take them to the best outfitters in Pretoria and buy them clothes that they would be proud to wear.

At the hospital, Manjeebapoo was diagnosed as suffering from anthrax and was quarantined in a tent in the grounds because there was no cure yet for that highly infectious disease. Ismail was perplexed because his father had spoken to him in the ambulance and had not appeared to be that seriously ill. Back home, he told Goolam what the doctors had said, but they kept the news from their mother as, in addition to her nervous disposition, she was not well.

Manjeebapoo spent the weekend in quarantine. On 13 March, 1917, his family were at jamatkhana in Marabastad when the news reached them that he had died, at the young age of 38 years. The family and the community were in a state of shock because they had not fully understood the gravity of the illness.

Before Manjeebapoo passed away, he had made a will leaving half his estate to Naranbapoo as an outright bequest and the other half in trust for his wife Noorbai Jamal and their eight children, with Naranbapoo as trustee. Naranbapoo carried out that task with diligence till his death in 1927.

Manjeebapoo was one of the first Ismailis to die in South Africa. The community sank into a miasma of gloom and Manjeebapoo's family and friends in Prinsloo Street went into mourning. During the funeral procession, all of Manjeebapoo's male family members took turns carrying the bier, but his closest friend, Tarmohamed Peermohamed of Carolina, insisted on carrying it all the way to the grave. Years later, their friendship was further sealed when he and another close friend of Manjeebapoo, Essa Hassim, were buried on either side of his grave.

Naranbapoo took on the responsibility of guiding the family while Ismail and Goolam were still in school. Each day after school, both brothers would go to 256 Jerusalem Street in Marabastad for a quick meal. Akoobhai's wife (related to Cassam Noormohamed) whom they called Masi, lived at the back of the premises and each day she would chop up a tomato and some onions, spice them and prepare a tomato chutney which she would serve with freshly made rotis. She would then pack them off to Prinsloo Street where they would help Naranbapoo with the family business.

Naranbapoo was a man of deep religious conviction and was the moral anchor of the jamat. Despite generational differences, he strengthened the spiritual life of the Ismailis. He got up each morning for meditation, without fail, inculcated moral habits in all the youth of the first generation, and, in close collaboration with Ebrahim Virji Vally, looked after all the waezeen who came to South Africa to deepen the jamat's knowledge of the the Ismaili religion.

Ismail and Goolam found it somewhat difficult to work with Naranbapoo as he was unworldly and rather stubborn. However, they respected the fact that their father had trusted him unreservedly and they obeyed his wishes. While his ways may not have suited their new outlook on life in South Africa, which was distinct from traditional life in India, he did instil in them religious and ethical values. Goolam left the shop for a year, during which he was employed at V Keshavjee and Sons, because he found it difficult to work with Naranbapoo. Ismail stayed on and did Naranbapoo's bidding until he was ready to take on the leadership of the business himself many years later.

Naranbapoo had multiple responsibilities. In addition to being the paterfamilias of the Manjee Keshavjee family, he had also brought with him from India his late sister Santok's son Ebrahim Kanjee Kassam, who was also his wife Prembhabu's nephew. In typical Gujarati fashion, Naranbapoo arranged for his ward Sakina, Manjee's eldest daughter, to be married to Ebrahim, which brought Ebrahim closer to the Manjee Keshavjee family. In addition, he helped his son Hassan to set up his own business on Boom Street in Marabastad. Hassan became a very successful businessman; he also learned the Qur'an and was respected as an *alim* (religiously knowledgeable person) by other Muslims in the area. He performed the *nikah* (recital of the Muslim marriage contract) at many marriage ceremonies in the 1940s. Meanwhile, M Keshavjee and Company continued to thrive for the next few years on the reputation established by Manjeebapoo coupled with the new ideas Goolam learnt through his business association with the Velshi Keshavjees.

In 1918, as a highly virulent strain of influenza swept through the world, decimating populations wherever it surfaced, thousands of people died in South Africa. In scenes reminiscent of the European plague of the Middle Ages, there were so many corpses that they had to be placed in hessian bags and buried in mass graves. Jivanbapoo's cousin, Chagan Jiwa, and his nine-year-old nephew, Hassim Manjee Keshavjee, went from house to house in a horse-drawn cart, picking up bodies for ablution and burial. In the Ismaili community, the first to die was Alibhai Velji, married to Jivanbapoo's daughter Hirbai. He was followed by one of Naranbapoo's twin sons, Noormohamed, and the son of Allibhai V Keshavjee, Aladdin.

Two other deaths, which touched most people very deeply because they occurred in quick succession, were those of my maternal grandmother Mongi Kassam Panchaan and Jivanbapoo, both highly respected members of the community. Mongi was Kassam Panchaan's second wife and mother of three children aged between two and six. She was pregnant again when she contracted the flu and passed away in October 1918. Her husband was left with three young children to look after. Mongi's two daughters, Sakina and Koolsam, were playing in the yard of the house behind the shop in Bloed Street when her son, Habib, aged six years, saw the female relatives in the room administer the last rites to his ailing mother. When they covered her face with a white sheet with moans of bereavement, he realized that his mother had passed away, ran to Sakina and Koolsam, put his arms around them and told them, "Look, Ba has gone. She will not come back again." That did not make sense to his sisters, as they could still see their mother on the bed in the house.

Habib then started sobbing inconsolably and made a promise that Koolsam—who would later become my mother—and Sakina were to remember throughout their lives: "Don't worry, I will look after you. I will be your Ba." Even when his sisters became adults, Habib kept his vow and remained their mentor. Kassam Panchaan also showed great fortitude and faith, accepting what he considered to be his destiny. He grieved, but, conscious of his responsibilities to his young family, refused to succumb to depression.

A communal outpouring of sorrow ensued after Jivanbapoo's death on 22 October 1918, but many of the community members were too ill to attend the funeral. The few who did make it to the cemetery included Chagan Jiwa and Hassim. For Chagan, burying his cousin was a poignant reminder of the impermanence of life. A tall lanky man himself, he had measured Jivanbapoo's grave, and then lain down in it to ensure that it was the right size. He had even prepared the shroud and stitched it, and he performed the burial rites himself. After placing the incense on the grave, he muttered with deep stoicism, "*Allah, Allah che!*" ("God is present everywhere!")

The passing away of the two patriarchs within such a short time heralded a new phase in the development of the Ismaili community in South Africa. The end of the First World War and the beginning of a new decade gave rise to fresh challenges and needs. Jivanbapoo left an estate worth £8000. Manjeebapoo's estate at that time amounted to about £3000. It was now time to develop additional businesses as the youngsters in families had grown up and had families of their own. Jivanbapoo and Manjeebapoo had instilled in them a sense of service, wanting them to play a role in the institutional framework that the Imam had set up for the jamat. This, they felt, would provide strong support for the community when it faced the challenges to come. It now devolved upon Velshi Keshavjee to steer the destiny of the family and the jamat. He had established himself in business and was known in the country as well as outside. Effectively, he had become the head of the entire Keshavjee family, a responsibility that he carried out till his death in October 1952, when he was knocked down by a bus while crossing the road in front of the jamatkhana, which he had built with the approval of the Imam, and whose foundation stone he had laid some twenty years earlier.

Chapter 6

Gandhi in the Transvaal

THE KESHAVJEES WERE EXPANDING AND STRENGTHENING their trading activities amid continuing efforts by the Whites to carve up the population into a racial hierarchy, with the Africans at the bottom, Whites at the top, and Indians and Coloureds in the middle. At the same time, Gandhi was persevering in his crusade to end racial discrimination against the Indians. After setting up the Natal Indian Congress in 1894, he contacted Dadabhai Naoroji, the first British Asian MP, to inform him of the problems facing the Indians in South Africa. He wrote to Naoroji almost every week, receiving a personal handwritten reply each time, encouraging him to continue fighting against discrimination in South Africa.

Gandhi also sought support in India, returning there in 1896 to write and distribute a pamphlet entitled "The Grievances of the British Indians in South Africa." A Reuters news agency report on the pamphlet was published in South African newspapers and created an uproar among the Whites. Gandhi returned to Natal at the end of the year in the *SS Courland*, a steamer owned by Dada Abdulla, the Indian businessman whose court case had been the reason for his going to South Africa in the first place. On his arrival, Gandhi was told that the local Whites had convened a meeting calling for him and his fellow Indian passengers to be prevented from landing. To protect his family from possible violence, he sent them to the home of Parsi Rustomji, a wealthy Parsi friend, before disembarking.

Gandhi was accompanied by a friend named Laughton, who hoped that his presence would deter the crowd from using violence, but they were set upon by a mob of Whites who pelted them with various objects including pebbles and also beat up Gandhi. The wife of Natal Police Superintendent

Alexander came to their defence, using an umbrella to ward off missiles until constables arrived to rescue them.

When the Anglo-Boer War broke out, Gandhi felt that the Indians, as British citizens, should be loyal to Britain, even though his personal sympathies, as he wrote later, "were all with the Boers." He offered to organize Indians as medical orderlies and stretcher-bearers for the wounded, but the Natal government spurned him. Nevertheless, Gandhi began to train a team of volunteers as nurses. Heavy casualties suffered by the British forces soon caused the Natal government to sanction the formation of an Indian Ambulance Corps and they served the British army for about six weeks. For their services, Gandhi, RK Khan and several other Indian volunteers were awarded the War Medal and the corps was mentioned in despatches. In October 1901, unable to practise law in Natal because of the war, Gandhi returned to India to practise there.

The Indians' support of the British did not lead to amelioration of their conditions after the Boers were defeated. Instead, their situation became even worse, particularly in the Transvaal. The Indians decided to petition Secretary of State for the Colonies Joseph Chamberlain, who was due to visit South Africa to collect a war debt of 35 million pounds from the Boers, and they requested Gandhi to return and speak to him on their behalf. Gandhi arrived in South Africa towards the end of 1902 and wrote a long petition about the grievances of the Indian population. The Transvaal government did not allow Gandhi to accompany an Indian delegation to visit Chamberlain, which was led by George Godfrey, an Indian barrister from Natal. Chamberlain, who was briefed by the newly established Asiatic Department, used various excuses to exclude Gandhi from the discussions. Anti-Asian laws remained on the statute books but Indians managed to survive somehow.

Gandhi then applied for and received admission to the roll of attorneys of the Supreme Court of the Transvaal. He opened a practice in Johannesburg, enlisting Louis Walter Ritch as his legal clerk. Ritch worked for Gandhi for two years and then went to England to continue his legal studies. Gandhi also set up a printing press at a farm and school that he had established in Phoenix, Natal. All seemed to be going peacefully when, in 1906, he clashed with the Transvaal government over a new law affecting the Indians there.

The Asiatic Law Amendment Ordinance of 1906 was designed to force all Indians above the age of eight years to be fingerprinted for a registration document they would have to carry on their person at all times and produce on demand. The police could even enter the home of any Indian without a warrant and demand the registration certificates of the occupants. This was designed to harass the Indians in the province. Any Indian who did not register could be fined, imprisoned, or deported. At a meeting of leading Indians to discuss the ordinance, Gandhi pointed out that it would lead to similar laws in other parts of the country and was calculated to "strike at the very root of our existence in South Africa." The meeting resolved unanimously to oppose the proposed legislation.

On 11 September 1906, three thousand Indians from across the Transvaal attended a meeting to oppose the proposed legislation, which they termed the "Black Ordinance." It was presided over by Abdul Gani, a Muslim businessman who was chairman of the Transvaal British Indian Association. Sheth Haji Habib, a prominent public figure, asked the audience to take an oath. Those present took the oath not to comply with the ordinance should it become a law. Gandhi explained to them the full implications of this decision. A few hours later, the venue of the meeting, the Empire Theatre in Johannesburg, was destroyed by a fire, the cause of which remains a mystery to this day.

Gandhi sent off a series of memoranda and petitions to the government and a deputation called on the colonial secretary, who assured them that the government would consider the bill's proposals. In the end, the Transvaal Legislative Council deleted only a single clause, which related to women, before passing the ordinance. Since the Transvaal was still a crown colony in 1906 and needed royal assent to all laws, the Indian community authorized sending Gandhi and HO Ally to London to present a petition urging rejection of the legislation to the Secretary of State for the Colonies, Lord Elgin.

Once Gandhi arrived in London, he contacted Dadabhai Naoroji, who put him in touch with Sir William Wedderburn, chairman of the British Committee of the Indian National Congress, and Sir Henry Cotton, an MP who supported Indian nationalism. Gandhi also met the only other

Indian MP in Britain, Sir Muncherjee Bhownagree. With the assistance of English friends and Indian students, Gandhi and his colleagues sent out about five thousand letters and addressed sympathetic MPs during the next six weeks.

Lord Elgin informed Gandhi and Ally that the registration of Indians in the Transvaal was for their own benefit. They were to be fingerprinted because most Indians in South Africa were illiterate and used a thumb print instead of a signature. Even when Gandhi pointed out that all ten fingers were to be printed, as was done with criminals, Elgin refused to change his position. Gandhi next appealed to the Secretary of State for India, John Morley, for a royal commission to enquire into the grievances of Indians in South Africa but once again received sympathy but no action. Morley argued that there would be no use in appointing such a commission since the Transvaal would soon become self-governing and would then be able to ignore any decision made by the British government. Gandhi, Ally, and a few MPs called on Prime Minister Henry Campbell-Bannermann, who assured them that he would speak to Lord Elgin. Gandhi also met with the Under-Secretary of State for the Colonies Winston Churchill, who reiterated the argument used by Morley but promised to do what he could. Gandhi and Ally had to be content with these assurances and left Britain on 1 December 1906.

When they reached the Portuguese island of Madeira on their way back to South Africa, Gandhi found two telegrams awaiting him, with the news that the ordinance had been refused assent. However, when they arrived in Cape Town, they found that Lord Elgin had already notified the Transvaal commissioner in London that if the Transvaal re-enacted the ordinance after 1 January 1907, when the territory would no longer be a crown colony, royal approval would not be withheld. Gandhi was indignant about this duplicity on the part of Elgin.

A general election was held in the Transvaal in February 1908 and Louis Botha became the prime minister. He appointed General Smuts as colonial secretary, with the responsibility of resolving the "Asiatic Question." At the first session of the newly constituted parliament, the government introduced the Asiatic Law Amendment bill, which basically reproduced the earlier ordinance, and it was rushed through all its stages in twenty-four hours and became effective on 1 July. Terming the law the "Black Act," Gandhi and his followers formed the Passive Resisters Association and started a campaign urging all Asians not to register even if it meant being sent to prison.

On 31 July, the final deadline for registration at the permit office, two thousand Indians from all over the Transvaal attended a meeting outside the mosque in Pretoria, which was presided over by Yusuf Ismail Mian, acting chairman of the British Indian Association. The overall mood of those present was summed up by Ahmed Muhammad Kachalia, a trader from Marabastad, who declaimed, "I swear in the name of God that I can be hanged, but I will not submit to this law!"

As the struggle advanced, Gandhi decided that the term "passive resistance" needed to be changed since it suggested weakness, and he offered a prize to anyone who could suggest a good alternative. One of his nephews, Maganlal Gandhi, suggested *sadagraha* (firmness in a good cause) but Gandhi preferred a slightly different word, *satyagraha*. *Satya*, meaning truth, also implies love, while *graham*, meaning firmness, generates power. Thus, satyagraha is the power that is born of truth, love and nonviolence.

With very few Indians registering, the government extended the deadline several times, but a mere 5% of the community responded. Many Indians did capitulate over time, but Gandhi remained steadfast. He was arrested and asked the court for the heaviest penalty provided by the law, which was six months' hard labour and a fine of £500. The magistrate sentenced him to two months' imprisonment without hard labour. Before long, a number of fellow satyagrahis, including a few members of the local Chinese community, joined him in the Johannesburg prison.

While Gandhi was in prison, Smuts sent him a draft agreement aiming to settle their differences. Gandhi consulted his fellow prisoners, who did not like the vague and pretentious language of the proposed pact. Thambi Naidoo, a Tamil satyagrahi, and Leuing Quinn, president of the Chinese Association, amended it slightly and Gandhi and his colleagues then signed it.

A few days later, on 30 January 1908, Gandhi was taken from his police cell to Pretoria for a meeting with General Smuts, who received him courteously and congratulated him on the firmness of the Indian community despite his imprisonment. Smuts promised to repeal the new law "as soon as most of you have undergone voluntary registration." After about two hours of discussion, Smuts told Gandhi he was free to leave and that he would instruct the prison authorities to release his colleagues.

Gandhi contacted Yusuf Mian and explained the situation to him. That night a meeting was held outside the mosque, attended by a thousand people, where Gandhi outlined his agreement with Smuts and asked everyone to register, pointing out that that there was no more question of coercion. Most agreed, but a minority were doubtful about trusting the authorities before the Act was repealed. However, Gandhi told them that a satyagrahi should never be afraid of trusting an opponent even after the trust had been betrayed many times.

A week later, when Gandhi, accompanied by Yusuf Mian and Thambi Naidoo, was walking from his office to the registration office less than a mile away they encountered some of the doubters. Gandhi tried to persuade them to join him, but they beat him senseless. Gandhi was rescued by passing Europeans, most notably Reverend Doke, later to become his first biographer, who also captured his assailants and handed them over to the police.

Smuts characteristically failed to carry out his promise and Gandhi called a meeting to burn the certificates of voluntary registration. About two thousand certificates were set alight in a cauldron outside the Hamida Mosque in Johannesburg by Yusuf Mian.

The Asiatic Registration Amendment Act was followed by the Immigration Restriction Act, which had a provision that people unable to speak a European language would not be allowed to immigrate, which made it clear that it was aimed against Indians. The Satyagraha Committee decided to test the right of educated Indians to enter the Transvaal by asking Parsi Rustomji and Sheth Daud Mohamed, two Indians who had established domicile rights in that province but were living in Natal and had some knowledge of English, to make a border crossing. When they arrived on the Transvaal-Natal border, they were arrested and deported back to Natal. Two weeks later, when they tried again and were arrested and fined £50, they refused to pay the fine and were jailed. More Indians from Natal followed and were also jailed. Some Transvaal Indians, including Gandhi's son Harilal, began to hawk goods without a licence and joined the others in prison. Gandhi was jailed twice for not having a registration certificate.

The South African government continually found new ways of harassing the Indians in order to force them to comply with its racist legislation. Deportation from one province to another, or to India, was a common tactic even before Gandhi's lobbying visit to the UK in June 1909. Gandhi helped the deportees to make arrangements for their return to India and managed to get volunteers to accompany them on their journey.

Other forms of harassment included degrading treatment of Indian prisoners and denial of adequate facilities to them during winter, which led to a few deaths. Despite the difficulties, the satyagrahis did not give up and went on hunger strikes when they needed to. The Transvaal Indians were particularly courageous. In *Satyagraha in South Africa*, Gandhi singles out two outstanding volunteers, Thambi Naidoo and Ahmad Muhammad Kachalia, both from the Transvaal. Kachalia lived initially in Marabastad and Naidoo's family lived in Marabastad and Doornfontein, Johannesburg. The children and grandchildren of both these freedom fighters played a major role in the continuing struggle against apartheid in the twentieth century. Five generations of Naidoo's family were incarcerated during the hundred years of struggle for human rights in South Africa.

Naidoo was a strongly built man who placed duty before self. "He shone equally, whether he had to take the chair at meetings and lead them [the people], or whether he had to do porter's work," Gandhi recalled later. He had little formal education but managed to speak English quite well. He had a keen intelligence with an ability to grasp new subjects quickly and so acquired some knowledge of Tamil, Hindi, Telugu, and a few African languages as well. His wit was edged with a sharp sense of irony and humour.

Of Kachalia, Gandhi wrote, "I have never come across a man who could surpass Mr Kachalia in courage and steadfastness. He sacrificed his all for the community's sake. He was always a man of his word." Born in Surat, India, Kachalia was a strict orthodox Muslim and treated people of all faiths and affiliations equally. Humility and simplicity were his particular trademarks.

Kachalia kept his promise to resist the Black Act, which he had made publicly in Johannesburg on 31 July 1908 at the anti-registration meeting attended by two thousand Indians. During the struggle against the Act, his European creditors peremptorily called up their loans at the instigation of the Transvaal government, intimating that they would not press for their loans if he withdrew from the satyagraha movement. Kachalia's assurances went unheeded, and he declared bankruptcy. A year later, however, he repaid his creditors in full and limited his enterprise considerably to protect himself from any further vulnerability.

Kachalia's quality of courageously sticking to his principles was inherited by his children. His sons, Maulvi and Yusuf, were active in the freedom movement in the 1940s and 1950s. His daughter-in-law, Amina, was also active in the freedom struggle and played a prominent role in the Transvaal Indian Youth Congress and Transvaal Indian Congress. Together with Helen Joseph, Lillian Ngoyi, and Ida Mtwana, she founded the Federation of South African Women, which in 1956 mobilized about 20,000 women to march to the Union Buildings in Pretoria to protest against the Pass Laws. Amina was placed under house arrest, imprisoned and banned at various times, but the government was unable to break her spirit and she continued her political activities.

She and her husband were close friends of Nelson Mandela. When she passed away on 31 January 2013, the Nelson Mandela Foundation issued a statement on that friendship, noting, "On 1 June 1986, when he was in Pollsmoor Prison, Mandela wrote her a letter saying: 'I love you and Yusuf very much and you are always in my thoughts . . . There is, therefore, no danger whatsoever of me forgetting you.'" She became a Member of Parliament after South Africa's first democratic elections in 1994 and was awarded the Order of Luthuli for her contribution to the freedom struggle.

It was against this background, with Botha and Smuts about to travel to England for discussions on creating a White-ruled Union of South Africa, that Gandhi was asked by the Indian community to lead a deputation to London to lobby on their behalf. The other members of the deputation were Sheth Haji Habib, Kachalia, and VA Chattiar, chairman of the Tamil Benefit Society. Unfortunately, Kachalia and Chattiar were arrested, so

Gandhi and Haji Habib sailed without them on the *Kenilworth Castle* on 23 June 1909.

By that time, the conflict between the Indians and the government in South Africa had reached a stalemate. The government had lost some court cases brought by Indians, but many Indians were getting tired of the satyagraha and regarded the satyagrahis as misguided idealists. One reason for this was that many of the Transvaal Indians were passenger Indians and wanted to get on with settling down in their chosen country. Some were supporting relatives in India.

In England, Gandhi and Haji Habib did a considerable amount of lobbying and had discussions with Lord Ampthill, a former governor of Madras and president of the South Africa British Indian Committee, who acted as a go-between for them. After conferring with the South African leaders, Ampthill brought back a message that "General Botha appreciates your feelings in the matter, and is willing to grant you minor demands. But he is not ready to repeal the Asiatic Act or to amend the Immigrants Restriction Act. He also refuses to remove the colour bar which has been set up as the law of the land." Ampthill then exhorted compromise and urged them to postpone their demands to a later, more opportune time.

Haji Habib told Lord Ampthill that he represented the majority of the community, which "also holds the major portion of the community's wealth," and was willing to accept Botha's offer in order to end their suffering. Gandhi translated his sentences faithfully word by word and then, on behalf of the satyagrahis, said, "The Indians for whom I speak are comparatively poor and inferior in numbers, but they are resolute unto death."

While in London, Gandhi happened to share a platform with an extremist fringe inspired by the firebrand Indian nationalist Vir Damodar Savarkar, who was disdainful of nonviolence as a strategy against oppression. Years later in India, in one of those remarkable coincidences that pepper history, it was one of Savarkar's disciples, Naturam Vinayak Godse, who assassinated Gandhi.

It was on his way back from this visit to England that Gandhi wrote his booklet *Indian Home Rule* on board the *SS Kildonan*, which became the blueprint for India's freedom.

Back in South Africa, the satyagraha movement was flagging and the satyagrahis had been reduced to a small group of people, largely Tamils, whose families were dependent on the Passive Resistance Council for support. Shortly after Gandhi disembarked in Cape Town, he received a telegram from his friend Gopal Krishna Gokhale, the Indian nationalist leader and member of the Viceroy's Imperial Council in India, informing him that RJ Tata, the illustrious industrialist and philanthropist, had donated 20,000 Rupees (£1500) to the satyagraha movement in the Transvaal. It could not have arrived at a better time. Then came Hermann Kallenbach's gift of Tolstoy Farm, which became the site of Gandhi's school as well as commune.

In 1910, the government of India, on Gokhale's advice, made a strong recommendation to Downing Street that the recruitment of indentured labour for Natal should be discontinued. Lord Ampthill, too, put pressure on the British government to take action. Consequently, indentured emigration to Natal was prohibited from 1 July 1911. In February 1911, the South African government introduced a bill to repeal Act 2 of 1907 (which forced all Indians to register themselves) in all parts of the Union except the Orange Free State, which was unyielding in its determination to maintain race-oriented laws.

Deportations, beatings, jail sentences, confiscation of property, and a number of other penalties made it increasingly difficult for Gandhi to hold on to his followers.

Chapter 7

Tolstoy Farm, Gokhale and Accord With Smuts

WHILE CONTINUING THE SATYAGRAHA STRUGGLE, GANDHI set up a commune for satyagrahis, incorporating a small school at Lawley, twenty miles from Johannesburg. It was named Tolstoy Farm. Gandhi admired Tolstoy's ideas, which he had expounded in *The Kingdom of God Is Within You*, and had an ongoing correspondence with him. It was then that our family came into contact with him, largely through that school, to which Velshi Keshavjee sent his second son Rajabali as a pupil.

It is not clear why Velshi Keshavjee sent ten-year-old Rajabali to Gandhi's school in 1912, but there are various explanations that seem plausible. One is that the original members of the Ismaili community were concerned about maintaining the cultural identity of their children who had grown up in South Africa. They wanted particularly to ensure that their children could speak their mother tongue, Gujarati. Since much of the Khoja Ismaili religious education material was in Gujarati, they also feared that if their children did not learn that language, they would lose their religious identity.

The young generation did not live as their parents had done in India. For example, Jivanbapoo's eldest son, Madhavjee, then in his early twenties, was a natty dresser who was fond of barrelling along the road between Pretoria and Germiston on his motorcycle with his cousin Allibhai, Velshibapoo's eldest son, as a pillion passenger. While that could be attributed to the exuberance of youth, some of his other habits were difficult for the older generation to brush away. Kanjee Kassam Panchaan, who was employed by Jivanbapoo in his Bloed Street shop, was particularly incensed about Madhavjee's practice of using the phone in the shop to instruct the domestic servant to bring him tea in a bone china cup and saucer. He cautioned Madhavjee's mother, Ladoobai Varin (who was his cousin) that the young man was falling prey to the egregious excesses of affluence.

Velshi Keshavjee may have been influenced to choose Gandhi's school by the satyagrahi Kachalia, who sent his eldest son Ali to Tolstoy Farm. Another person who may also have extolled the virtues of Gandhi's school was Jetashanker Pranshanker Vyas, a bookkeeper who was in charge of Gandhi's business affairs in Pretoria. Gandhi used to stay at his home on Vermeulen Street whenever he was in Pretoria. Vyas, who had migrated from Rajkot in 1896, owned a general dealer's business as well as a bookkeeping agency. He was also bookkeeper to the Keshavjee family and taught Gujarati to their children. Rajabali was not the only Muslim pupil at Gandhi's school. Among the others were Mohamed Abed, whose family originated from Lachpur in India, and Mustapha Mossam, whose family lived in Nelspruit in the Transvaal.

Tolstoy Farm comprised 1,100 acres with two wells and a spring, and about a thousand orange, apricot, and plum trees. It had been bought by Hermann Kallenbach, a rich architect of German Jewish origin who was a friend of Gandhi and had offered it to him rent-free to further the satyagraha movement. It was Kallenbach who had suggested naming it Tolstoy Farm. The farm had only basic facilities, in keeping with the spartan ideals of Tolstoy and Gandhi.

The farm had separate accommodations for men and women, a schoolhouse and a workshop for carpentry and shoemaking. All the buildings were simple corrugated iron structures. Some skilled workers were hired for the more specialized aspects of the construction, while the satyagrahis did all the unskilled work themselves under the supervision of a European mason engaged by Kallenbach. A Gujarati carpenter, Narayandas Damania, volunteered his services free of charge and persuaded other carpenters to work on the project for a minimal fee.

The population of the farm fluctuated from time to time, depending on who was arrested by the government. The community grew its own food and ground its own wheat for bread baked by Gandhi each day. Some of the wheat was toasted to make caffeine-free caramel coffee, using a recipe provided by Gandhi. Marmalade was prepared from the farm oranges and the settlers made their own peanut butter.

The meals were frugal. For breakfast, there was wheaten coffee and bread at 6 a.m. Lunch was rice, daal, and vegetables. Supper, at 5.30 p.m., was normally wheat pap and milk, or bread and coffee. Each person ate from a simple bowl with a wooden spoon made on the farm and washed up his or her own bowl and spoon after the meal. Cooking pots were cleaned by different people in turn.

The daily routine ended with singing of bhajans and readings from the Hindu, Muslim, and Christian scriptures. There was very little furniture. The satyagrahis were provided with two blankets each, one on which to sleep on the floor and the other to cover themselves. Care was taken not to foul the environment. Rubbish was buried in trenches and waste water collected in buckets and used to water the trees. Food and vegetable refuse was utilized as manure. Night soil was deposited in shallow pits, covered with earth and left to be transformed by anaerobic bacteria into odourless dry fertilizer that could be sold.

Small workshops were started to help make the community self-supporting. Kallenbach had spent some time at a Trappist monastery in Natal to learn sandal-making, which he taught to Gandhi, who in turn taught it to the others. Kallenbach, who knew basic carpentry, was in charge of the woodwork department. Gandhi learnt to make school benches, chests of drawers, and other items. Self-reliance was the cornerstone of the commune. Men shaved each other and cut one another's hair. Since they all laboured, they wore workmen's trousers and shirts stitched from coarse blue cloth by the women. Velshibapoo often wrote to Gandhi, who, despite his busy schedule, replied to him as well as to others. Gandhi kept a meticulous diary in which he noted whom he had met each day and to which letters he had replied.

There were two teachers at the school, Gandhi and Kallenbach. Gandhi was also involved in legal work and Kallenbach had his own architectural office in Johannesburg, so they went on foot to Johannesburg in the morning and returned to teach in the afternoon. They would be totally exhausted by the end of the day. Gandhi imparted moral education to the children, largely by acquainting himself with the Qur'an, the Vedas, the Bible, and the Avesta. Velshibapoo was so confident of the knowledge and intentions of Gandhi, a Hindu, that he also entrusted him with the responsibility of teaching Rajabali Ismaili devotions, in Gujarati, a language which was common to both Gandhi and the Ismailis hailing from Gujarat.

Gandhi used to send the children on errands to Johannesburg, which they loved to visit even though it meant a twenty-two-mile walk. As a matter of principle, he allowed rail travel, in a third class compartment, only when the journey was on farm business. Anyone wishing to go on a recreational trip had to walk and carry their own provisions with them. No one was allowed to spend money on themselves in the city. The walk would begin at 2.30 a.m. and the group would reach Johannesburg six or seven hours later. On one such journey, Rajabali was too exhausted to continue and Gandhi then carried him on his shoulders for part of the journey. My cousin Murad Velshi recalls his father showing him the route along which Gandhi carried him.

Rajabali doubtlessly found Tolstoy Farm a unique and enjoyable learning experience. On his return, he became a volunteer religion teacher in the Ismaili community in Pretoria and Velshibapoo's right-hand man in the business of V Keshavjee and Sons. The ethic of service was central to his values as was the practice of social engagement that Gandhi had instilled in him. Throughout his life, he remained a vegetarian due to Gandhi's influence. He cared for lepers in Pretoria, visiting them regularly, and also did a great deal for prisoners and helped them to rehabilitate. One abiding testimony to his association with Gandhi was that he willed both his eyes to charity and, on his death in 1960, parts of them were used to help four people to regain their sight. That noble act some twenty-eight years later inspired his nephew Madat, Jivanbapoo's grandson, who like him was a vegetarian, to do the same, enabling other people to regain their sight after he died in an accident in Dallas, Texas.

Gokhale visited South Africa in the autumn of 1912 and held talks with Botha and Smuts, after which he reported to Gandhi that the Black Act would be repealed, the three-pound poll tax on formerly indentured Indians would be abolished and restrictions on Asian immigration would be based explicitly on social and economic grounds rather than race. Gandhi was doubtful that Botha and Smuts would keep their word. When Gokhale left South Africa a few days later, he requested Gandhi to return to India within the year and join the struggle for that country's independence, but Gandhi declined to do so since he felt he was still needed in South Africa. Soon after Gokhale's visit, Smuts announced in Parliament that the Whites of Natal were not willing to end the three-pound poll tax.

In March 1913, a court judgment added fuel to the fire. It involved the right of one Bai Mariam to join her husband, a Muslim who had migrated from India to the Cape. Justice Malcolm Searle of the Cape Provincial Division of the Supreme Court ruled that only marriages that were celebrated according to Christian rites and recorded by a registrar of marriages were legally valid. When Gandhi told his wife Kasturba about the ruling, she was so incensed that she decided to join the satyagraha struggle, which until then had attracted only men.

The government's failure to abide by its undertaking to Gokhale was the last straw for Gandhi, and he once again asked Indians to defy the racist laws. In September, a group of twelve men and four women left Durban for Volksrust to cross the border into the Transvaal. They included Kasturba, two other women from Gandhi's family, Parsi Rustomji, Ramdas Mohandas Gandhi, Gokuldas Hansraj, and Revashankar Ratansi Sodha. They were prevented from crossing the border, tried under the new Act as prohibited immigrants, and deported to the Natal border. When they attempted to cross into the Transvaal again, they were sentenced to terms ranging from one to three months with hard labour.

Soon thereafter, a group of eleven women from Tolstoy Farm crossed the border from the Transvaal into Natal without immigration permits. One of them was pregnant, while six others were accompanied by infants. All but one were Tamils.* For unexplained reasons, the police did not arrest them and they marched thirty-six miles to Newcastle, the mining centre of Natal. There, they persuaded some 3000 indentured Indian miners to go on strike to protest against the three-pound tax and the Searle judgment. The police then arrested the women and they were sentenced to three months with hard labour each.

During their incarceration, Gandhi stayed in Newcastle with an Indian couple, Mr and Mrs DM Lazarus, who also played host to the other satyagrahis. Soon, some 2000 strikers were camped within sight of the Lazarus home. In October 1913, Gandhi set out from Newcastle for the Transvaal with his "army of peace" consisting of 2037 men, 127 women and 57 children. At Volksrust, Gandhi was arrested and sentenced to a £60 fine or nine months' imprisonment with hard labour. He chose the latter and was sent to prison in Bloemfontein in the Orange Free State. He thus became one of the very few Indians in twentieth century history who could boast of having been able to stay overnight in the province! Soon, two other marchers, Kallenbach and Polak, were also sentenced to three months behind bars with hard labour. The remaining satyagrahis continued their march.

Gandhi's plan was for the demonstrators to march into the Transvaal and, if they were not arrested, to converge on Tolstoy Farm. The marchers were stopped when they reached Balfour, a town near Johannesburg, and herded into special trains to be returned to Natal. The indentured Indians among them were sentenced to various terms of imprisonment, to be served by working in mines, which were designated as outstations of the Dundee and Newcastle jails. However, the prisoners refused to descend to the coal face despite beatings. As the news of their mistreatment spread, Indian workers all over Natal went on strike in sympathy, only to be set upon by mounted military police. On one occasion, the military killed and wounded several people.

The passive resistance campaign began to attract support in India and internationally. After the Viceroy of India took the unprecedented step of publicly criticizing South Africa, the Union government established an enquiry commission to look into the issue. On the commission's recommendation, Gandhi, Polak, and Kallenbach were released on 18 December 1913. Gandhi was dissatisfied with the composition of the commission because of the anti-Indian bias of two of its members, but Smuts refused to reconstitute it, so Gandhi boycotted its proceedings.

While the commission was conducting its enquiry, White railway workers went on strike for higher wages, bringing the entire South African rail network to a standstill. Gandhi was reluctant to take advantage of the government's predicament and announced that the passive resistance actions would be suspended for the duration of the strike. His decision lightened the atmosphere between the parties, and through a number of letters and conversations he was able to negotiate an agreement with Smuts. He was helped in that by Charles Freer Andrews, an emissary sent by Gokhale, and Sir Benjamin Robertson, an emissary of the Viceroy of India. According to the agreement, the satyagraha would be suspended and all satyagrahis would be released from jail. The enquiry commission issued a report recommending acceptance of the Indians' main demands. The agreement was then incorporated into the Indian Relief Bill and submitted to the Union Parliament.

Under that legislation, all monogamous Indian marriages solemnized by Hindu, Muslim, and Parsi traditions were recognized as valid, the three-pound tax was abolished, and tax arrears were cancelled. A domicile certificate bearing the holder's thumbprint was made sufficient evidence of the right to enter the Union. However, the main provisions of the Black Act still remained in force, banning Indians from moving freely from one province to another, and the entry of Indian labourers into South Africa was to stop totally after 1920. The Union Immigration Restriction Act also remained in force, but six educated Indians were to be allowed to immigrate into South Africa every year.

It was when Gandhi travelled to Pretoria for his negotiations with Smuts that his contact with the Keshavjee family was renewed. CF Andrews used Velshibapoo's home to prepare some of his paperwork. Often, he and Gandhi needed transportation to and from Pretoria town for the meetings as well as for discussions with Indian leaders, some of whom lived in the Prinsloo Street area in downtown Pretoria while others lived in Marabastad. Velshi Keshavjee was one of the few people who had a dray, and he made it available to Gandhi and CF Andrews.

By that time, Marabastad had become an unglamorous ghetto. One square mile in size, it was on the margins of the White areas geographically but light years away from the consciousness of the Whites. It was divided by a number of dusty murram roads running from north to south and numbered consecutively from one to twelve. At equal distances between these roads and parallel to them were three paved streets: Von Wielligh in the extreme west, which was well maintained; Jerusalem, which was badly tarred; and Cowie Street, a little further to the east. Intersecting all these roads were four poorly maintained tarred streets running east to west: Bloed, Grand (also known as Aurangazeb), Boom, and Barber. Boom was a feeder road for all the major traffic from the town centre to Pretoria West, so it was relatively better maintained than the other three. There was yet another street running from east to west named Mogul Street, but for some reason it did not warrant tarring.

On a clear day, the residents of Marabastad could see a grand set of colonial buildings perched on top of Meintjieskop hill overlooking their part of the town. Designed by the British architect Sir Herbert Baker, who also designed the Law Courts in Nairobi and the Parliament building in New Delhi, the Union Buildings were an intrusive expression of the swollen pride of Empire and had been chosen as the administrative seat of the Union government. In spring, their beautiful red sandstone merged with the bluish mauve of the flowers on the hundreds of jacaranda trees around it, creating a marvellous pattern of stone and vegetation under the azure summer sky. Jacaranda trees could also be found all over the town, making Pretoria one of the most beautiful urban areas in the world.

To the north of Marabastad stands the Magaliesburg mountain, like a giant wall between Marabastad and the White areas beyond. At its foot runs the Apies River, which Winston Churchill swam to escape from the Boers during the Anglo-Boer War, with the dense vegetation on its banks infested by grasshoppers and baboons. On cold winter mornings in the early part of the twentieth century, the high veldt plateau exuded a sharp aroma of mint, combined with charcoal smoke wafting from the braziers used by Africans to keep themselves warm. Occasionally, one could see an African watchman, wearing a warm brown overcoat and a balaclava, slowly crossing the veldt with his dog.

By 1914, Velshibapoo, who was the same age as Gandhi, had established himself in a single-storey building of wood and corrugated iron at 349 Grand Street in Marabastad. The building, on the northeast corner of Grand and Sixth Streets, consisted of a shop at the front and a house at the back. The corrugated sheets were painted a dull grey, and in front of the house was a *stoep* (verandah). Velshibapoo lived here with his wife Jabuma, four sons, and two daughters.

Velshibapoo traded largely with the Coloureds to the south of Marabastad and the Africans to the north. Some Whites also came to the shop. Africans from the outskirts of Pretoria were beginning to provide cheap labour in the centre of the city, which was becoming prosperous on account of the gold rush in the Transvaal. They would often spend as much as a guinea coin, which was the normal means of wage payment. Ndebele women, wearing necklaces and armbands of brightly coloured beads, came from outside Pretoria to buy beads.

During the final days of negotiation with Smuts, Gandhi and Andrews used to turn up at Velshibapoo's house, where Jabuma would serve Gujarati food to them and their colleagues. Gandhi would also visit Kachalia on Boom Street. After spending some time there, he would return to Velshibapoo's shop for a ride back to Pretoria town or the Union Buildings, where he would meet Smuts. By then, Gandhi eschewed all material possessions and no longer dressed like a dapper lawyer. He had already taken his brahmachari vows relating to lifestyle and behaviour, and was optimistic about the future of the Indians in the country.

He spent much time arguing with Velshibapoo, asserting that everything would work out well in the end. However, Velshibapoo complained about the conditions under which they had to trade and the continuing crippling restrictions confronting Indian businessmen. Despite Gandhi's assurances, he remained sceptical and reminded Gandhi that Smuts was first and foremost a politician with his own constituency to satisfy.

While Gandhi, Andrews, and Velshibapoo chatted, Velshibapoo's eldest son Allibhai, aged seventeen, and his nephew Goolam, aged seven, would sit respectfully and listen intently, impressed by the *vakil* (lawyer) who went to the Union Buildings to hold discussions with the government. When Velshibapoo asked them whether they would like to accompany Gandhi and Andrews for the ride to the Union Buildings, they seized the opportunity to do so with youthful enthusiasm.

♦

Some three-and-a-half decades later, on the south-west corner of the same Grand Street in Marabastad, a tall, imposing, athletically built African boxer-cum-lawyer, dressed in a blue worker's overall with a cap set jauntily on his head, knocked on the door of a house as he had been in the habit of doing for some time. While waiting on the stoep, he looked around furtively to see whether anyone had spotted him. The owner of the house, Mrs Thayanayagee Pillay, daughter of Thambi Naidoo, looked out of the front window, and after verifying that the visitor was Nelson Mandela she opened the door. Inside, he was greeted by friends and colleagues, including an Afrikaner jurist named Bram Fischer, a charismatic Indian doctor smoking a pipe whose name was Yusuf Dadoo, and a twenty-four-year-old student recently returned from London named Rhemtulla Velshi Keshavjee, who was the grandson of Velshibapoo.

Mrs Pillay's cooking, particularly her crab curry and lamb tripe, which was a favourite of Mandela's, was normally on the table for her visitors. After the meal, Mrs Pillay and her brothers-in-law Sooboo, Govind, and Naran, together with the visitors, went into a room at the back of the house where they looked over flyers and pamphlets printed by a Tamil named Sathya before discussing the activities planned for the next few days. The meetings were normally preparations for the Defiance Campaign that Mandela, as head of the African National Congress Youth League, was masterminding in collaboration with Dr Dadoo, Dr Naicker of the Natal Indian Congress, and activists from a number of other institutions.

Both, Gandhi's satyagraha and the later resistance by Mandela and his colleagues, may be described as "failures" initially. Gandhi's failure was due to satyagraha being out of place. Despite his overt optimism about what he had achieved, Gandhi's philosophy and strategy did not work in South Africa at that time. However, South Africa was the crucible in which he developed the art of the mobilizational politics that he would use with consummate skill later in India. As for his encounters with Smuts, although he was respectful of him at that time and for long afterwards, he was aware of his darker side. "First, he has some principles in politics, which are not quite immoral. Secondly, there is room in his politics for cunning and on occasions for perversion of the truth," he wrote. Smuts, for his part, was equally ambivalent, remarking at the time of Gandhi's departure with some irony, "The saint has left our shores, I sincerely hope for ever."

In the case of Nelson Mandela, arguably, his was a "failure" of time. South Africa was not yet ready for him in the fifties, sixties, seventies, and eighties of the twentieth century and considerable sacrifice would still be needed before apartheid, as a creed, imploded under the weight of its own contradictions and cruel absurdities. Thousands of people still had to suffer and pay the price for freedom, and Mandela had to spend ten thousand days in jail and undergo a comprehensive personal transformation before apartheid was finally jettisoned. It could only happen, as Desmond Tutu put it, quoting St Paul, "in the fullness of time." Meanwhile, of the millions of people struggling against apartheid, some died, others fled, some lived in exile and eventually returned to the country only to find that "tomorrow was another place." Some were "disappeared." Some of my family members emigrated.

The struggle, hard as it was, was not devoid of a silver lining. While India gave South Africa the lawyer Gandhi, South Africa reciprocated by sending back a Mahatma in the making. The struggle continued, and in its wake it produced another moral giant in Nelson Mandela. Thus, the fight for human dignity in South Africa produced two of the greatest men of the twentieth century, and the beauty was that neither of them embodied any bitterness or hatred towards any person. They became the moral icons of our times.

Chapter 8

Early 1920s: Emigration and Consolidation

WITH SOUTH AFRICA HAVING EFFECTIVELY CLOSED ITS DOORS to Indian immigrants by the end of the First World War, economic difficulties in Kathiawar continued to be an imperative for villagers to emigrate to other parts of Africa. As we have seen earlier, all of Keshavjeebapa's sons had migrated to South Africa, but his two daughters, Santok and Manek, remained in India even though their sons, Ebrahim and Valjee, had joined their maternal uncles in Pretoria.

Santok's daughter, Hirbai, was married to one Ismail Jinnah, of the Bhadiani family in Gondal. Manek had two daughters, for whom she found husbands in the village of Mengri near Rajkot. One of Manek's daughters, also named Hirbai, was married to Lalji Mangalji, whose father was a respected trader and the chief purchaser for the princely family of Rajkot. Lalji and Ismail emigrated separately in the early part of the twentieth century and settled in British East Africa and Portuguese East Africa respectively.

Indians had begun to settle in Portuguese East Africa in the early sixteenth century and it was still open to immigrants, who were allowed to trade relatively freely and live in European areas. Some Asians went into the interior to open small shops. One large leading Ismaili family, the Babools, who were in trade, were responsible for encouraging some members of our family to settle there and many Ismailis had established themselves by the beginning of the twentieth century.

In East Africa, a major railway line had been constructed from the Kenyan port of Mombasa to the border with Uganda by 1901and Indians were able to settle in Kenya as well as Uganda. There, too, Asians went into the interior and opened small shops. They played an important role as middlemen, introducing a monetary economy into the subsistence areas of East Africa.

The Indian migration to Africa eventually gave rise to large business families who came to play an important role in the commercial life of the colonies in which they settled as well as of the metropolitan areas in the Western world to which they moved decades later. An example was the migration from Gondal to Lourenço Marques of Ismail Jinnah with his nine-year-old son Gulamhussein around 1918. They went to the province of Inhambane where the Ismaili families of Jamal Hemraj and Jiwa Hemraj had already settled and were engaged in business with some success. Ismail worked with them and after some time set up his own shops in Inharrime and Jangamo districts. From that modest base, he started to deal in two products, cashew nuts, which he bought from African farmers, and textiles, which he imported from Portugal and India.

In the early 1940s, Ismail's son Gulamhussein (known as Gulamo) branched out and set up his own business in Lourenço Marques, supplying cashew nuts to an Ismaili industrialist, Jiwa Jamal Tharani, who had started the first cashew nut processing factory in the territory. Tharani had a streamlined factory, processing and packaging cashew nuts in small flat tins, labelled Amendoa de Cajou, for export to Portugal. In the late 1940s and early 1950s, Gulamhussein started trading directly with Portugal and also opened a business in Bombay which was run by his wife's nephew, Kamruddin Shivji. In the early 1960s, Gulamo was one of the first Ismailis to settle in Portugal, from where he started exporting raw textiles to Mozambique and Angola in partnership with Portuguese entrepreneurs.

The Lalji Mangalji family were equally adventurous and started a business in Mombasa in the early twentieth century. After a while, they ventured north into Wajir, in the semi-arid north-west part of Kenya, selling produce to the indigenous population there. Lalji Mangalji's three sons, Jafferali, Akbarali and Hassanali, continued the business activities in Wajir during the Second World War even though it was an area of direct conflict between Italian and British forces. Later, as part of their diversification activities, the Lalji Mangalji family moved to Uganda and purchased large coffee estates. In the late 1960s and early 1970s, they entered the hotel trade. When Idi Amin expelled the Asians from Uganda, they had already partly settled in Canada, owning some well-placed businesses there, including some buildings housing important Canadian government ministries, which they rented back to the government on 25-year leases. The *Ottawa Citizen* once summed up their story as moving "from tenants to landlords of the Canadian government." Their generosity matches their wealth and, as a family, they have contributed to many civic causes in Canada and elsewhere, including the developing world to further the causes of health and education through the AKDN network.

Gulamaly Nanji Bhaloo of Paanch Dwarka migrated to Masaka, Uganda in the early 1920s. Before doing so, he went to Rajkot in search of a bride, attracting the attention of Manekfaiba, who suggested her granddaughter Jena, (daughter of her own younger daughter, Sankubai) who was in her late teens. Gulamaly and Jena raised a family in Uganda, and later, following the expulsion of Asians from that country, their descendants settled in Australia, England, and Canada. Their eldest son, Rajabaly, gave unstinted support to many Ugandan expellees, personally filling out the forms needed for their departure and attending to their other needs till the last few refugees left.

The Sacoor brothers are another entrepreneurial family. Originally from Keshod in Gujarat and then Inhambane in Mozambique, they are descended from Naran Keshavjee, whose daughter Poori was married to Sacoor Alibhai. They arrived with very little capital in Lisbon in the 1970s, after the revolution in Mozambique, and established an enterprise that became a leading clothing company. Today, their name is synonymous worldwide with high-quality clothing. Their boutiques are found in nine countries, with seventy-five stores in, among other cities, Dubai, Singapore, Kuala Lumpur, London, Doha and Lisbon. Their grandfather, Sacoor Alibhai, after establishiing himself in business in Inhambane in the 1920s, invited his nephews from Keshod, Gulamhussein Esmail Kassam and Sadruddin Kassam, to settle in Mozambique. Gulamhussain married Khatija, Naran Keshavjee's youngest daughter, and Sadruddin married Sakerkhanoo, Naranbapoo's granddaughter. They settled in Zawalla, a town between Lourenço Marques and Inhambane and ran small shops catering to Portuguese settlers and the local African clientele.

Another important family that came to be related to the pioneer families in South Africa was that of Guiga Janmohamed, originally from Oona in India. Most of the Guiga Janmohamed males married into the Keshavjee family. Following the outbreak of revolution in Mozambique, Sultanaly Guiga and his family emigrated to Portugal, and through their Mozambican and Portuguese business connections they were able to establish a successful crockery store in the heart of the Portuguese capital. Madat, the eldest brother, who had been the mainstay of the family in Lourenço Marques, arrived in Lisbon in 1974. He opened a large shop in central Lisbon that he named Socoeuropa, where he sold some of the finest kitchenware in the country.

A family that is legendary in Mozambique is that of five Babool brothers from Oona—Vasanji, Pardhan, Noormahomed, Somji and Rawjee—who migrated to Mozambique in the last quarter of the nineteenth century and were well established in business by the early part of the twentieth century. They mainly exported produce to India and imported spices, which they sold in the hinterland of Central Africa. They also traded with neighbouring countries such as Northern and Southern Rhodesia and Nyasaland. Another section of the family arrived in South Africa in 1938, when Goolamali Rawjee Babool, known by the nickname Hoxie, after the American movie cowboy of that name, settled there. Although handicapped by an apartheid law that denied them the right to have refrigerators in their premises in the Asiatic Bazaar, the family set up a sea-food business, selling any stocks left at the end of the day at give-away prices. Later, they branched out, first into the produce business and then into the refrigeration of trucks, becoming the leading truck refrigeration company and fourth-largest fish distributors in South Africa. Today they have extensive business interests in South Africa and Mozambique, where they also run the first private medical university in the country.

It was through the Rawjee Babool family that Ahmed Keshavjee, a well-known social worker in the Portuguese East African Ismaili community, came to the notice of Naran Keshavjee in Pretoria. (They were not related.) Ahmed's family had started a business in Lourenço Marques in the early 1930s, selling coir mattresses, and later expanded into furniture, eventually developing their own furniture for sale to hotels and offices. In 1926, Ahmed married Naran Keshavjee's second daughter, Rahemat, who was known to be a lady of fashion and good taste. In 1974, the family moved to Lisbon, where they opened the first Indian restaurant in the capital.

While families from Kathiawar were looking for fresh opportunities in other parts of Africa, the Ismailis of South Africa, having won the right to remain in the country, consolidated their permanent residence by working hard to strengthen their business activities and sending their children to schools that provided them with secular education in the mornings, which was supplemented by basic education about their faith and heritage at a community school in the afternoon.

Velshibapoo and Naranbapoo as community elders played an important role in this. While Velshibapoo helped to establish the basic infrastructure for the community by leveraging his position in and outside the community, Naranbapoo provided the moral authority for the community to grow and develop. Among the key accomplishments of the Keshavjees during the 1920s were the acquisition of a bakery by the Velshi Keshavjee family; marriage of children who had either been born in the country or had grown up there to women largely from India; construction of a cinema by the Manjee Keshavjee family in close association with Kanjee Kassam Panchaan; and the acquisition of a Caltex petrol station by the Velshi Keshavjee family. For the Ismaili community at large, there was the construction of a purpose-built jamatkhana in the centre of the Asiatic Bazaar. The jamatkhana, which became the focal point of the Ismaili community's identity, has since been declared a heritage site.

During their lifetime, both Jivanbapoo and Manjeebapoo made sure that their children—sons as well as daughters—attended school. However, non-White children had access only to basic education, which was far below the level required for entry to university. The prevailing culture required boys to get a grounding in basic numeracy so that they could earn a living in the business world, while girls were expected to learn cooking, sewing, and housekeeping. Notwithstanding the restrictions, many young girls from the Ismaili community in South Africa, among them Kanjee Kassam Panchaan's daughters Sakina and my mother Koolsam, were sent to school, as were Velshibapoo's daughters Kulsam and Sherbanoo and Naranbapoo's daughters Rahemat and Khatija.

The only available educational institution was the Ferguson School on Lorentz Street in Marabastad, known popularly as the "Coloured school," which had been established by Miss Ferguson, a spinster from New Zealand. She was a Church Mission Society missionary and her mission was realized through teaching. As mentioned earlier, she was helped by her sister, Miss Emily, and a cousin, Miss Tarlton. They created a moral, though limited, educational universe for most of the youth in the Ismaili jamat and many others in the Asiatic Bazaar. Later, another school was allocated to Indians in the area and, predictably, it became known as the "Indian school." The pupils at Miss Ferguson's school were taught the Bible, which the parents did not mind as it imparted good values to their children. However, the moral and spiritual education of Muslim children attending the school was firmly embedded in their own faith of Islam as imparted to them by their community. Ismaili religious education was given by elders in the community, particularly Mongi Kassam Panchaan, my maternal grandmother, who was a teacher and whose brother VN Hooda in India had the responsibility of printing books for use in Ismalii religious schools. Hirbai, widowed daughter of Jivan Keshavjee, also imparted religious education to the younger generation, as did Saboor Chatoor Hooda, another of Mongi's brothers. Later, Manibai Kanji Nanji Hooda joined the team, as did Rajabali Velshi. Velshibapoo was constantly in touch with his cousin Merally Harji in Bombay, from whom he used to receive books on Ismaili religious education for the children. Merallybapoo occasionally visited South Africa and, during his visit, handed out silk handkerchiefs, as gifts to the children who attended religion classes.

In 1923, Velshibapoo decided to travel to Chotila. He had two main reasons for doing so. First, he wanted to fulfil his promise to repay all his father's financial debts. He is said to have gone from village to village to ascertain who was owed money and then repaid them. The second reason was the building of a jamatkhana in Chotila, on a piece of land owned jointly by him and Manjee Keshavjee. Velshibapoo approached Manjee's widow, Noorbai Jamal, and she agreed that he would have approved of such a donation, provided the Imam was happy to accept it. In India, Velshibapoo engaged local masons and supervised the construction of the building. Members of the Chotila jamat also pitched in to help with physical work. After ensuring that all the title deeds were transferred to the Imam, Velshibapoo returned to South Africa.

By the mid 1920s, many of the Ismailis between 15 and 23 years old had grown up in South Africa, and those in the upper part of that age group were regarded as being ready for marriage. The Ismailis, being a small endogamous group, wanted to find brides from within the community and, while there were a few marriages between cousins in South Africa, by and large brides had to be found among Ismailis outside the country. For that, the Keshavjees turned to their indomitable matchmaker Manekfaiba in India. She knew many people in the villages of Gujarat and could arrange the necessary introductions.

In 1927, Velshibapoo wanted his youngest son Habib, who was then about nineteen years old, to marry Amrath, the daughter of his friend Mohan Anandjee, the Ghee King of Chotila. He asked his maternal cousin Merally Harji to represent him in the negotiations and instructed Habib to seek his help in securing Amrath's hand.

However, Merallybapoo's negotiations with the Anandjees seemed to go nowhere. At one stage, Merallybapoo unfortunately slighted the Anandjee family in the course of the discussions, with the result that they suspended the negotiations. Velshibapoo became impatient for Habib to return and work in the growing family businesses in South Africa and wrote an impatient letter to him urging him to make up his mind and return as soon as possible. He exhorted his son not to waste time waiting for a simple Gujarati village girl, thus denigrating all Gujarati village girls. The letter was sent to Habib at the Anandjee home, where he was a house guest, and somehow the Anandjee family were apprised of its contents. The result was that they refused to let Habib marry Amrath.

Amrath was not only physically beautiful, she also had other appealing attributes. When she grew older, she emigrated to South Africa, where she married Jivanbapoo's eldest grandson, Noormohamed, and showed great business acumen, working side by side with her husband in addition to bringing up thirteen children. She ran a business, owned property, and managed the family accounts. Despite the race-based odds against her and her family, she managed to send her son Shawkat to Dublin to study medicine.

After the breakdown in negotiations with the Anandjees, Velshibapoo asked his cousin and friend in South Africa, Chagan Jiwa, to find a bride for his son. Chagan told him that he had a well-brought-up niece named Sakina in Vinchia, a town a few hours' train journey from Rajkot in Gujarat. She was the daughter of his sister Manibahen, whose husband, Chagan Meghji Pirbhai, was a prominent trader in the area. The Meghji Pirbhai family were advisors to the Maharaja of Jasdan. Chagan Jiwa offered to write to them. Velshibapoo then wrote to Habib, urging him to visit the Meghji Pirbhai family in Vinchia. Habib did so, in a specially decorated bullock cart, part of a marriage convoy known as a *jaan*, with musicians on horseback playing the shenai flute as they entered the town. He was received like the proverbial princely bridegroom from a distant land of opportunity and wealth. As was the custom, he was not allowed to see his wife, not even a photograph of her, until after their marriage. Manekfaiba might have disapproved of that, but she had probably been sidelined after the Anandjee debacle.

By the time Habib went back to South Africa in 1927, Velshibapoo had already acquired the ABC Bakery, which in the years to follow would become an important business enterprise as well as a social and political meeting place in Marabastad. The bakery had been started by a Chinese businessman, perhaps in the early part of the twentieth century, but in 1923, for reasons that are not clear, the business went bankrupt and Velshibapoo purchased it. Velshibapoo also acquired a few more plots of land with the bakery.

With Velshibapoo's four sons all married, he wanted to give them responsibilities in different parts of his growing business projects. He allocated the bakery to Rajabali, who was methodical and disciplined and whom he considered to be most likely to make a success of it. Rajabali, in turn, trained his two younger brothers, Cassim and Habib. Cassim learnt the art of baking and became chief baker, while Habib looked after the marketing and was responsible for sales and delivery. In addition, Habib worked in the Boom Street shop of V Keshavjee and Sons.

Around that time, Velshibapoo also bought a Caltex petrol station situated next to his wholesale business in Boom Street. It had been established by AC Kassam, a Memon, who planned to go into another business. After acquiring the petrol station, Velshibapoo added car repair facilities to it and named the enterprise Kay's Garage, which was run by his son Allibhai, for many years thereafter. It was the only Indian-owned garage in the Pretoria area for decades. Thus, by the middle of the 1920s, Velshibapoo was a successful businessman in Marabastad, owner of some prized enterprises which he was intent on expanding.

The Manjees, too, with the ascetic Naranbapoo as paterfamilias, were doing well, largely through the diligence of Ismail and Goolam, who by then were married. Their mother, Majeebapoo's widow Noorbai Jamal wanted to have her two eldest sons married and constantly spoke about it to her brother-in-law Naranbapoo, so he made arrangements for her to sail to India to assess possible bridal candidates. Noorbai wrote to Manekfaiba, her sister-in-law in Chotila, for help in her quest.

Manekfaiba asked around and then decided to approach the Hooda family of Tithwa, the village from which Noorbai originated. They had a daughter named Kulsum, a winsome young woman with light brown eyes, and Manekfaiba duly put forward a proposal that she be married to Ismail. For the younger Goolam, she approached the family of Nazaraly Vasta in the village of Wankaner for the hand of their daughter Jena. She then wrote back to Noorbai for photographs of her two sons, properly suited and booted, for submission to the two families.

In 1923, the Ismaili Imam, Sir Sultan Mahomed Shah Aga Khan, decided to visit his followers in Rajkot. It was customary to celebrate marriages on such occasions and Noorbai Jamal viewed it as an excellent opportunity to take her children to India to see the Imam. It would also enable her to meet some of her siblings who had been born after her departure from the country two decades earlier. Most of her family had adopted the Ithna Ashari persuasion of Shia Islam and consequently her contact with them had attenuated over time. The trip would also enable her to check out other potential brides for Ismail and Goolam. However, Noorbai needed to convince Naranbapoo, who had been named trustee of her inheritance by her husband, to give her the money for her seven children to accompany her. Naranbapoo was careful with money and difficult to persuade, so she asked Velshibapoo to talk to him. Velshibapoo, together with Kanjee Kassam Panchaan, approached Naranbapoo and prevailed upon him to agree to her request. Noorbai then started making arrangements to take her children, ranging in age from seven to twenty-three, as deck passengers aboard the *SS Karapara*.

They were accompanied by a few members of the community who had also decided to make the trip to India to see the Imam. They first went by road to Durban, where they stayed with the family of Amod Bayat, a generous full-bearded Surti Muslim businessman who was known to the Manjee Keshavjee family. Then they took the ship to India, spending a few days en route in Zanzibar with Aitmadi Jiwan Lalji, a leader of the Ismaili community who was known to Velshibapoo.

When they arrived in Bombay, Noorbai fell ill and they had to stay there while she recuperated. Once she was able to continue the journey, they hired a Ford pickup and made their way along the dusty track, first to Rajkot and then to Chotila. The trip took some fifteen hours. In Chotila, people were amazed by the large self-propelling "metal cart" packed with relatives from Africa. It was modern science coupled with affluence, perhaps the equivalent today of a space tourist arriving on the moon in a capsule.

Noorbai was told that her sister, whom she had not seen for twenty-three years, had passed away in Bombay and the news saddened her deeply. However, over time her grief lessened and was finally replaced by happiness when she saw her two sons married during the Imam's visit. She placed her younger children in a religious school in Chotila, where her husband's niece, Jivanbapoo's daughter Hirbai, who had been widowed during the flu epidemic, was a teacher, and spent two blissful months in the village. Then she visited her ancestral home in Tithwa before going back to South Africa in the *SS Karapara* with her children and two daughters-in-law. After their return, Ismail and Goolam were given a more settled role in M Keshavjee and Company, which was growing and beginning to compete with V Keshavjee and Sons in the wholesale trade.

In 1927, a major development occurred in the US that was to have a dramatic effect on cinemas all over the world. Until then, speech in films had been conveyed through subtitles. Then Hollywood came up with talkie films and people flocked to see the first full-length one, *The Jazz Singer*, in which Al Johnson, with his trademark blacked-up face, promised, "Wait a minute, wait a minute, you ain't heard nothin' yet." The words proved prophetic, not only for Hollywood but also for the Keshavjee family thousands of miles away. Together with their brother-in-law Ebrahim Kanjee Kassam (known as KK), the M Keshavjee and Company partners decided to go into the cinema business and embarked on building what was in South Africa called a bioscope.

There was already a cinema on Boom Street in Marabastad, the Bombay Star Bioscope, which had a brass band playing outside to attract passersby. It was run by some members of the Kanamia community under the leadership of two Muslims who were prominent in commerce, Sheikh Ahmed, who was also a flamboyant politician with good connections among government officials, and Ismail Vally.

Goolam and KK decided to build their celluloid dream palace, to be named Royal Kinema, on a plot of land at the corner of Fifth and Grand Streets, in front of the Manjee Keshavjee residence. Kanjee Kassam Panchaan, who was running his own business on Bloed Street with his son Ebrahim (KK), lent them £400 interest-free without security. They commissioned a group of Coloured builders to design and construct the building, but the project was denied building permits because only Whites were allowed to practise as architects. Ismail managed to persuade a local Afrikaner architectural firm, Dordrecht and Kie, to approve the plans prepared by his Coloured architect, and work on the cinema was resumed. The Royal Kinema opened its doors in 1928 amidst great fanfare, including a live band gloriously wending its way through the streets on a horse-drawn cart.

Meanwhile, Habib Velshi Keshavjee found the ABC Bakery did not provide him a sufficient income to feed his family, so he, too, decided to go into the cinema business, but part-time. A group of Whites were screening silent movies at a community centre called Dougal Hall on the outskirts of Marabastad, largely for Africans, but they were making losses. Habib took over the management of that enterprise and made it viable. He hired a horse and cart with a live brass band to go through the streets of

Marabastad to advertise the films with colourful posters.

Whites did not go to the Marabastad cinemas, because they had their own rather smarter ones in downtown Pretoria. Consequently, the Royal Kinema and Bombay Star were competing for the same non-white clientele. In the late 1920s, at around the same time as the Royal Kinema was being constructed, the owners of the Bombay Star began a project to build a modern cinema on Boom Street east, to be named Empire Bioscope. However, midway the owners ran out of funds. Banks refused to give loans because of insufficient collateral. Sheikh Ahmed and his partners therefore approached Suleiman Ebrahim Jalalpore, a Muslim Surtee businessman from Broederstrom, for a loan of £3000, interest-free and with the new cinema as collateral. However, once the cinema was built, Sheikh Ahmed and his partners fell out and Jalalpore found himself the owner of a fully constructed cinema which he could not operate, did not understand, and did not even want. Furthermore, the global Great Depression made the cinema a white elephant that no one wanted to buy. Finally, Habib Keshavjee rented the cinema from Jalalpore for about £16 a month and used it as a dance hall for the first three days of the working week and a cinema for the other three days. That resolved his own financial problems.

With the passage of time, the Bombay Star folded and the non-White cinema business in the Pretoria area came to be owned by Ismailis. The Royal Kinema belonged to the Manjee Keshavjee family in partnership with Ebrahim Kanjee Kassam. The Empire Cinema, owned by Suleiman Ebrahim Jalalpore, was eventually sold to Habib Velshi Keshavjee. The third cinema, the Orient People's Palace, was partly financed by Madhavjee Jivan Keshavjee and Kanji Vally in partnership with Rambhai Patel and Jiwa Barber, a Hindu and a Sunni Muslim respectively.

The government restricted what could be shown to non-Whites in cinemas. For example, films with scenes in which people of different races mixed socially were considered abhorrent because they might encourage miscegenation in South Africa. Similarly, scenes of violence might lead to murderous behaviour among the "lesser" races, that would be turned against the Whites. Therefore the owners of cinemas in Marabastad found it safer to screen films that had already been shown elsewhere in the country, with "objectionable" scenes cut out, or purely educational ones, for example on subjects such as health. Thus, in addition to providing temporary relief from the harshness of daily life in South Africa, the cinemas contributed to social life when the inhabitants had few civic services.

In the early 1930s the Royal Kinema became a venue for community gatherings of South African Indians. The Indian Women's Organisation (IWO) prepared food and knitted jerseys to be auctioned to raise funds for charity at the cinema. The IWO was run by far-sighted Tamil women in Pretoria, such as Archiamal Pillay and Athiamal Chetty. Sakina KK Khoja was an active member and played a leading role. Among those attending the events were enlightened Whites such as the mother of the deputy prime minister, Mrs Hoffmeyr, and the wife of the director of immigration, Mrs Kincaid, who were concerned about the wellbeing of Indian women and contributed to the IWO. Mrs Maharaj Singh, wife of the agent-general of India to South Africa, also attended some functions. Through Sakina, most of her daughters got involved in charitable work.

Additionally, the cinemas were a safe place for political meetings where activists like Yusuf Dadoo and Maulvi Kachalia had discussions with local people when they came to Pretoria. At first they met at the ABC Bakery, but later they started doing so at the cinemas.

The cinemas gave the Keshavjee family a reliable cash flow. It was not very much, because the takings could not have been that great with the tickets for stalls starting at 9 pence and for gallery seats at 2 shillings and 11 pence. However, the steady income enabled the family to find new ways of creating wealth. Even the apartheid government received some—unintended—benefits from cinemas: the police often waited in their nylon-meshed trucks for the cinema audiences to come out and conducted inspections of the pass books that all Africans were required to carry. Anyone whose pass book was not in order was arrested.

Naranbapoo died in 1927, leaving M Keshavjee and Company in the hands of his three nephews, Ismail, Goolam, and Ebrahim (KK). Velshi Keshavjee, the only senior Keshavjee left, became leader of the Ismailis of Pretoria, working closely with other pioneers such as Chagan Jiwa, Kanjee Kassam Panchaan, and Cassim Ali. By then, the jamat had established its presence. It had ties with the Ismaili institutional leadership in Zanzibar, and most of the community members who had come from India were successful businessmen. The Jamat felt it was time to seek permission of the Imam to build a jamatkhana that would represent the growing importance of the Ismaili community in South Africa. They felt that it should be constructed on a plot of land next to the original jamatkhana on Boom Street, which had been built by Jivanbapoo many years previously. Wishing it to be the most striking building in Marabastad and one of the finest jamatkhanas in Africa, the Council, after gaining the requisite permissions from the Imam's representative in Zanzibar, commissioned an architectural firm in which Gandhi's close friend Kallenbach was a partner, to design the building.

Under Velshibapoo's direction, Ismail Manjee Keshavjee spent considerable time personally supervising the construction of the jamatkhana. The entire jamat was involved in the process in one way or another. The foundation stone was laid on 9 November 1929 by Velshi Keshavjee and the jamatkhana was formally opened on 2 July 1930 by Rai Fazal Mahomed Ebrahim of Zanzibar, accompanied by Moloo Alarakhia Dossani and attended by the whole jamat. To mark the occasion, Velshibapoo called the jamat together for a communal feast.

While the South African jamat was being consolidated, relatives of the Keshavjee clan who had settled elsewhere in Africa had various travails and problems of their own, depending on the colonial policies of the European powers in thier region. Velshi Keshavjee's daughters, Kulsam and Sherbanoo, who had married into the Guiga Janmohamed family, were settled in Mozambique, as were Naranbapoo's three daughters and other women from some of the pioneer families. The Great Depression made the lives of these new arrivals to Africa difficult and perilous.

Though racial segregation was prevalent in all the African colonies, it would be fair to say that none of them faced the stringent and often inhuman restrictions that non-Whites did in South Africa. In Portuguese East Africa, Indians were allowed to live and trade in European areas. In Uganda, Asians successfully became important middlemen in the economic system and helped to monetise the subsistence economy over time. That was in contrast to South Africa, where successive governments first tried to deny citizenship to Indians and then relegated them to the status of second-class citizens. Many years would pass before Indians could enjoy the privileges of equal citizenship in a free country.

FAMILY TREE

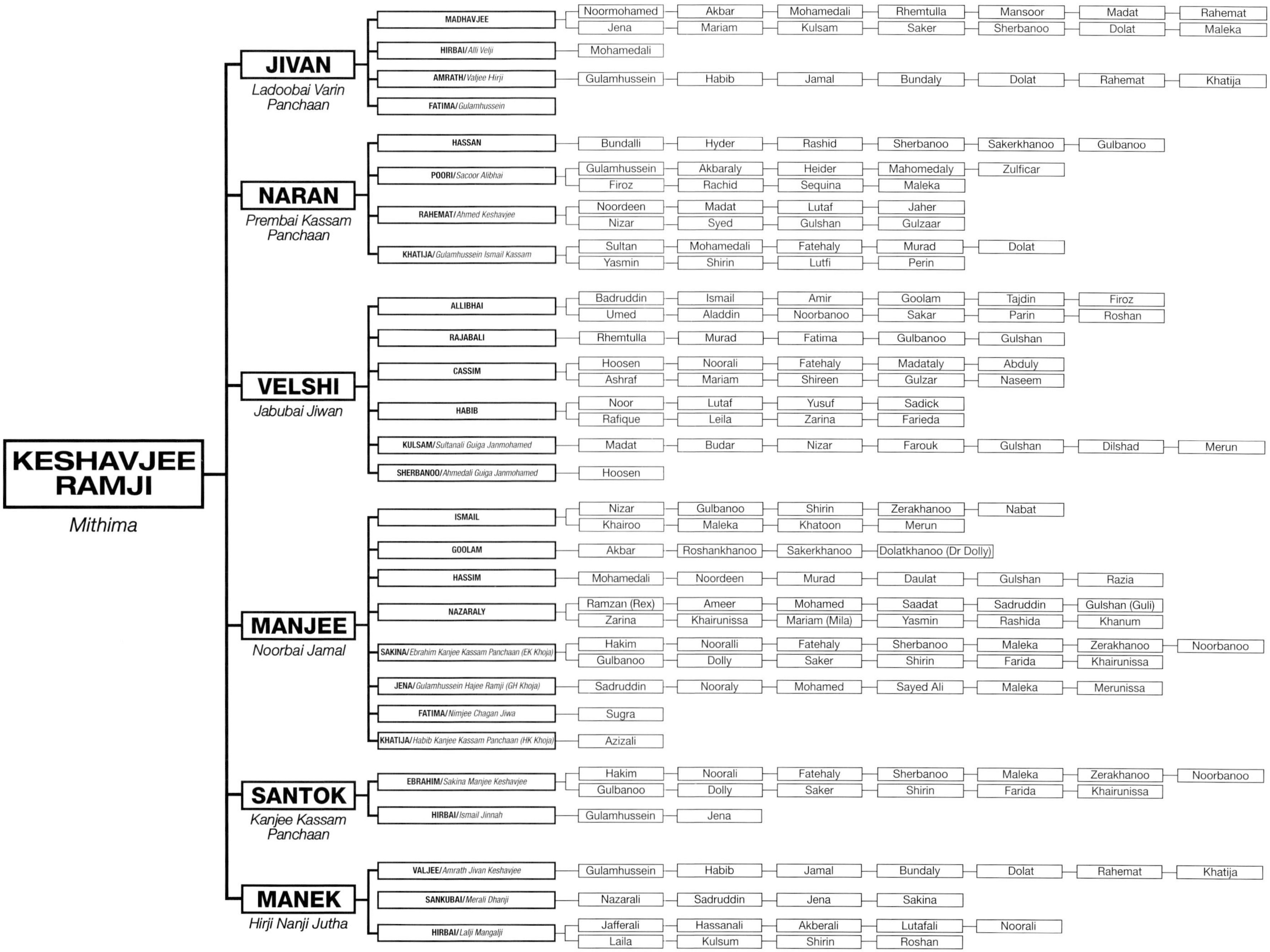

KESHAVJEE RAMJI
Mithima
JIVAN
Ladoobai Varin Panchaan
MADHAVJEE
Noormohamed
Akbar
Mohamedali
Rhemtulla
Mansoor
Madat
Rahemat
Jena
Mariam
Kulsam
Saker
Sherbanoo
Dolat
Maleka
HIRBAI/Alli Velji
Mohamedali
AMRATH/Valjee Hirji
Gulamhussein
Habib
Jamal
Bundaly
Dolat
Rahemat
Khatija
FATIMA/Gulamhussein
NARAN
Prembai Kassam Panchaan
HASSAN
Bundalli
Hyder
Rashid
Sherbanoo
Sakerkhanoo
Gulbanoo
POORI/Sacoor Alibhai
Gulamhussein
Akbaraly
Heider
Mahomedaly
Zulficar
Firoz
Rachid
Sequina
Maleka
RAHEMAT/Ahmed Keshavjee
Noordeen
Madat
Lutaf
Jaher
Nizar
Syed
Gulshan
Gulzaar
KHATIJA/Gulamhussein Ismail Kassam
Sultan
Mohamedali
Fatehaly
Murad
Dolat
Yasmin
Shirin
Lutfi
Perin
VELSHI
Jabubai Jiwan
ALLIBHAI
Badruddin
Ismail
Amir
Goolam
Tajdin
Firoz
Umed
Aladdin
Noorbanoo
Sakar
Parin
Roshan
RAJABALI
Rhemtulla
Murad
Fatima
Gulbanoo
Gulshan
CASSIM
Hoosen
Noorali
Fatehaly
Madataly
Abduly
Ashraf
Mariam
Shireen
Gulzar
Naseem
HABIB
Noor
Lutaf
Yusuf
Sadick
Rafique
Leila
Zarina
Farieda
KULSAM/Sultanali Guiga Janmohamed
Madat
Budar
Nizar
Farouk
Gulshan
Dilshad
Merun
SHERBANOO/Ahmedali Guiga Janmohamed
Hoosen
MANJEE
Noorbai Jamal
ISMAIL
Nizar
Gulbanoo
Shirin
Zerakhanoo
Nabat
Khairoo
Maleka
Khatoon
Merun
GOOLAM
Akbar
Roshankhanoo
Sakerkhanoo
Dolatkhanoo (Dr Dolly)
HASSIM
Mohamedali
Noordeen
Murad
Daulat
Gulshan
Razia
NAZARALY
Ramzan (Rex)
Ameer
Mohamed
Saadat
Sadruddin
Gulshan (Guli)
Zarina
Khairunissa
Mariam (Mila)
Yasmin
Rashida
Khanum
SAKINA/Ebrahim Kanjee Kassam Panchaan (EK Khoja)
Hakim
Noorалli
Fatehaly
Sherbanoo
Maleka
Zerakhanoo
Noorbanoo
Gulbanoo
Dolly
Saker
Shirin
Farida
Khairunissa
JENA/Gulamhussein Hajee Ramji (GH Khoja)
Sadruddin
Nooraly
Mohamed
Sayed Ali
Maleka
Merunissa
FATIMA/Nimjee Chagan Jiwa
Sugra
KHATIJA/Habib Kanjee Kassam Panchaan (HK Khoja)
Azizali
SANTOK
Kanjee Kassam Panchaan
EBRAHIM/Sakina Manjee Keshavjee
Hakim
Noorali
Fatehaly
Sherbanoo
Maleka
Zerakhanoo
Noorbanoo
Gulbanoo
Dolly
Saker
Shirin
Farida
Khairunissa
HIRBAI/Ismail Jinnah
Gulamhussein
Jena
MANEK
Hirji Nanji Jutha
VALJEE/Amrath Jivan Keshavjee
Gulamhussein
Habib
Jamal
Bundaly
Dolat
Rahemat
Khatija
SANKUBAI/Merali Dhanji
Nazarali
Sadruddin
Jena
Sakina
HIRBAI/Lalji Mangalji
Jafferali
Hassanali
Akberali
Lutafali
Noorali
Laila
Kulsum
Shirin
Roshan

Notes to the Family Tree

1. To facilitate ease of connecting, only the spouses of females of the third generation are mentioned, and where there are double relationships through marriage then the sons of the females of the second generation (Valjee and Ebrahim Kanjee Kassam) are also indicated.

2. Mention of siblings are not necessarily in any chronological order, with males followed by females.

3. All names, where spellings were not easily available, are spelt phonetically.

4. The chart extends to only 4 of the 7 generations of the larger family, but has sufficient details to help members from all 7 generations to make the necessary connections.

5. E and O excepted.

Sadruddin Khimani
Mithima Keshavjee
Valjee Hirji
Mohandas K. Gandhi
Nelson Mandela
Ahmed Mohamed Cachalia
Guiga Janmohamed
Noormohamed Babool
Cassamali Ahamed
Jivan Keshavjee
Velshi Keshavjee
Naran Keshavjee
Gulamhussein Kassam
Ahamed Keshavjee
Chief Justice Ismail Mahomed
Manjee Keshavjee
Kanjee Kassam Panchaan
Manekfaiba Hirji
Sidney Poitier
Thayanagee Pillay
Ebrahim Karsan
Nana Sita
"MAKING THE CONNECTION"
"INTO THAT HEAVEN OF FREEDOM" BY MOHAMED M. KESHAVJEE
The Old Mill, Toronto, Canada, 7th June 2009
Tharia Topan
Mohamed Ali Veljee
Rahemtulla Kanjee Vally
Cassimaly Ismail
Rahim Karim Khan
Lalji Mangalji
Jadavjee Hajee
Goolam Sarif
Allibhai Ananjee
Janmamod K. Kamula
Sacoor Allibhai
Rawjee Babool
Chagan Jiwa
Kanjee Nanjee
Gulamhussein I. Gina
Baberbhai Patel
Miriam Makeba
Ebrahim Virjee
Gulamali Nanji
Jenabai Nanji

Mithima (seated) with sons Jivan (*left*) and Velshi (*right*). Madhavjee is on extreme left and Allibhai on extreme right. *Circa* 1904.

Gandhi and Kallenbach at Tolstoy Farm school with the family of Thambi Naidoo and others, *circa* 1911. (Photo courtesy of Museum Africa, Johannesburg).

Rajabali Velshi Keshavjee in his Tolstoy Farm outfit. He often walked to Johannesburg with Gandhi and Kallenbach. *Circa* 1912.

Manjee Keshavjee, founder of M Keshavjee and Co. *Circa* 1912.

Jivan Keshavjee, beloved grand old man and pioneer of the Ismaili settlement in South Africa. *Circa* 1914.

C F Andrews (*centre*) with a number of South African Indian leaders. Allibhai Keshavjee to his immediate left. A I Kajee at extreme left. Sorabji Rustomji standing behind Andrews. *Circa* 1914.

Jivan and Velshi Keshavjee with delegates from the Aga Khan Supreme Council from Zanzibar. Seated (*L-R*): Jivan Keshavjee, Missionary Gulamhussein Merally of Zanzibar, Aitmadi Jiwan Lalji, Moloo Allahrakhia, Rawjee Babool. Back row (*L-R*): Rahemtullah Kanji Vally, Ebrahim Virjee Vally, Velshi Keshavjee, unknown person. Reclining on the floor: Mohamedaly Kanji Vally. *Circa* 1916.

Naran Keshavjee, the ascetic who brought up the Manjee Keshavjee children, *circa* 1920s.

Noted Ismaili lawyer RK Khan, close friend of Gandhi and secretary of the Natal Indian Congress after Mohandas Gandhi. He left his estate to charity which established the RK Khan dispensaries and an urban hospital for the relief of the poor. *Circa* 1920. (Photo from *Aga Khan and Africa*, courtesy of Habib V Keshavjee).

Ismail Manjee Keshavjee in a 5-image photograph in Bombay, which Manekfaiba used to get him a bride. 1923.

ABC Bakery in 1925. Bought in an auction, it became the hub of activities in the Pretoria area. Cassim Keshavjee was the master baker and is seen in front of the wagon.

H H Aga Khan Volunteer Corps Pretoria with Instructor Mr White. Seated *L-R*: Cassim V Keshavjee, Allibhai V Keshavjee, Mr White, Hassan N Keshavjee, Mohamedali Alli Velji. Back row: Kamruddin Saboor Nanji, Habib V Keshavjee, Kanjee Nanji (Khoja), Habib Kanjee Kassam (Khoja), Nazaraly Manjee Keshavjee, Akbaraly Madhavjee Keshavjee, Noormohamed Madhavjee Keshavjee. Inset *left*: Gulamhussein Valjee Hirji (Khoja). Inset *right*: Habib Vajee Hirji (Khoja). *Circa* late 1920s. (Photo from *Aga Khan and Africa*, courtesy of Habib V Keshavjee).

Harji Bhanji, the clove king of Zanzibar (paternal grandfather of actor Ben Kingsley) dressed in his cultural attire and hat, with members of the Pretoria Ismaili community. Velshibapoo (in full beard) is seen standing at the back. *Circa* 1929.

Opening of the South African Jamatkhana in Boom Street, Marabastad, on 2 July 1930 by Rai Fazal Ebrahim of Zanzibar (garlanded, centre) and Rai Moloo Allarakhia (standing at the back, garlanded). Velshi Keshavjee in black frock coat and black kofia with white beard, third to the right of the flagpole.

Kanjee Kassam Panchaan (KK Khoja) who helped the Keshavjees acquire cinemas, *circa* 1930s.

Velshi Keshavjee, friend of Mohandas Gandhi, in his cultural attire, *circa* 1930s.

Chagan Jiwa, a close friend and cousin of Jivan Keshavjee, *circa* 1930s.

South African Indian Congress Emergency Session with Sir Kurma Reddy Indian Agent General (front row in white triangular turban), A I Kajee to his right. Also in front row is R K Khan (in black coat and white waistcoat, 7th from left). Goolam M Keshavjee, standing 4th from left, middle row. *Circa* 1930s.

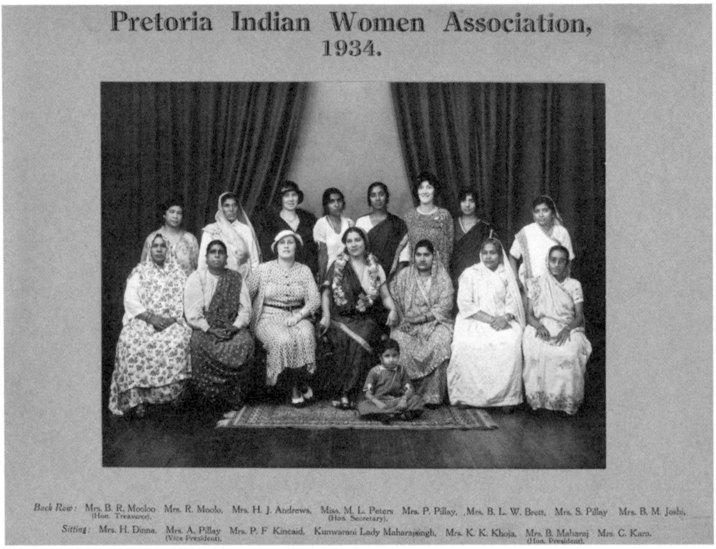

The Pretoria Indian Women's Association 1934. Sakina Khoja played an active role for many years. (Photo courtesy of Pillay Family).

Nazaraly Manjee Keshavjee, a pioneer of the notion of recycling in Pretoria in the 1940s. (Photo: Van Kalker Studio, Cape Town).

H H Aga Khan Ladies Committee, Pretoria, 1941-42.

H H Aga Khan Education Board 1941-42.

Royal Kinema (bioscope) in 1942. The first cinema built jointly by Ebrahim Kanjee Khoja and the Manjee Keshavjee family with help from Kanjee Kassam Panchaan. The author's birthplace is immediately behind the cinema.

The Aga Khan Welfare Society, 1942-1944. The younger women were all born in South Africa.

The Aga Khan (religious) school Pretoria *circa* 1944/1945. Seated on the floor, *left to right*, Zainul Rawjee, Lutfunissa Rawjee, Leila Ebrahim Virji, Saker Ebrahim Kanjee, Guli Nazaraly Keshavjee, Tajdin Allibhai Keshavjee. Row behind, seated (*L-R*), Roshanbahen (teacher), Gulshan Rajabali, Leila Noormohamed, Shirin Noormohamed, Leila Habib Velshi, Roshan Allibhai Velshi, Daulat Gulamaly Rawjee, Dolly Ebrahim Kanjee, Sherbanoofaiba (teacher). Row immediately behind, (*L-R*): Badruddin Noormohamed, Noordeen Hassim Keshavjee, Lutaf Habib Keshavjee, Murad Velshi Keshavjee, Rex Manjee Keshavjee, Hoosen Ahmedali Guiga, Sadruddin Alibhai Anandjee (Khoja). Back row, (*L-R*): Amir Allibhai Velshi Keshavjee, Mamdoo Hassim Keshavjee, Bundaly Valjee Hirji (Khoja), Ali Noormohamed, Noorali Ebrahim Kanjee Kassam (Khoja).

The Pretoria Ismaili jamatkhana illuminated for their Highnesses' visit in 1945. Omarjee Suleiman, Marabastad's creative electrical genius played a pivotal role in the decorations. August 1945.

Chapter 9

The Great Depression, Forerunner of the Apartheid State

THE 1930S WERE THE DECADE OF "THE GREAT DEPRESSION." All across the globe, jobs were lost, industries closed, companies went bankrupt, and hunger and poverty became rampant. In South Africa, both Whites and non-Whites were affected, though not equally. The desperate plight of the indigenous population was more or less ignored by the government. Indians relied on their business acumen and well-honed family and community networks to soften the hardship. The Hertzog government that was in power introduced welfare policies such as free medical services, subsidized low-cost housing and free education for the Whites. It also protected Whites by reserving a number of skilled and semi-skilled jobs for them.

Africans were allowed to live in the cities only as long as their labour was needed. Any African who lost a job had to return to his or her homestead in the rural areas. The government regarded the dire economic situation as a threat to White supremacy and began to focus on plans to segregate the races even further. As South Africa's economy eventually took a turn for the better and the position of the Whites improved, the position of non-Whites deteriorated commensurately, both economically and politically. Africans became the worst off in this process.

It was against this backdrop that, sometime in 1929, Harji Bhanji, an Ismaili businessman known as the Clove King in Zanzibar, visited South Africa for several months. A man with a benign chubby face set off by a sleek pencil moustache, he had a pleasant smile but also exuded authority. The reason for his visit is not now known, but in Pretoria he had discussions with the leaders of the Ismaili community, particularly Velshibapoo, who was the head of the community. He was also a friend of Ismail Manjee

Keshavjee, who had met him on an earlier visit to Zanzibar to discuss the building of the Pretoria jamatkhana. Interestingly, and by one of those amazing twists of fate, Harji's connection to South Africa turned out to be greater than this mere visit.

Harji married twice. He had four children by his first wife, one of whom was a son named Rahemtullah who, at the time of his father's death, was still in high school and was planning to go to England to study medicine. He practised medicine in Manchester for many years. Rahemtullah's son, Ben Kingsley, became the world-famous actor who played the title role in Richard Attenborough's film, *Gandhi*.

Many businessmen in South Africa went into liquidation during the Depression. However, other more astute and entrepreneurial souls saw opportunities and took advantage of them. One of those was Habib, the third-youngest son of Velshi Keshavjee. As outlined earlier, in the 1930s, Habib rented the Empire Bioscope from Suleiman Ebrahim Jalalpore. Later, he rented the loss-making old Osrin Cinema in Fereirastown, Johannesburg, and made it a money-earner by screening films that mainly catered to the rank and file as well as some that appealed to a higher class of patrons. In order to manage the cinema on a daily basis personally, Habib moved permanently to Johannesburg in 1937, with his first wife Sakina and their four young children, while still continuing his bread deliveries and cinema business in Marabastad, which is about thirty-five miles from Johannesburg.

Over the years, Habib developed a deep sense of social justice and shared his business know-how with indigenous entrepreneurs. He became acquainted with various leading lights in the African community, men such as Professor Jabavu, Dr Tsele, Dr Moroka and Dr Dube, who were then leaders of the African National Congress. Dr Alfred Bitini Xuma, who had a PhD from the London School of Tropical Hygiene and was later elected president of the African National Congress, became his family doctor. Habib discovered that African businessmen were being exploited by middlemen wholesalers who charged them exorbitant prices, and arranged for them to receive favourable terms from Asian businessmen such as the Parekhs of Glendale Sugar Company, and AI Kajee, a leading manufacturer's representative, both based in Natal.

During his daily trips into the townships to sell bread, Habib saw the suffering of the African population at first hand. Living in tin shanties without electricity or running water, they endured hunger often to the point of starvation. Outstanding people among them, such as Dr Moroka and Dr Xuma, who had trained overseas at some of the best institutions of higher learning, were relegated to an inferior status simply on the basis of colour and race. He did whatever he could to help them improve their lives, for example by employing African tutors to teach his children subjects such as mathematics.

Other Ismailis in Johannesburg at that time included Habib's brother Cassim. In 1939, Cassim had decided to move away from Marabastad as he was finding it difficult to eke out a living in the V Keshavjee and Sons family enterprise. He had nine teenage children by then and his eldest son, Hoosen, was at school in Marabastad. Cassim moved to Johannesburg with all his children, and settled in the Doornfontein area, where he soon became aware of the plight of the Coloured population. He was drawn to the South African Coloured Blind Association, a cause to which he thereafter devoted the better part of his life. On his arrival in Kenya years later, he served on the Kenya Council for the Disabled till the end of his life.

Cassim's business initially was grossly undercapitalized and he was constantly on the lookout for opportunities to increase his income. He started a little printing press, Mercantile Printers, servicing the needs of various small businesses in the Johannesburg area. He also became friendly with a Jewish baker who needed a responsible person to run his small bakery for him, but under his name. Cassim had no objection to that because the bakery was in a Whites-only area and he would not be able to operate there under his own name. He came to an arrangement to purchase the bakery over a period of time, but to leave the business in the original name. As his sons grew up, Cassim placed them one by one in his enterprises. Young Hoosen attended school in the mornings and worked in the bakery retail shop in the afternoons. Cassim's other sons worked in the printing press. Cassim acquired another small bakery in the heart of the Afrikaner city of Potgietersrust in Northern Transvaal and installed another of his sons, Abduli, there. He also embarked on a small venture to produce metal beds for the African market. That was followed by a suitcase-manufacturing factory, which was a large enterprise employing a number of people.

Life in the Johannesburg area was not easy for Cassim. However, through hard work and perseverance he helped Hoosen, who matriculated in 1945, to be admitted to the premedical study programme at Witwatersrand University. The move was farsighted, and as the years went by, Hoosen, as a qualified doctor, supported his father in sending a second brother, Fatehaly, to the Royal College of Surgeons in Dublin. They also sent one of Cassim's daughters, Shireen, to Witwatersrand University to become a midwife, and she was among the first Muslim women in the Johannesburg area to qualify in this field. Hoosen ran a medical practice in Alexandra township, where his clients were mostly Africans, who received him with warmth and affection because of the compassion he showed to them. In 1967, he set in process the move of our family to Canada, where he opened a medical practice in Toronto's fashionable Fairview Mall. The practice is still running, with his brother Fatehaly, known as Fred, working there full time. One of Hoosen's daughters is also a doctor in Canada.

While some members of the Velshi Keshavjee family branched out and settled in Johannesburg, the Manjee Keshavjees concentrated on the Pretoria area. M Keshavjee and Company, started by my grandfather Manjee Keshavjee, continued its wholesale business in Prinsloo Street, where African traders from far and wide in the Transvaal purchased goods on credit for their retail shops. AM Masike, a short, pot-bellied teacher from Hebron who also ran a retail shop in that town, used to come all the way by bus to purchase goods. Since there was no place for an African to stay in Pretoria, he was put up at our family home in Marabastad. That stone house had accommodated a number of visitors from as far away as Zanzibar, Tanganyika, Uganda, and India. Among the many people who stayed there were Hassim Kassam-Lakha from Uganda, and PJ Bharwani and AG Abdulhussain, two leading businessmen from Tanganyika who visited South Africa in the 1940s. The family narrative has it that one Chief Sibasa, head of the Venda tribe in the Northern Transvaal, also stayed for a while at our home.

Having established themselves in the wholesale and cinema businesses, the M Keshavjees also tried their hand at extracting oil from sesame and other edible seeds, opening a small oil-extracting plant on 8th Street in Marabastad in the early 1930s. It was called the South African Oil Company. The venture, owned largely by my uncle Ismail, was run by my father Nazaraly on behalf of the family partnership. The oil was sold to wholesalers and retailers, as well as marketed through the main shop on Prinsloo Street.

Ismail Manjee was part of that project, though, for reasons that are not clear, he was no longer a part of the M Keshavjee partnership. The oil business did not engage Ismail's full attention as he was interested in setting up a shirt factory in the Pretoria area. There was only one shirt factory in the Transvaal not owned by a White at that time, run by Hassam Haji Habib, whose father had accompanied Mahatma Gandhi on the1909 lobbying mission to London.

Ismail learnt the dynamics of the trade from the Haji Habib enterprise and started manufacturing shirts in the later part of the 1930s, just before the beginning of the Second World War. His factory, named Universal Shirt and Clothing Manufacturers, was in the building that had once housed the Bombay Star Bioscope. Ismail's specialty was khaki shirts, which he sold to large Jewish wholesalers in the Johannesburg area. The quality of his clothes was second to none and one of his biggest outlets was Shubits and Co., a leading store in Johannesburg. He provided employment for about forty women.

Ismail's factory thrived, but in the early 1940s he had serious financial difficulties and the business was liquidated. However, he hung on to the property lease, which he kept till the mid 1950s with intermittent court cases in between for possession. In 1957 he converted the building into the Universal Dance Hall, and for the first time after many years, Marabastad once again had its own dance venue. Here, the Essop Moosa boys, Hassan and Issie, entertained patrons with their musical talent till the early hours of the morning.

In the 1940s, the M Keshavjee enterprise acquired some valuable properties in the Cape and other areas of the country, but often found itself facing a liquidity problem. That was overcome by networking within the Indian business community. For example, Glendale Sugar Estates in

Natal, owned by the Parekhs, had overproduced sugar for some years and was looking for an outlet in the Transvaal for the surplus. Through the mediation of an enterprising employee named Mr Olla, M Keshavjee and Company was given the exclusive agency for Glendale Sugar in the Transvaal area. The company could purchase the sugar on credit, to be paid for when the partners had the cash.

The other branches of the Keshavjee family developed their own wholesale activities. Manjeebapoo had left half of the assets of M Keshavjee and Company to Naranbapoo in his will, and with the help of that company, Naranbapoo established his only son, Hassan, in a business, HN Keshavjee and Sons, on Boom Street. Jivanbapoo's estate (not insubstantial) had gone to his son Madhavjee, who moved out of Prinsloo Street after transferring his shares in Keshavjee Ltd to a Kokanee family enterprise, Aly Ismail and Sons. Madhavjee then opened a number of shops in various suburbs of Pretoria, where he placed his older sons. Over a period of time they all branched out on their own as his businesses were not able to sustain the expanding needs of a growing extended family. Madhavjee purchased the Orient Cinema with Jiwa Barber of Pretoria in the 1930s. No one in the Keshavjee family knows how long he kept the cinema and why he eventually sold it.

Many other Ismailis established themselves during the Great Depression years. For example, Kanji Nanji started his Khoja's Corner shop on Vermeulen Street in the late 1920s. The Hajee Ramjee family also developed their business empire in Louis Trichardt in the Northern Transvaal in 1915 with a string of shops in the heart of town serving a largely White clientele. AA Khoja established his enterprise in Pretoria West, opposite the Iron and Steel Corporation, in the 1920s.

By the early 1920s, Kanjee Kassam Panchaan had entrenched himself in business as Kanjee Kassam Khoja. Initially he had worked for the Keshavjees in Bloed Street, but in the early years of the settlement, even before the First World War, he started his own corner shop, KK Khoja and Company on Bloed Street. He was helped by Rahemtullah Kanji Vally, who was in the timber business and provided the materials to build his shop and gave him a loan. A benign man with strong principles, Kanjee felt strongly that to work for someone else was to sell out one's own prospects, and he decided to build his future with his young son Ebrahim.

By 1927, KK Khoja and Company was a leading wholesale and retail enterprise, competing with well-known wholesalers such as Moshal Gevisser, Katzenelenbogen and M Bulkin in the Pretoria area. Kanjee had money, but he was a man of simple tastes and had a spartan lifestyle. In 1929, he dissolved his partnership with Ebrahim and branched off on his own with his younger son Habib. As part of the dissolution agreement, he acquired a few stands at 329 Bloed Street. Kanjee then started another shop, HK Khoja and Company, on Grand Street and spent the remainder of his life building up that shop with Habib.

Rawjee Babool's two sons left Mozambique in 1937. Aladdin, the elder one, went to Pretoria, and Goolamaly went to Nairobi, Kenya, where he set up a macaroni factory and stayed for two years. In 1939 he went to South Africa and laid the foundation of an enterprise that in early 2000 was the fourth-largest fish distribution company in the country. The Babools diversified their business interests, which are now in both South Africa and Mozambique, and they have family connections in the US and Portugal. Noormohamed Babool's grandson Nazir is in the hotel business in South Africa and Kenya.

The decade of the 1930s saw the development of Ismaili community institutions such as the Women's Committee and the Volunteer Corps in Pretoria. In 1936, Ismailis around the world celebrated the Golden Jubilee of the Imam, His Highness Sir Sultan Mahomed Shah Aga Khan. A huge ceremony was held in Nairobi, Kenya, and some members of the South African jamat travelled there to attend it.

After the Second World War, the White South African government began to project itself as a bastion against communism in Africa and further curtailed the rights of the majority indigenous population. That period also witnessed the rise of the icons of the freedom struggle—individuals such as Nelson Mandela, Walter Sisulu, Oliver Tambo, Yusuf Dadoo, Maulvi Kachalia, and Ahmed Kathrada. For South Africans, the decade was a crucible for creative thinking, producing writers such as Ezekiel (Es'kia) Mphahlele and Bloke Modisane, singers such as Miriam Makeba and Dorothy Masuka, jazz artists such as Hugh Masakela and lawyers such as Ismail Mahomed, George Bizos, Vernon Berrangé (himself an Afrikaner), and Ismail Meer. The 1940s were a decade in which the non-Whites were able to mobilize world opinion and make the world aware of the deprivations and degradation of apartheid and how it was dehumanizing millions of people. As the next chapter will show, this was done in a variety of ways.

Chapter 10

The Turbulent Forties

THE 1940S WERE TURBULENT YEARS IN SOUTH AFRICA, WITH the South African government systematically finding protean ways of keeping non-Whites in their place. However, the country faced a major conundrum: the mining industry and related industrial development, which formed the backbone of the national economy, depended on cheap African labour, but White South Africans were not willing to ensure even the basic needs of that workforce.

Africans from the rural areas flooded into cities in search of work to enable their families to survive. Alan Paton's classic *Cry, the Beloved Country* succinctly encapsulates the social upheaval caused by that population movement. Lamenting the fear that characterized the racially torn country, Paton writes with intense poignancy:

> Cry, the Beloved Country, for the unborn child that is the inheritor of our fears. Let him not love the earth too deeply. Let him not laugh too gladly when the water runs through his fingers, nor stand too silent when the setting sun makes red the veldt with fire. [...] For fear will rob him of all, if he gives too much.

For millions of Africans, the only source of income was the gold mines, which provided dangerous work for wages that did not reflect its lethal risks. They left their families in South Africa, Mozambique, Nyasaland, and Northern and Southern Rhodesia because racist policies there left them with no other choice. Many died in cave-ins, identified only as statistics. Their bodies were interred in unmarked graves, dishonoured even in death. While Africans suffered most under the inhuman laws, Asians also felt the deprivation, as did many Coloureds. In Natal, the conditions of the children of indentured labourers were dismal and poor Indians lived cheek by jowl with Africans in squalid ghetto conditions.

The decade was marked by certain milestones that are important to this narrative: the end of the Second World War in 1945, the visit to South Africa by His Highness the Aga Khan in the same year, and the celebrations marking the sixtieth anniversary—Diamond Jubilee—of the Aga Khan's accession to the Imamate which because of the war, were held in 1946.

The year 1946 also witnessed a global stirring of conscience when India, under the leadership of the prime minister-in-waiting, Pandit Jawaharlal Nehru, raised the issue of the inhuman treatment of Indian South Africans in the newly established United Nations Organisation. Simultaneously, Indians in South Africa, mainly from Natal, organized the Passive Resistance Campaign under the leadership of Dr Yusuf Dadoo and Dr Monty Naicker, supported by two young law students from Natal studying at the University of Witwatersrand, Ismail Meer and JN Singh, who interrupted their studies for a year to organize the campaign. It marked a major shift in the Indian contribution to the freedom struggle and was a turning point in the history of both the Natal Indian Congress and the Transvaal Indian Congress, which was run by Dr Dadoo, who later became President of the South African Indian Congress, then Chairman of the South African Communist Party. Both these men saw the need for a new vision, with Indians and Africans working together for political changes.

The African political movement, too, experienced a major shift in its approach, with the coming on the scene of activists such as Nelson Mandela, Walter Sisulu, and Oliver Tambo, working under the moral leadership of Chief Albert Luthuli. The young African radicals were also frustrated with what they regarded as appeasement by their old-guard leadership and wanted change.

The decade ended with Afrikaner nationalism capturing the state. The National Party received fewer votes than Smuts's United Party, but its alliance with the Afrikaner Party created a slim majority of five votes. With each succeeding election in the years to come, White support for the government increased and the National Party remained in power for over forty years, refining the racist legislative apparatus that it had inherited into a sophisticated machine, making South Africa the epicentre of world racism.

By 1948, there were some ten thousand Afrikaner-owned businesses, mostly small trading operations, dairies, and garages. The small shops had to compete with large chain stores such as OK Bazaar, which were beginning to set up branches in rural towns, offering goods at a much cheaper price, and the shopkeepers started agitating against them as well as against Indian traders.

During their election campaign, the Nationalist candidates had promised to restrict the rights of Indians until they were "repatriated" to India. A South African Indian Congress delegation, which included Habib and Goolam Keshavjee, called on Dr Theophilus Ebenezer Donges, one of the high priests of apartheid, to protest against the Nationalist stance, but he told them, "If you wish to live in South Africa, you will have to reduce your population to an irreducible minimum." In 1950, soon after the National Party came to power, it passed the Group Areas Act, which prevented Indians and other non-Whites from residing, owning property, or trading in White areas.

In 1944, a group of young African activists in the Rand, among them Walter Sisulu, Anton Lembede, Oliver Tambo, and Nelson Mandela, began to form the Congress Youth League. The League pressed for change in the African National Congress (ANC), feeling that it was too influenced by middle-class White values and not close enough to the ordinary African people whom it was supposed to represent. In July 1949, the leadership of the ANC was voted out of office and the new leaders pledged to work for "political independence" and to reject both racial segregation and White domination.

By the early 1940s, the Ismaili community in Pretoria had developed its own institutional framework under the guidance of the Imam, and many families were heavily involved in providing voluntary service through these institutions. In the early part of that decade, as the youth of the jamat were growing up, the earlier generation built on the work in religious education that had been done by people such as Jivanbapoo's daughter Hirbai; Velshibapoo's son Rajabali; and an elder brother of VN Hooda,

Saboormama. VN Hooda was a prominent Ismaili community leader in India, who was involved in the producing of religious education material for Ismaili children in India and Africa.

Saboormama was assisted by his sister-in-law, Manibai Kanji Nanji, who was a teacher from India and an expert in Gujarati. Rajabali, who was also fluent in the Gujarati language and culture and had a good knowledge of the Ismaili tariqah, taught its principles to the first generation of Ismailis born in South Africa.

Immediately after the Diamond Jubilee celebrations, Sir Sultan Mahomed Shah Aga Khan appointed two daughters of Kanjee Kassam Panchaan, Koolsam Manjee Keshavjee and Sakina Velshi Keshavjee, as members of the Pretoria Provincial Council. Born in South Africa and fluent in English, they brought a perspective on women's issues and maternal and child health to the Council. Sherbanoo Velshi Keshavjee, Velshibapoo's daughter, played a pivotal role in setting up a number of social development programmes by harnessing the skills of all the young women in the jamat. Sherbanoo—addressed by the community's youth as Sherbanoofaiba—had attended Ms Ferguson's school with Koolsam and Sakina. The Council was made up of senior leaders such as EK Khoja, Allibhai Keshavjee and Chagan Jiwa.

Sherbanoofaiba had an open and enlightened mind. Even as a young girl, she had shown an indomitable spirit coupled with a compassion for those less fortunate than herself. In a culture where girls did not aspire beyond the status of wife and mother, Sherbanoofaiba had other ideas and was intent on getting education. With Velshibapoo's backing, she had completed Standard 6, the highest level of schooling available to girls in those days, with outstanding grades.

In the early 1930s, Sherbanoofaiba had married Ahamedaly Guiga of the Guiga Janmohamed family of Mozambique. They had lived in Lourenço Marques at first, but had to move to the rural areas of Mozambique for business reasons. There, the young Ahmedali contracted blackwater fever, a severe form of malaria, and was transported by van all the way back to Lourenço Marques but died there in June 1934, leaving Sherbanoofaiba with an eight-month-old son named Hoosen. Sherbanoofaiba, who was only eighteen, was distraught but she was not one to indulge in self-pity and decided to rescript her life. Seeing no future for herself in Portuguese East Africa as a widow, she returned to Pretoria with her father's help and, in the late 1930s, established a small café in the precincts of the newly constructed Empire Cinema.

Sherbanoofaiba was a disciplinarian and had a deep sense of service, which she imbued in the young women of the jamat, encouraging them to serve on various committees set up by the Council. Although she worked long hours, she also found time to enjoy the world of art, becoming an adept in decorative art herself, using tinsel of different colours on satin and other cloth for her creations.

She considered education and health, twin vectors of community development that the Imam had constantly emphasized in his Farmans, to be very important. Initially, she set up a small school on the ground floor of the Pretoria jamatkhana and taught the principles of the Ismaili tariqah to a group of young boys and girls. She was helped by Roshan, the eldest daughter of her cousin Goolam Manjee Keshavjee. Roshan, then in her late teens, had just passed the Junior Certificate examination at the Pretoria Indian High School, where she had distinguished herself as a serious and hard-working student who consistently received the highest grades. The Aga Khan Education Board in Pretoria helped them to enlist the services of a Master Patel. Although a strict teacher, Master Patel was soft-spoken, very respectful, and embodied the Gujarati characteristic of humility and respect, which he inculcated in all his students. He taught the children the Gujarati alphabet, poems, songs, and proverbs.

In addition to teaching her students the principles of the tariqah, Sherbanoofaiba also instructed them in hygiene, first aid, and art. She taught the girls to do embroidery and paint on cloth. Under her tutelage or influence, a new cadre of female volunteers emerged, notable among whom were Fatima Jamal, who became a teacher at the nursery school after it was set up; Noorbanoo Esmail, who worked in the educational field and distinguished herself years later as the first non-White female inspector of schools in the Transvaal Education Department; Zeri Aziz from the KK Khoja family; Amina Habib Chagan, known as aunty MIM; Saker Ebrahim Virji; Dolly Madhavjee; Gulbanu Esmail Cassim; Laila Umedaly (nee Habib Keshavjee) Parin Allibhai Keshavjee; Gulshan and

Gulbanoo Rajabali Velshi; and a host of others whose children today are settled in different parts of the world and are holding important positions. Sherbanoofaiba and Roshanbahen ran the school from 1944 till around 1947.

Other Ismailis also volunteered their services to the jamat, through institutions such as the the education board, the welfare society,and the ladies and gents volunteer corps. Women cleaned the jamatkhana each day and volunteers cared for the old and infirm. Chagan Jiwa, mentioned earlier, was not only a one-man funeral service; he also cooked for the entire jamat on high days and holidays.

Habib Keshavjee returned to Pretoria from Johannesburg with his family in the early 1940s, wanting to be close to the community due to the failing health of his wife Sakina, who had just given birth to a daughter, Farieda. Sakina, who was suffering from dropsy and rheumatic heart disease, died at the age of 29 soon after their arrival, leaving him with five children ranging in age from one to thirteen years. After her death, Habib decided to remain in Pretoria. He married Sakina Kanjee Kassam, who had been widowed recently in Mozambique and coincidentally had the same name as his first wife. By yet another coincidence, her late husband had been named Habib!

With the worst of the Depression over, Habib Keshavjee wanted to strengthen his economic base with a cinema of his own. He had turned the Empire Bioscope around after renting it from Old Man Jalalpore, and many Indians from as far away as Durban had covetous eyes on it. Habib wanted to buy the cinema but did not have enough money to do so outright, so he asked his new father-in-law Kanjee Kassam Panchaan, who was a friend of Jalalpore, to negotiate a financial arrangement that would enable him to make the purchase. Old Man Jalalpore, generous as always, told Kanjee that Habib could have the cinema for the same amount that he had lent to Sheikh Ahamed, and that he could pay the sum in instalments. Habib was later able to do for others in South Africa and Kenya what Jalalpore did for him in Marabastad in the early 1940s.

Ownership of his own business, coupled with the experience he had gained in Witwatersrand during the Depression years, gave Habib a new sense of confidence to leverage his contacts and help strengthen the excellent jamati structure underpinned by the cadre of volunteers that was already existent in Pretoria. He acted as a catalyst, bringing his professionalism to bear on the task. Habib's contribution to the community was seminal in the field of education, particularly early childhood education, for which he had a passion.

He was joined in his educational activities by Manjeebapoo's son Goolam, who was a successful businessman by then. A senior partner in M Keshavjee and Company, Goolam had been visiting East Africa as a member of various delegations from the Aga Khan Provincial Council of South Africa since the 1930s. In the 1940s, he and Habib were both members of the Aga Khan Education Board in Pretoria, together with Mohamedali Alibhai Velji, Noormohamed Madhavjee, Mrs Dolat Hassan Keshavjee, a teacher from Kenya, and Gulamaly Nathoo, and they set up an educational programme for the community and those around it that lasted till the end of the century.

The Empire Bioscope continued to contribute to the development of African talent. Among those gracing its stage were a Marabastad Muslim animation artist, Omarjee Suleiman, the penny whistler Kippie Moeketsi, and Miriam Makeba who, at the age of 15, had sung solo before the British royal family in 1947. Habib made the stage available to her free of cost on a Friday evening and gave her an honorarium that helped her sustain her family. She went on to become the world-famous artiste who used her songs to protest against apartheid, and the South African government revoked her passport in 1960. She lived in exile until the 1990s.

When the Second World War ended in 1945, His Highness the Aga Khan announced, to the joy of the jamat, that he would be visiting South Africa with his Begum sometime in August of that year. For Velshi Keshavjee, the news was a joyous occasion because he recalled his earlier request to the Imam to visit South Africa, and the Imam at that time had said that one day he will come. Preparations began in earnest for what was going to be a memorable event, not only for the Ismailis but for the whole of Pretoria. The South African government nominated JH Basson as a liaison officer to assist the Aga Khan Provincial Council in Pretoria with the arrangements.

On 7 August 1945, His Highness and the Begum, Ome Habibeh Mata

Salamat, arrived at the Pretoria station from Lourenço Marques, where they had been guests of the Portuguese government. The railway stations in both Pretoria and Johannesburg were decorated with flags and bunting, in which His Highness's colours, red and green, predominated. As their train pulled into Pretoria Station, a large crowd surged forward to see them being received by the civic dignatories of Pretoria. An hour later, the train arrived at Johannesburg Station, where Allibhai V Keshavjee, president of the Aga Khan Provincial Council for South Africa, and Ismail M. Keshavjee, a member of the reception committee, received Their Highnesses.

That afternoon, His Highness was driven to Pretoria, where he called on the governor-general and on Prime Minister Smuts. At 6 p.m., he arrived at the Pretoria jamatkhana to address the Ismaili community. Thousands of people had gathered to welcome him; some were even standing on rooftops to get a glimpse of him as he was escorted into the jamatkhana by community leaders.

The jamatkhana had been decorated for the occasion with the help of well-known artist Omarjee Suleiman. He had asked Habib for a symbol that would have meaning for the Ismailis and their Imam, and Habib had shown him the Imam's crest. Omarjee had reproduced it with lights reflecting the forty-eight Imams, going back to Hazrat Ali. He had then prepared an illuminated welcome sign that blinked on and off in coordination. Marabastad had never seen anything that resplendent before.

The next day, the Aga Khan visited members of the Ismaili community individually at their shops, mainly in Marabastad but also in downtown Pretoria and Hercules, and had photographs taken with each family. He also visited the jamat and had discussions with various members of the council about the progress in their areas of responsibility. The members of the education board informed the Imam of their wish to give Sherbanoofaiba and Roshanbahen a small token of gratitude for their sterling voluntary work and he expressed happiness that their work was being recognized.

When Habib and Goolam informed Sherbanoofaiba and Roshanbahen—their sister and daughter, respectively—of the award of about 100 pounds, they felt uncomfortable about being singled out from among the many people who had given services to the community, and refused to accept it. Habib and Goolam persisted, and the two women finally agreed, on the basis that the money would be used to purchase cupboards for a proposed clinic in the jamatkhana precincts. That gift was the nucleus of Sherbanoofaiba's dream to set up a modern clinic for the jamat. Their wish was accepted and the clinic was set up immediately after the Imam's departure from South Africa.

During the Imam's visit, Habib mentioned to him that there was a need for a nursery school for Ismaili as well as non-Ismaili children, a germinal idea for that time. The Imam asked if there was a plan for achieving that objective, and Habib replied that there was one problem, that the only available physical space was a piece of land abutting the jamatkhana that belonged to the Manjee Keshavjee family. The land was in the name of Manjeebapoo's eight children who anticipated that it would be used someday for an extension to the jamatkhana. The Imam supported the plan for a nursery school and asked Habib to discuss the matter with the Manjee Keshavjee family members. Ismail and Goolam, the two elder sons, immediately called a family meeting and, since the school was the Imam's wish, all of them agreed to gift the land unconditionally to the project. They also bought a small adjoining plot of land from a non-Ismaili neighbour and donated it for the school.

On the evening of 8 August, the Imam and Begum attended a banquet in Johannesburg, given in their honour by the Transvaal Indian Congress and attended by some 500 people, including Acting Prime Minister JH Hoffmeyr and several cabinet ministers. In his speech, the Imam advised the Indian community, "While keeping the cultural, intellectual, and religious heritage of India, you should look to this country as your home, for yourselves and your children always." He also reminded White South Africans that "to make cultural, economic and social barriers artificially can never lead to what is your ideal—a union of all civilized people in this vast land." The Aga Khan cautioned, "The one thing which causes suffering, misery, and strife is fear."

Thursday, 9 August was the high watermark of Their Highness' visit. It was the evening on which the Ismailis of South Africa hosted a banquet in Pretoria's City Hall. The function was attended by some 1300 people, including Prime Minister Smuts, Deputy Prime Minister Hoffmeyr and Indian High Commissioner RM Desmukh.

The hall was attractively bedecked with flowers. Thousands of fresh carnations adorned it and in the centre was a bed of primulas. At the foot of the stage was a flowery star of red and green. His Highness and his party were seated at a horse-shoe table from which radiated each of the seating rows. Every table had vases filled with fresh red roses. In addition, the main table had poinsettias and greenery. As the main table guests followed Their Highnesses into the hall, where the lights had been dimmed, the rows lighted up one by one. As the last row lit up, the beauty of the stage decorations stood out in splendid radiance. The Imam paused, looked around him and exclaimed, "This is most beautiful, wonderful!"

Presiding on behalf of the Ismaili Provincial Council, Allibhai V Keshavjee referred to the Imam as "the greatest spiritual leader of our time." He observed, "In the Bible there is a phrase, 'Through tribulations ye shall enter into the kingdom of heaven,'" and evoked a laugh when he added, "In this country, Your Highness, we feel we are very near to it." The next speaker was his brother Habib, organizing secretary of the visit. Habib commended His Highness for his international work and vision, "whether at Geneva, as leader of the Indian delegation, or as President of the League of Nations, or at the Disarmament Conference, or at a conference where any matter of international importance is discussed."

Representatives of the Indian community in South Africa also delivered addresses of welcome. They included R Mooloo, chairman of the Pretoria branch of the Transvaal Indian Congress; Hajee Joosub Hajee Mohamed of the Pretoria Indian Commercial Association; Adam Osman Ali, representing the Pretoria and District Muslim Council; and PM Joshi on behalf of the Pretoria Hindu Seva Samaj.

Prime Minister Smuts spoke next, presenting the face of moral reasonableness that he used in the international arena. That day the US had instantaneously vaporized a large part of the Japanese city of Nagasaki with an atomic bomb, three days after doing the same to the city of Hiroshima, and General Smuts, terming war the "greatest of all evils," urged His Highness to help "build up a society in which justice, fair play, common sense, and decent virtues will be triumphant and in which war will not be needed as an arbitrator of fate."

The Aga Khan started his speech by urging Indians to avoid sectarianism. He then reminded the gathering that there were many ways in which Indians could advance. Citing education as an example, he said that, while there were few opportunities for it in South Africa, the Indians could send their children to the United States, Britain and India, as well as Cairo.

On 12 August, His Highness addressed the Transvaal Muslim League at the Johannesburg City Hall. In his welcoming address, MA Dinath, vice-president of the League, extolled the Aga Khan's contribution to education, particularly to Aligarh College in India, which had been raised to the status of a university "mainly through Your Highness' efforts."

In his address, the Aga Khan once again cautioned against sectarianism of any type and added, "You have united as friends but there is a second danger—a division between rich and poor."

On 16 August, Their Highnesses flew to Durban. There, at a reception hosted in his honour by the Natal Indian Congress, attended by Parsi Rustomji, PR Pather, Sheik Abdulla, and others, the Aga Khan once again urged loyalty to South Africa.

The next day Their Highnesses left South Africa. An interesting footnote to the visit occurred when Allibhai V Keshavjee returned to the Transvaal. He was summoned to the Union Buildings in Pretoria and accused by a government official of having talked politics at the function held on 9 August, when he had indirectly referred to the adversities suffered by Indians in South Africa. Allibhai denied that he had violated any government instructions. "All I did was quote from the Bible, that through tribulations ye shall enter into the kingdom of heaven," he told the official, leaving him dumbfounded and speechless.

What was the impact of the Imam's visit to South Africa? Looking back, it was clearly an important watershed in the life of the jamat. It was a forerunner to the next phase of development, in which the younger members of the community, particularly women, were going to participate more actively. Secondly, it gave greater impetus to the tertiary-level education of community members. Some of the women went into professions such as medicine, nursing, and teaching, and the young felt inspired to go for university education. Among others who have been mentioned earlier, Alibhai Jadavjee from Louis Trichardt and Bundaly Kanji Vally of Johannesburg were admitted to Witwatersrand University to do a degree in science and languages, respectively.

Hardly had the memory of the Imam's visit faded, than Smuts and his United Party came up with the infamous Ghetto Bill to introduce in Natal some of the trading restrictions that had been in force against the Indian community in the Transvaal for some time. This led to India asking the United Nations Organisation to take up the issue of the treatment of South African Indians.

As the chapters to come will show, the struggle against apartheid was underpinned by high drama on the international stage. In a way, it led to Smuts's political downfall and the growing prominence of the South African racial situation on the international agenda. Furthermore, with the expansion of apartheid, the spirit of Gandhi and passive resistance emerged once again with renewed vigour in mid-1946.

Chapter 11

Stirring of the International Conscience

THE YEAR 1946 WAS ONE OF SHAME FOR SOUTH AFRICA. FROM the announcement of the drafting of the Ghetto Bill in January to a United Nations verdict on the colour bar in December, the country's image worsened considerably.

"Ghetto Bill" was the epithet given by South African Indians to the Asiatic Land Tenure and Indian Representation Bill, which not only aimed to segregate Indians in terms of where they could live and practise their trades and professions, but was also intended to prevent them from entering certain professions and industries and to deny them political rights.

The South African Indian Congress asked the Indian government to intervene on its behalf and to place the issue of the Ghetto Bill before the newly established United Nations Organization. On 24 May 1946, India recalled its High Commissioner from South Africa and on 25 June it ended its trade pact with the Union. The Indian delegation to the UN, led by the sister of Prime Minister Jawaharlal Nehru, Mrs Vijayalakhshmi Pandit, requested that the issue of South African Indians be placed before the UN General Assembly. In her address to the General Assembly, Mrs Pandit voiced India's determination to ensure "equal and honourable treatment of our people wherever they may go."

In a press interview, she contended that the Indian problem in South Africa was a test case not only of human rights but also of the very purpose and principles of the UN Charter. She also declared that Asia had a great role to play in shaping the future of the world, a prescient statement that is becoming a reality in the twenty-first century.

A steering committee was entrusted with deciding whether or not the issue of South African Indians should be placed on the General Assembly agenda, and it was there that Smuts went on the attack on 1 November. He argued that Articles 17 and 27 of the UN Charter specifically excluded domestic matters from discussion by the Assembly, so India's request should be rejected. However, MC Chagla, a leading Indian jurist speaking on behalf of the Indian delegation, questioned the very basis of the discussion. He said that only the General Assembly, not the steering committee, had the right to decide whether or not the Indian issue was a domestic one. A resolution to that effect was approved by five votes to three. When the decision was communicated to the General Assembly, it resolved unanimously to refer the matter to its Joint Political and Legal Committee. Eventually, on 8 December 1946, the General Assembly affirmed in resolution 44 (I) that the treatment of Indians in South Africa should be in conformity with the UN Charter.

While the UN was grappling with the issue, for the better part of that year Indians in South Africa were continuing their passive resistance campaign against racist laws. The campaign played a vital part in the history of Marabastad, where two prominent freedom fighters, Mrs Thayanayagee Pillay and Nana Sita, were among its key leaders. The significance of the campaign can be better understood against the background of the change in leadership in the Natal Indian Congress and Transvaal Indian Congress.

As mentioned earlier, Dr Yusuf Dadoo and Dr Monty Naicker led a movement for change in the Indian leadership. Naicker had been elected president of the Natal Indian Congress in the early 1940s and Dadoo became the leader of the Transvaal Indian Congress. They gave the freedom movement a new dimension by building bridges with African leaders, to forge a common front against the increasingly intransigent government.

In February 1946, the entire Indian political leadership met in Cape Town to discuss the best way to present and protect the interests and rights of the Asian community in South Africa. Habib and Goolam Keshavjee attended as delegates. The conference resolved to fight the Ghetto Bill through passive resistance and to send delegations to the US, UK and India to influence world opinion against the racism in South Africa.

The passive resistance movement immediately attracted support in Natal, where the Anti-Segregation Council enlisted some 30,000 paid-up members in twenty-nine branches, most of which were trade unions. The indigenous people were also mobilizing against their exploitation, and 50,000 African mineworkers went on strike in 1946. They were fully supported by the Transvaal Indian Congress (TIC) and the Passive Resistance Council, which suspended other activities and started mobilizing resources to help the strikers. Dadoo, Ismail Meer, and others worked closely with the African leaders, among whom were JB Marks and David Bopape. However, using violence the government crushed the strike within three days. Dadoo, JN Singh and Mohamed Vania were among those arrested.

The Indians held mass meetings and open-air rallies to mobilize protesters for the passive resistance. Ismail Meer and JN Singh had excellent connections in the Johannesburg Indian community, with whom they had spent considerable time as students. In the Pretoria area, they were helped by Roy Naidoo of Doornfontein, son of Thambi Naidoo, who introduced them to the Sooboo family into which his sister Thayanayagee had married. Nana Sita, a veteran Gandhian politician and president of the Transvaal branch of the Indian Congress, was based in the Pretoria suburb of Hercules, and he, too, supported the campaign.

The first recruits in Pretoria were Nana Sita's eldest son Ramlal, Sooboo Pillay, and BR Mooloo. Thayanayagee and Nana Sita's daughter Maniben contacted the TIC leaders and offered to mobilize women for the campaign. Mooloo and Mohamed Jeeva, known as Jeeva Barber, were so committed to the resistance campaign that they also encouraged their daughters to enlist. A total of ten women enlisted. They were Thanga Dharmalingam, Beeta Mooloo, Raji Mooloo, Shamugam Pillay, Gowrie Bharoochi, Maniben Sita, Ameena Jeeva, Thayanayagee Pillay, Muniamma Pillay and Jasoobehn Desai. The oldest, Thayanayagee (Thaylamay) Pillay, daughter of Thambi Naidoo, was in her thirties, while the youngest, Gowrie Bharoochi, was under 16 years of age. A number of men were also recruited: Ahamadoy Khan, Dicky Bhana, Ismail Allibhai Velshi Keshavjee, Jeeva Mohamed, Thayanayagee's husband Perumal (Fisher) Pillay, and Charlie (Govidasamy) Pillay.

Krishna Pillay, head of the Tamil community and an executive of the Pretoria branch of the TIC, designed a uniform for the recruits that would also be a reminder of the Indian freedom struggle. For women, it consisted of a white sari with the map of India as a motif and a border in the colours of the Indian flag; the men wore a Nehru cap in addition to white clothing with the same motif and borders as the saris.

In Durban, the first group of resisters, comprising some 6000 people under the leadership of Dr Naicker and Dr Goonam, held a mass rally on 31 March 1946 at Nicol Square (which was renamed Red Square by the activists). The Ghetto Bill became law on 2 June and the next day the Natal Indian Congress (NIC) met and decided to launch the passive resistance on 13 June.

On that day, about 20,000 resisters gathered at Red Square and marched five kilometres to a vacant plot of land at the corner of Umbilo Road and Gale Street, in a designated White area, which they intended to occupy as a symbolic repudiation of discrimination. They pitched tents and camped on the site until arrested. Resisters from all over the country converged on Durban from June 1946 till the end of 1947, ready to replace those arrested by the police, thus maintaining constant occupation of the site.

The arrested women were incarcerated in Pietermaritzburg, the prison where Thayanayagee's mother Veerammal and her sister Seshammal had been jailed during the Satyagraha march in 1913. Maniben Sita recalls the daily interaction with the female wardens, who were by and large fairly benign and left the resisters alone for most of the day. The men were imprisoned in Ladysmith and their experience, as will be seen later, was different.

In the Transvaal, when Yusuf Dadoo and Maulvi Kachalia called upon protesters to join the passive resistance, among those who responded were Aminabai Pahad, who left five of her young sons in the care of her husband to participate in the 13 June resistance action in Durban, together with Zainab Aswat, Zubaida Patel, Mrs PK Naidoo, Lutchmee Govindar, Veeramah Pather, and Jamila Bhaba.

On 17 June, with the police looking on passively, a group of White thugs rampaged through the Durban occupation site, tearing down the tents and destroying whatever they could reach. Leaders of the protest urged their cadres not to answer violence with violence. Additional police arrived on the scene at last and the destruction ended. On 20 June, the resisters were arrested and charged under the Riotous Assemblies Act, even though they were the victims. Goonam and Naicker were sentenced to six months' imprisonment with hard labour. Others, including Zainab Aswat, who was injured during the attack, were sentenced to three months.

Dadoo was arrested too, and during his court appearance he said he hoped the protesters would "continue their struggle with renewed vigour, but in a nonviolent manner in keeping with their code of passive resistance and do what men and women have done in the War just concluded, a war that was fought for democracy and decency." His reference to the moral reasons underpinning the Second World War was astute, reminding people that there were ethical values worth fighting for, and it intensified support for the resisters among non-Whites as well as Whites. A council for human rights was set up to support the resisters and advocate their case among the White population. Thousands of people visited the resistance camps in Durban and elsewhere and money poured in. As the protest got reported globally, governments and people in the developed world, too, became more aware of the plight of the Indians in South Africa. In India, Mahatma Gandhi called upon the South African government to stop thugs from attacking the resisters.

On 22 June the nature of the resistance changed when the first White protestors, Michael Scott and Benny Sischy, joined a march led by Goonam. Hooligans attacked again and Scott and Goonam were arrested. On 23 June, there was another onslaught by White hooligans, which left many people injured. Despite the violence and arrests, the movement continued to grow. In August, Cissy Gool led the first group of resisters in the Cape and 594 people were arrested in September.

On 23 October, to coincide with the opening of the General Assembly session in New York, 355 volunteers resisted in South Africa, opposing discrimination against *all* non-Whites in the country. The speakers at the Red Square rally were arrested and brought before a court appointed specifically to deal with the passive resistance. They were sentenced to one month's imprisonment with hard labour.

The hard labour consisted of work such as repairing roads and disposing rubble and excrement. Ismail Allibhai Keshavjee was given the task of collecting buckets of human excrement from the cells, placing them in a wheelbarrow and pushing it up a steep hill for disposal. After some trips up and down the hill, he was exhausted and sat down for a rest. "*Dit is baie swaar*" ("This is very heavy") he explained in Afrikaans to a burly Afrikaner policeman, only to be told in succinct and idiomatic Afrikaans that if he did not resume work, the policeman would take a red hot chilli grown in the province by Ismail's ancestors and use it as a suppository to energize him. The threat was sufficient for Ismail to feel a sudden surge of energy to push the wheelbarrow up the hil.

The passive resistance movement was still going strong in the early part of 1947. In March 1947, Mrs Sarojini Naidu, former president of the South African Indian Congress, became the chief organizer of the Asian Relations Conference in New Delhi. The NIC and TIC wanted Dadoo and Naicker to participate, but the Smuts government introduced new measures denying passports to opponents of the government. This provoked international protests, to which Mahatma Gandhi added his voice. The government gave in and issued the passports. In India, where the freedom struggle was coming to a climax with independence only months away, the South African Indian leaders were welcomed as heroes and promised full support.

Years later, Nelson Mandela wrote that the peaceful resistance campaign by the Indians became an inspiration for activists from the indigenous community. The 1946 passive resistance campaign moved South Africa's racism from the domestic sphere to the global one, with the issue continuing to be debated annually at the UN.

♦

It was in 1946 that Habib Keshavjee, assisted by carpenters and the youth of the Ismaili community set up a nursery school with modern facilities behind the Pretoria jamatkhana. Members of the jamat funded the construction and provided materials. The teachers, all volunteers, were to be trained at Union College, Pretoria, in the Montessori method of early childhood education. The first batch of trainee teachers were Noorbanoo

Esmail (mentioned earlier) from the Cassim Ally Ismail family of Pretoria; Mrs Gladys Ismail (no relation to Cassim Ally), wife of Ismail Barber; and Ratu Gulab, a young Hindu girl. A young African girl, named Margaret, who was taken on as a teaching assistant, also registered for the Montessori course, as did three of Rajabalikaka's daughters, two of whom were still studying at the Pretoria Indian High School.

Among non-Ismailis who sent their children to the nursery school were Joosub HS Ebrahim, Hajee Ebrahim, Cassim Osman Ali, the Maharaj Singh family and the Chiba family. The children of a Chinese family in Marabastad also attended. In the early days, Habib was helped by his sister Sherbanoo, who had some practical experience in teaching. She enlisted the help of various volunteers, among them Ebrahim Virji's daughter Saker and AA Khoja's daughter Gooly. The school was rated "A" grade and was credited to allow training for six teachers. Of these, three were non-Ismailis and three Ismailis. The non-Ismailis were a Hindu, a Sunni Muslim, and an African.

Legally, the school had to have a White supervisor, but the law forbade Whites to work for Indians, so Habib was unable to find one willing to take the job. Luckily, he was told about Miss Martins, a trained European nursery school teacher who was recuperating from a bout of tuberculosis and so was unable to get a job. Habib offered her the supervisory position, and after she was given a clean bill of health, she accepted and held the position for two years, with Miss Peacock, a Coloured woman, as her deputy. Habib then heard of Glennie Tomlinson, a newly trained specialist supervisor in Cape Town. He travelled there and recruited her after assuring her parents that their daughter would be treated with the highest respect and that she would be teaching in a professionally run school. Eventually, she left South Africa to work at the multiracial United World College in Mbabane, Swaziland, and lived in that country until her death in the early 2000s.

Habib realized that two basic conditions needed to be met if non-Whites were to survive and ultimately flourish in South Africa. First, proper meals had to be provided to the young, who were malnourished and occasionally went hungry. Moreover, they needed to have vigorous play-time activities as well as time to rest and recuperate. The second necessity was education to provide the intellectual tools, knowledge, and skills to enable them to succeed. Habib viewed the nursery school as part of the survival strategy, providing both early education as well as nutritious meals consisting of vegetables, fruit, soup, milk, and cheese. The children thrived physically and mentally and in due course became responsible and successful adults. One of the alumni, Sue Singh, became an ambassador for South Africa many years later.

Children's health was also ensured by the clinic that was set up. Infants were inoculated and each week mothers brought them to the clinic for health checks. Mothers were also given advice on basic hygiene, nutrition and maternal and child health care. People who were ill were seen by a doctor who visited the clinic from downtown Pretoria one day a week. Among the White doctors who provided their services were Dr Rudolph, Dr Epstein, Dr Kaplan, Dr de Villiers and Dr Botha. Referrals from the clinic were made to the Pretoria Indian Hospital, particularly the Cassim Adam Ward, named after the leading Memon businessman who had donated it some years earlier.

In early 1946, Rhemtulla Velshi Keshavjee, Rajabalikaka's eldest son, left for London immediately after matriculating from high school. Rhemtulla intended to study law at the London School of Economics, but it was then giving priority to returning war veterans and he was unable to gain admission. He was impressed by the work that Krishna Menon was doing for the India League and joined Menon's team. Together, they produced a small newsletter publicizing the treatment meted out to non-Whites in South Africa.

While delivering bread in Black townships, Habib came into contact with Father Trevor Huddleston, an English Anglican priest (and later Bishop of Stepney in London) who worked in Sophiatown, the major hub of African settlement in the Rand. Huddleston, who had arrived in Sophiatown in 1943, was well known for his anti-apartheid activism. Since, unlike their European counterparts, African children were not provided with food at schools, Huddleston started the African Children's Feeding Scheme, mobilizing private donations to give each child a peanut butter sandwich every day. When Habib met him, he immediately pledged a dozen loaves of bread a day on behalf of Rajabalikaka, who was managing the ABC Bakery and was already involved in a number of philanthropic activities.

At the bakery, Rajabalikaka provided employment to a number of people, including Whites, particularly ex-convicts who were unable to secure jobs in White enterprises. He thus helped them to rehabilitate. He also visited patients at a leper asylum near Johannesburg as well as at a mental asylum and was on a committee to oversee their wellbeing. During the 1940s, when extreme poverty was widespread and flour was being rationed, he sold half-loaves so that poor families could eat fresh bread every day. In addition, he opened his bakery ovens for one day a week to African and Coloured people who had flour. Hundreds of women from Marabastad and Bantule flocked in on the given day, carrying pots of risen dough on their heads, to bake it free of charge after the bakery's bread had been produced and the ovens were still hot.

Later in his life, Rajabalikaka joined the Moral Rearmament Movement and visited the MRM centre for post-War European reconciliation at Caux in Switzerland with Dr William Nkomo, one of the first Black medical doctors from the Pretoria area, who often frequented his home in the 1940s.

Rhemtulla's involvement with anti-racism and left-wing peace organizations created problems for Rajabalikaka, especially with the advent of the Cold War. The Special Branch frequently raided the bakery and Rajabalikaka's home. They banged on the door in the early hours of the morning, and as soon as he opened it they barged in, ransacked the cupboards, pulled all the clothing out of cupboards and chests of drawers and left the house in a mess. Their excuse for the raids was that some of the bakery's yeast stock was being used by indigenous people to make illicit beer. The trauma of the predawn raids haunted his wife and daughters for years. Despite all these difficulties, Indians continued to trade, coming up with new ideas each day in order to survive.

Because of the competition between the two major cinemas in Marabastad, their owners used various methods to attract clientele, and that was where Marabastad's creative electronics genius Omarjee Suleiman played an important role. For example, when screening *Mighty Joe Young* at the Empire Cinema, Habib asked Omarjee to create a big animation for it. The film was about a gorilla going on the rampage in a Hollywood nightclub, and its twenty-four-foot poster displayed the gorilla clutching a woman in its paw. Omarjee cut out the gorilla, mounted it on hardboard, and used an electrical mechanism to move the paw and open the woman's mouth in a scream for help. The screams were provided by Habib's young daughter Farieda. Thousands of people came from as far away as Atteridgeville, Lady Selborne, Bantule, Mooiplaas, Pretoria North, and other African locations to view and listen to this spectacle of terror and then pay the entry fee to view the film. For Tarzan films, Habib had his young son Lutaf dress the stage with a lion skin, some bush effects and images of muscular African warriors with spears.

Habib's novel attractions helped to increase revenues, which enabled him to purchase a modern Rex Westrax movie projector, the type used in the White movie theatres of Johannesburg. It was typical of Habib that every month he donated one day's takings to a charitable fund that provided blankets to African families in the townships—something that his nephew, Noordin, continued for years, earning him the nickname "Blanket."

The circumstances in which urban Africans lived in the South Africa of the 1940s were reflected in the casualties who ended up at the Baragwanath Hospital in Johannesburg. It was there that Dolly Keshavjee, as a medical intern—the only female Muslim doctor from Pretoria at the time—and Dr Ronnie Pillay, who followed her at Wits University some years later, ministered to humanity in the raw: people who had been beaten up by a police officer, shot by a gangster, or had tried to commit suicide in order to escape the purgatory in which they lived. It was this South Africa that incensed activists like Nelson Mandela and Oliver Tambo. They established one of the first African legal practices in the country, in Johannesburg, to help the downtrodden to the extent possible through the legal system.

Chapter 12

March Towards Apartheid and Defiance

AS THE 1940S UNFOLDED, HABIB, AS HEAD OF THE EDUCATION board, realized that there was an urgent need to replace Sherbanoofaiba, who had passed away after having done much to provide spiritual and intellectual education to the Ismaili youth. The banalities of American pop culture, coupled with the deleterious effects of apartheid, were infiltrating the entire country, and in Marabastad the absence of libraries and other cultural services left young Ismailis vulnerable to such influences. However, the religion lessons had to be mentally stimulating, not learned by rote, and in English, since young Ismailis now had limited knowledge of Gujarati.

Habibkaka wrote to the Aga Khan outlining the situation and asking for a teacher to be sent to Pretoria to help the jamat. The Imam told him to get in touch with VM Nazarali, who was the education administrator of the Ismaili community in Tanganyika. Through Nazarali, he got in touch with the Ismaili leadership in India, who recommended Sadruddin Khimani, a bright young matriculant in Karachi who was fluent in English. There were very few English-language books on the Ismaili tariqah, so Habibkaka requested Khimani to bring along all those in Gujarati, which he could translate in Pretoria. Khimani arrived in South Africa in January 1948 with his wife Malek, who was also a teacher, and his baby daughter Yasmin.

The V Keshavjee family helped Master Khimani—as he was addressed despite his youth—to set up his school and home in Barber Street, opposite the veldt at the base of the Magaliesburg Mountain. Master Khimani was very well versed in Islamic studies and the Ismaili tariqah, having studied the Qu'ran and worked with Ismaili scholars such as Kassamali

Mohamed Jaffer and the well-known Gulamali Shah. Master Khimani became a pillar of the community, playing a vital role in the education board and assisting in the work of the nursery school as well as the council. He eventually migrated to Vancouver in Canada.

In mid-1947, a major development took place in the M Keshavjee family that was to have a significant impact on my life and the lives of my siblings. The M Keshavjee & Company partnership was dissolved, with many issues that took decades to resolve. That unfortunate event led to our inability to access our share and the massive dissipation of my father's assets over a period of time. Despite that difficulty, the later generations have maintained or restored a sense of family and friendship. As is often the case, the women played an important part in the healing process.

Following the dissolution of the partnership, my father started a business as a manufacturers' representative on Pretoria's Prinsloo Street under the name Manbro Proprietary Limited, selling flour, soft drinks and brand-name chocolates to retailers in the Pretoria area. He also had a small office on Commissioner Street, in a poorer area of Johannesburg, in a building called New Court Chambers. On the same floor were two young African lawyers operating under the name Mandela & Tambo – Attorneys. Every day, the corridors leading to their office were crowded with Africans with cases to plead in court.

In 1948, Prince Sadruddin Aga Khan, then aged 15, the younger son of the Imam, visited South Africa. He was accompanied throughout the country by Goolam Manjee Keshavjee. He visited all the social development institutions of the community and on his return reported the progress to the Imam.

By 1948 it had become apparent to those in power that the world needed South Africa's gold, diamonds, and other resources more than South Africa needed the world. That unpleasant reality had also dawned on the non-White population of the country, who were intimidated and insulted on a daily basis by the police.

The 1948 Malan government, the first all-Afrikaner administration in the country's history, built on such racism and gave priority to protecting the White population through legislation to segregate the races, prevent miscegenation and reserve the best or crucial parts of the economy for Whites. Millions of non-Whites were uprooted from their homes and transported to barren ghettos without electricity or running water and very often without shelter of any kind, while Whites lived in great comfort in areas reserved for them.

The apartheid policies of the Afrikaner regime deepened resentment among non-Whites and caused outrage among decent-minded liberal South African Whites. They were catalytic years in which the Campaign of Defiance of Unjust Laws was launched jointly by the African National Congress (ANC), South African Indian Congress (SAIC) and Franchise Action Council, a Coloured organization in the Cape, who demanded the repeal of certain discriminatory laws by 1 March 1952, failing which they would embark on mass action. They also resolved to carry out country-wide protest meetings and demonstrations on 6 April, the 300th anniversary of the arrival of White settlers in South Africa, as the prelude to the Campaign of Defiance of Unjust Laws.

The government's response was to threaten to "make full use of the machinery at its disposal to quell any disturbances, and, thereafter, deal adequately with those responsible."

On 6 April, tens of thousands of non-White South Africans and some White supporters demonstrated their abhorrence of racism and apartheid in a way never before witnessed in the country. The meetings, held in almost every city and town, were among the largest ever organized by Black movements. Alarmed by the unity and determination of the protesters, the government confined a number of leading Congressmen and trade unionists to their provinces and ordered them to resign from their organizations. This failed to intimidate the protesters and their leaders set 26 June 1952 as the date for commencing the Defiance Campaign. The leaders who had been restricted to their provinces would also defy the order. The government thereby arrested several ANC and SAIC leaders.

On 26 June, acts of defiance against the newly passed racist laws were carried out by groups of volunteers in all the main centres of the country. On the first day of the campaign, prominent leaders such as Walter Sisulu, Nelson Mandela, Yusuf Kachalia, and Raymond Mhlaba were arrested and detained, but the defiance actions continued. By that time, Rhemtulla Velshi Keshavjee had returned to South Africa and started working closely with Sooboo Pillay and Thayanaygee Pillay. Borrowing his cousin Noor's car without telling him what he planned to do, he joined Sooboo and others in entering the Pretoria railway station through the front entrance, which was reserved for Whites. The Special Branch noted the number plates of all the cars parked at the station, and since Noor's was registered in his name, they assumed he had participated in the defiance action. In the course of that year, Rhemtulla, like thousands of others who were part of this protest movement, broke the law at various other public locations.

Defiance Campaign participants throughout the country were arrested and fined, but they refused to pay the fines and were imprisoned. The courts, which had initially handed out light sentences, began to impose maximum sentences in almost all the protest areas.

Even though more than 5,000 participants were imprisoned during the first three months, the campaign grew in popularity among non-Whites all over the country. It also won the grudging respect of many White English-language newspapers. Then riots broke out. There was evidence that they had been instigated by the police to give them an excuse for increased violence against the campaigners, but the government brushed aside demands for a judicial commission of inquiry. A number of people were killed. In 1952, the government banned all meetings of more than ten people and passed the Criminal Law Amendment Act, which enabled the courts to sentence campaigners to be whipped and imprisoned. It also passed the Public Safety Act, which empowered it to declare a state of emergency anywhere in the Union and suspend all laws there. Lawbreakers could be given any penalty, including confiscation of goods and property as well as death.

Within a week of the enactment of that legislation, one of the most dramatic defiance actions took place on 8 December 1952, when a group of non-Blacks—whose ranks included, among others, Patrick Duncan, son of the former governor-general of South Africa, Manilal Gandhi, son of the Mahatma, Sooboo Pillay, Thayanayagee Pillay, Mosie Moola, Rhemtulla Keshavjee, and Percy Cohen—entered the African township of Germiston without a permit. They were arrested and jailed.

It was then, in mid-April 1953, that Chief Albert John Luthuli, who had been elected president-general of the ANC in December 1952, declared that in the light of government proclamations and the new draconian laws, it was necessary to call off the Defiance Campaign and take stock of the situation.

In the autumn of 1951, about a year before all this happened, Habib Keshavjee migrated to Kenya, which was then a largely agricultural British colony. He left his cinema in the care of his eldest son, Noor, instructing him to run it until he found a buyer and then to join him. Racial discrimination in terms of allocation of living areas, schools, and other amenities was a daily fact of life for non-Whites in Kenya, though not on the same scale as in South Africa. White settlers had appropriated land in the fertile highlands and resentment had been building to the point where an armed struggle for freedom was about to break out. An African nationalist, Jomo Kenyatta, was one of the moderate voices urging political action, but radicals within the highland tribes formed the Land and Freedom Army (later termed the Mau Mau) to launch guerrilla warfare from bases in the forests.

At the time of Habib's arrival, certain professions, particularly commercial farming, were reserved for Whites. Indians were largely in trade but were allowed to practise some professions and fill posts at certain low levels of the civil service, such as teaching. The Africans, largely living in the "reserves," were considered to be an inconvenient and potentially threatening blot on the generally cosy landscape of the White population.

One day, while Habib was sitting in a plane deep in conversation with a South African Indian journalist named Ronnie Peters, an air hostess accidentally dropped a tray of food on his suit. She apologized profusely and asked him to send the dry-cleaning bill to the airline. Immediately on his arrival in Nairobi, he went to a few dry-cleaners and was astounded to learn that none of them provided same-day service.

Habib found that all the dry-cleaners in Kenya, including long-established British firms, used antiquated equipment and inefficient processes. That sector was obviously the opportunity he was looking for. Early in 1952, at the then ripe age of 42, he imported state-of-the art machinery from Baker Perkins in South Africa and set up White Rose Drycleaners and Dyers, with the motto "Your clothes' best friend." He had never run a dry-cleaning enterprise, so he began to learn the rudiments of the business and used his contacts with White businessmen in South Africa to enable his sons and nephew, who were still in that country, to learn the necessary skills.

Through the business connections that he built up in Kenya, Habib was able to meet prominent people in all the communities. One such contact was JM Desai, an Indian in the insurance business who was very close to Apa Pant, India's high commissioner to East and Central Africa. Pant encouraged Indians to invite Africans to social gatherings in their homes, which was highly unusual in colonial Kenya. JM Desai and another well-known businessman, Suryakant Chhaganbhai Patel, responded positively, and over two or three years they invited more than three thousand Whites, Africans, and Indians to their homes. It was at one of those parties that Desai introduced Habib to Jomo Kenyatta as a man who had worked closely with Africans in South Africa. Habib was drawn to Kenyatta's immense energy and warmth and told him that he would like to help with the African social cause in Kenya.

As the year progressed, the Mau Mau guerrillas began their campaign to drive out the Whites and the press reported a wave of killings of White farmers. The British response was brutal and thousands of Africans were taken to detention centres where they were raped, tortured, and maimed by interrogators. Many were hanged.

In October 1952, the British government declared a state of emergency. Kenyatta and five other prominent African politicians were charged with orchestrating the Mau Mau movement and detained. Two Asians, Makhan Singh, a leading trade unionist, and Pio Gama Pinto, a leftist political activist, were also imprisoned. Some Indian lawyers in Kenya offered their pro bono services to defend Kenyatta, with Achroo Ram Kapila, barely in his twenties, taking the lead junior position. He was joined by Fitzwell de Souza and Jaswant Singh. The more senior Asian lawyers in Kenya soon managed to secure the services of DN Pritt, a leading British QC with leftist leanings who had made his name defending political activists, mainly in pre-World War II Europe and later in post-war Africa. In addition, through his connections with Nehru, Pant was able to engage some outstanding Indian lawyers to work on the defence team. Diwan Chaman Lall, India's ambassador to Turkey, flew in to join the team, as did HO Davies from Nigeria and Dudley Thompson, a well-known barrister from Jamaica.

The Kenyatta case, as it was called, commenced in December 1952 in Kapenguria, a few hundred miles from Nairobi. The legal process was contaminated by perjury on the part of prosecution witnesses. On Christmas day in 1952, DN Pritt had an exchange on a matter of procedure with the magistrate, who charged him with contempt of court. Kapila successfully defended him against the charge. After the day's proceedings, the defence team could not find a local place that would serve drinks to a multiracial group, so they drove to Nairobi to celebrate. There, Kapila told his good friends Gulli and Hassan Rattansi of his success in defending Pritt, and Hassan then passed on the news to Habib, who was holding a Christmas party at his home that evening. Habib invited Hassan and Kapila to join him and to bring the defence team with them. Among the guests at the party were Diwan Chaman Lall, DN Pritt and a group of local African trade unionists. That evening of innocent multiracial festivity was to cause reverberations in far-off South Africa later.

⸻ ♦ ⸻

Meanwhile, back in South Africa, I was a young schoolboy, living in the heart of Marabastad with my nine siblings in a greystone house that was formally called Fazal Villa in memory of a cousin who had died in infancy. However, we simply referred to our home by its street address, 274. It had beautiful bay windows overlooking the street. The front door was partly glass with wooden latticework. The front garden had a small palm tree and beautiful sunflowers, which spread out their bright yellow petals like solar-powered satellite dishes always following the sun. Between the verandah, which had a regularly polished bright red floor, and the deep green of the sunken garden was a row of cement balusters on which rested a slate top, almost like a long table. The house was usually filled with laughter and fun.

My parents enrolled me at the Pretoria Indian Junior School in 1951and I was mortified to find that I had been placed in a class humiliatingly known as the "baby class." The teacher, Miss Bridgens, had very short blonde hair, wore black dresses and peered at us through rimless spectacles perched on her nose, all of which gave her a severe and forbidding appearance. She used the cane unsparingly and I do not recall her ever smiling. With unwitting humour, we labelled her "a strict madam."

That period of my life also coincided with my spending most of my time at my maternal uncle's home. Habib Kanjee, whom we called Mama, was a gentle and caring man and was married to my father's youngest sister Khatija. They had no children, while my mother was pregnant with her tenth child by then, so I was "lent" to them. They lavished enormous love and affection on my brother Ameer and me.

I did not like school, but every afternoon I was forcibly seated in a bombie to be taken there by Sonny, an African with a pleasant oval face topped with a crest of peppercorn hair. This was particularly humiliating because a bombie—a bicycle in which a big wooden box resting on two wheels replaced the front wheel—was generally used to transport goods. Sonny had strict instructions to deposit me in Miss Bridgens's hands at the gates of the school.

No sooner was I delivered into her firm grasp, than I would try to tear free. If I succeeded, I would run to 181 Grand Street, where I would take refuge under my maternal grandfather Kanjee Kassam Panchaan's black metal bed. If an irate Rex came running to ask Bapa (Kanjee Kassam Panchaan) if he had seen me, he would feign ignorance of my whereabouts.

One day, fed up with my antics, the principal, Mr Walters, threatened to expel me unless serious action was taken to ensure my attendance. My eldest sister Guli was then given the responsibility of taking me to school each day. She asked our cousin Saker to help her with the task, and every afternoon they would each take firm hold of one of my hands and march me off to school. Miss Bridgens, too, had decided that serious measures were needed to keep me in line and every time I tried to escape she would grab me and administer two whacks with her cane. After a while, I gave up and resigned myself to my fate, looking forward to the time when I would no longer have to attend that school.

On 30 April 1951, Bapa passed away at the age of 85. His life had been somewhat sad. He had left Gondal in India in 1898 against his father's wishes and had never been able to go back to visit his parents. He had lost his parents as well as his wife in a single year, which had been a source of great sorrow to him for the rest of his life. He had visited India to marry for a second time, only to lose that wife in the 1918 flu epidemic. Bapa had not remarried after that but had given his life to caring for his two infant daughters, my mother and her sister Sakina. My mother later described to me how, when she was a child, Bapa would wrap an egg in a wet cloth and boil it for her and her sister by placing the package on a paraffin-fuelled heater for some minutes. He was a kind and conscientious man and did his best to make up for their not having a mother.

I started enjoying school only at the beginning of 1952, when I was transferred to the morning session and assigned to a teacher marvellously named Mrs Human. She encouraged us to do things rather than simply learn by reading and listening. Among other things, we were taught to make a cloth satchel for our books, a big task for little boys but nevertheless fun.

As mentioned earlier, one of my cousins, Hoosen Cassim Keshavjee, around 1951 set up a one-man medical practice in Alexandra township, one of the biggest Black townships in the Rand. He worked there until 1957. Hoosen's African neighbours, because of his compassion to them, always treated him with respect and hospitality. In spite of widespread petty crime, he could enter the township at any time of day or night without fear of being mugged.

Later in the decade, Hoosen went to England for a year to pursue a paediatrics course at the Mile End Hospital in the East End of London and the Institute of Child Health on Great Ormond Street. He returned to South Africa in 1960 to continue his practice for another seven years. In 1967, he decided that, with apartheid increasingly encroaching upon the family's lives, South Africa was no longer a place to raise children, and he emigrated to Canada. He was not the first member of our family to do so, having been preceded a few months earlier by a niece named Izzat, who was Jivanbapoo's great-granddaughter.

The early 1950s also saw other members of the Keshavjee family looking for new pastures. Mamdoo Madhavjee, one of Jivanbapoo's grandsons, became a trader in the Congo, but his small venture failed. A quixotic, adventurous and determined character, he ended up in London, establishing the Keshavjee settlement in the UK in the early part of the decade. He was followed by Ismail Allibhai Keshavjee, who had participated in the Passive Resistance Campaign of 1946. Bundaly, Naranbapoo's eldest grandson, also left, going to Nairobi where he started a highly successful turf accountancy.

For my siblings and me too, 1951 was an important year, as our family acquired the Empire Café. Bapoo, (my father) who had by then parted company with M Keshavjee and Company, had left Pretoria to try his luck in the burgeoning city of Cape Town. My two elder brothers and eldest sister, together with my mother, took over management of the family in Pretoria during my father's absence in the Cape. That period saw the closing phase of Habib's businesses in South Africa, as within a little over a year of his departure all his children left the country for Kenya for good.

The first year of our tenure in the cinema was exciting. We were energized by the new business and worked very hard to make a success of it. My six sisters, ranging in age from 10 to 14 years, worked like beavers at home and at school and then at the café. My eldest brother, Rex, worked outside at a clothing store during the day and helped in the evenings at the café. Ameer, my second brother, managed the café while he was still attending school. I helped to pack the café fridge with soft drinks.

Towards the beginning of 1953, Noor managed to sell the cinema to the Chetty Brothers, four enterprising Tamils who were in the fresh produce business but wanted to branch out into new activities. Within ten years they took over both the Keshavjee cinemas, thus making themselves the cinema kings among non-Whites in Pretoria.

After selling the cinema, Noor started making preparations to leave South Africa. His passport had expired, and to apply for a new one he needed a clearance certificate from the police. He submitted his old passport to the Pretoria police, but when he returned to collect it, together with the clearance certificate, they kept putting him off. Finally, he was told that the ministry of the interior at the Union Buildings had decided to withhold his passport. When he asked why, the officer said he didn't know. Murad and Gulshan, Rhemtulla's two siblings, who were also planning to leave for Kenya, went into the office next and were given a similar response. After discussing their predicament, they decided to contact Habib for advice.

Habib, who by then had good contacts in the British colonial administration, got in touch with a Mr Hymers in the Kenyan immigration department, who informed him that his family members could enter Kenya for a short time on the basis of an identity card. However, Noor did not have an identity card. Habib then suggested that they should get in touch with Rhemtulla, whose contacts in Johannesburg might be able to suggest a way for them to fly to Kenya. A Jewish friend of Rhemtulla's, a Mr Gershon who was in the travel business, advised him to purchase three return tickets from Johannesburg to Tel Aviv via Nairobi. He said he could arrange for an immigration officer to let Noor, Murad, and Gulshan leave Jan Smuts airport in Johannesburg without a passport. So, on a specified day towards the end of June 1953, Noor, Gulshan, and Murad were driven to the airport by Ismail Abed, who was then working at the ABC Bakery. They presented their documents to the immigration officer, who nodded them through, saying in a matter-of-fact tone, "Have a good flight." A short while later, their flight was called and they boarded the plane.

Within a few days of their arrival in Nairobi, Habib gave them jobs in his dry-cleaning enterprise. Noor immediately made Kenya his definitive home, but he was not able to get a Kenyan passport until 1963 when the country attained independence. Gulshan married Amir Jamal of Kisumu, who was later elected to the first post-independence parliament. Murad wanted to return to South Africa to complete his studies, but Habib advised him to stay in Nairobi until the political conditions in South Africa improved.

To help Murad secure travel papers, Habib turned to Apa Pant, who arranged for him to obtain Indian citizenship as well as an Indian travel document, which was to be surrendered to the nearest Indian embassy after he retrieved his South African passport or acquired any other nationality. After a few months, Murad was able to slip back into South Africa by train through the Portuguese East African border. He was met at the station in Pretoria by Rhemtulla. At their home, they were all about to eat breakfast when there was a knock on the door. It was Mr Lagransie of the Special Branch paying one of his "friendly visits." "Welcome back," he said to Murad with a wily smile. "And how was Nairobi?"

In view of the difficulties experienced by Noor in leaving South Africa, Habib advised his second son Lutaf, then in the midst of his matriculation studies in Pretoria, to pack up and discreetly leave for Kenya. One morning in early 1953, Lutaf boarded a BOAC Comet that flew him to Nairobi. That was the end of his schooling, and within a few days of his arrival he joined the burgeoning new business, to the growth of which he and Habib's adopted son, Hoosen contributed in no small measure over the next decade.

Habib's passport had also been cancelled by the authorities, and he only found out why two years later when a friendly Afrikaner in the immigration department told him that his file contained information about his links with "communists" like DN Pritt. It had a photograph taken at his Christmas party, with Pritt, Achroo Kapila, and Chaman Lall wearing paper Christmas hats, all in a jubilant mood. There were also photos of Noor's car at the Pretoria railway station during the Defiance Campaign a year earlier. Apparently, that had been enough for the Special Branch to conclude that Habib and his family were trying to overthrow the South African government with the help of "communist" and "terrorist" opponents of colonialism in Kenya!

Chapter 13

Snapshots of Marabastad in the 1950s

ONE COULD WALK FROM EAST TO WEST ACROSS MARABASTAD, from one boundary to another, in fifteen minutes, but despite its small size it was a microcosm of the linguistic and ethnic reality of South Africa. Most people spoke either English or Afrikaans, and one could also hear a range of African languages, including Zulu, Xhosa, Venda, Sesotho, Swazi, Ndebele, Tswana, and Mchaangaan. The mother tongue of the majority of the Indians was Gujarati, Hindi, Telegu, Malayali, Tamil, or Urdu. However, some spoke Memon, Cutchi, or Punjabi. The few Chinese spoke Mandarin or Cantonese.

A number of trades flourished, mainly conducted by the Indian community. The area was a patchwork of small shops selling everything that a small household would need, such as flour, paraffin, candles, butter, bread, milk, tea, coffee, lentils, cold drinks, and matches. Homes were attached to shops, some of which had been built in the late 1920s and 1930s, others later.

Marabastad had its share of barbers, butchers, and bicycle shops. Butchers were run mainly by Kookni (Kokanee) Muslims and had names such as Medina Butchery and Master Butchery. All displayed "Bismillah" or "786" in Arabic, indicating that the meat was Islamically pure. The shops were kept fastidiously clean, the floors covered with sawdust and the knives washed and sharpened frequently through the day. Electric saws were used to cut through bones.

Bicycle shops were characterized by the clutter in their windows, often displaying diverse products, from torch batteries and Swiss knives to ball bearings and bicycle pumps. All had a bicycle frame hung upside down on an outside wall with music blaring from the inside. The two best-known in the area were Kalla's and Adam's shops. They were mainly frequented by Africans, for whom a bicycle was the most convenient and cheapest mode of transport.

Barbershops generally enjoyed brisk business, but competition forced them to keep their charges low and the income was just enough to live on. One of the Muslim barbershops was that of Ahmed Barber, diagonally opposite the Ismaili jamatkhana. Ahmed, a short man with a dark complexion and sparkling eyes, always wore a red *kofia* over his sparse hair and was helped in the shop by his many sons. The shop was suffused with a sweet smell that came from Brylcream, Brilliantine, Vaseline hair tonic, and hair pomade. In addition to cutting hair, Ahmed performed all the circumcisions of Muslim boys, a lucrative and necessary sideline. He never anesthetized a child; instead, he distracted the child's attention by saying "Hey, look at the golden bird up there," and before the unsuspecting boy knew what was happening his foreskin had been cut off. Predictably, that led to mothers referring to male circumcision as "flying the golden bird."

Other barbers, too, coupled their barbering with other work to supplement their income. Ebrahim Sabi, a thinner version of Bob Hope and with a similar smile, was an excellent photographer. From the early 1940s, he shot professional-quality portraits of people in the area and recorded many significant family events. Every wedding celebrated in Marabastad was photographed by him. His photo business thrived until the late 1990s and his rubber stamp mark appears in the photo albums of many families in South Africa and wherever former residents of Marabastad have migrated.

Another barber, Jeewa Mohamed, who played an important role in the 1946 Passive Resistance Campaign, was an excellent singer of devotional songs in praise of the family of Prophet Muhammad. He also carried out exorcisms—which, curiously, were not banned by the apartheid regime. Thus, while the government had to use considerable force to evict people from their homes, Jeewa Mohamed evicted ghosts with incantations! Even some Whites turned to him when they needed to rid their houses of a stubborn White ghost.

Another colourful barber was Abu, a tall, handsome man with dark hair and dark intelligent eyes who wore a gold ring in one earlobe. He was also the drum major of a ceremonial band called the Muslim Brigade and led their marches, dressed in a resplendent uniform with a leopard skin draped over it, and carrying a glinting brass mace.

Marabastad had several restaurants. My favourite was Rah's Restaurant on Boom Street West, owned by the Bhaktavers. It had a billiard room and was famous for Mrs Kate Bhaktaver's delicious, juicy, heart-attack hamburgers. Pema's Restaurant, owned by Naran Pema, was known for its rich milkshakes in five flavours—chocolate, strawberry, vanilla, banana, and lime. The home-made ice cream used in the milkshake had a granular quality that gave wonderful body to the drink.

The Kit Kat, a spacious restaurant run by the grandchildren of Cassam Noormohamed, with whom Jivanbapoo had emigrated to South Africa, was adjacent to the Empire Cinema and provided upmarket snacks such as Goldfield's fresh cream pastries and samosas that put our own more plebeian product at the Empire café in the shade. However, Kit Kat charged double our price, so we did not lose clientele.

Sooboo's Café, on Boom Street, was run by the Pillay family, renowned for their contribution to the freedom movement. Its main culinary delight was the Dagwood sandwich—two thick slices of bread enclosing a large piece of fried fish—thought up by Vissoo, Thayanayagee's eldest son, who was also known as Pepe. He also pioneered a delicious toasted spicy mince sandwich. Like Rah's, the restaurant had a billiard room, which was also an important meeting place for political activists. Mohideen's, also on Boom Street, was a corner establishment whose main specialty was its Steak and Roll, the filling of which was curried steak with a unique sauce. It was owned by a Kokanee Muslim family who had originally run a butcher shop in the early 1950s.

Itinerant food sellers added to Marabastad's flavour with their own individuality. One example was Moosa Samosa, so-called because he sold that triangular spicy delicacy, which he carried in a basket. Aptly, his face was also triangular, a thin beard stretching from ear to ear across his chin, and a stalactite of straggly hair at its lowest point. He sported a short red *kofia* and sold his samosas to students at the Indian schools in Pretoria.

Then there was a Memon woman referred to simply as "Papadwaridossi" ("Old woman with the papadums") who walked down through the streets with a wicker basket of papadums on her head. A short woman with grey hair tied in a bun and a broad, friendly face, she wore a *shalwar khameez* and was a regular part of the street scene.

Another familiar figure was Manchimasi, a tall Gujarati woman with high cheek bones and a flat nose who balanced a basket of fresh Indian vegetables on her head with statuesque elegance as she went from house to house. Each morning she came to our home and placed all her vegetables on the stoep for us to choose from.

Another welcome peddler was a girl called Chundri, a student at the Pretoria Indian Girls' School who sold lemons garnished with spices and left to dry out in the sun. Our parents prohibited this mouth-watering snack with warnings that the lemons probably contained bird droppings picked up while drying. However, the contraband nature of the pickle only added to its taste and Ismaili children always had a good supply of it secreted away in various places.

Different streets had different smells. For example, 4th Street, the only north-south one in Marabastad that was paved, was filled every morning with the aroma of fresh hot bread from the ABC Bakery. In the evenings, passersby could delight in the smell of freshly baked buns called apricoteens and cakes. If one walked a block east, a smoky, nutty smell filled the air where Mr Siripat, who was also a teacher, roasted peanuts using home-made machines and sold in small paper packets. Yet further east, Gora Bibi, so-called because she kept horses in a big yard, grew the best mint in town, and the pungent aroma of fresh manure mixed with a heady smell of mint. At the corner of Boom and Cowie Streets, Chagan Ghanchi and his African employee Mazaambaan prepared "curry balls" each evening. The aromatic, hot, spicy fritters, sold in a newspaper cone with a topping of hot *achaar*, were so delicious that people scraped the newsprint off the pages with their curry balls to get the last bit of *achaar*. Across the road, his cousin Chunibhai produced a rose syrup that exuded a wonderful fragrance.

Marabastad had become so congested that every square foot of land was used for housing, cottage industry, or storage space for products sold in the shops. Therefore, the only playground we had was the side streets, which were not paved and therefore had less traffic. That was where we entertained ourselves after school, playing games, or simply hanging around. The boys played marbles, *gili danda*, and football with competitive intensity, and the girls played *borretjie*, a kind of hopscotch, with as much focus and competitiveness as the boys but perhaps less aggressiveness. The victors received lucky charms. My sister Khairu was one of the hopscotch aces and she still retains her tokens of childhood victories.

Festivals were times of widespread jollity and celebration, enabling people to forget their troubles briefly. During the five days of Diwali, Hindus lit oil lamps in their homes and temples in honour of Lakshmi, goddess of wealth, and sent sweetmeats to their neighbours. At night, they set off spectacular fireworks, lifting everyone's spirits. Often, the festival was accompanied by the latest Hindi film music blaring out from Mukhtiar Singh's residence on 5th Street. Mukhtiar, whose hat and drooping grey moustache made him look very much like a frontier Boer farmer, had a stall in the Pretoria market and would leave for town early in the morning in his horse and cart and return after a full day's hard work in the same conveyance. His daughters Chinta and Sheila and his niece Rupee went to school with my sisters.

Eid was another occasion for communal enjoyment. While the main celebration was held at the mosque in Pretoria town, Marabastad also had its own celebrations. Muslim boys wore red *kofia*s and went to the local mosque to offer the Eid prayer. Then came kite-flying in the streets, with home-made kites made from reed and garishly coloured tissue paper.

In the afternoon the Muslim Brigade would go out in full force, assembling at the ABC Bakery, which was festooned with coloured lights and beautiful bunting for the occasion. The band would march through the streets of the Asiatic Bazaar amid hundreds of clapping onlookers. Abu, the drum major, would fling his brass mace into the air and catch it, or twirl it imperiously. My sister Zarina played a bugle in the brigade and Uncle Habib's children were also part of it. As the brigade marched through the streets, it developed a growing tail of happy people in its wake, drawn to it like pins to a magnet. They created their own spectacle, spinning and dancing to the beat of the drum.

November saw the Coloured community commemorating Guy Fawkes Night. Young men and women from the Coloured location, costumed in a parody of sixteenth-century pot-bellied English gentry, came to our homes and asked for money, chanting, "*Aunty gee pennie vir die gai gai.*"

Once a year at springtime, Pretoria, the Jacaranda City, celebrated the widespread profusion of the purple flowers with the Jacaranda Festival, in which one of the central events was a contest to select the Jacaranda Queen. She would then ride in a long procession of floats gloriously bedecked with fresh flowers of various colours, regally waving at thousands of admirers who lined Church Street. Alongside the floats walked well-known Disney characters, such as Mickey Mouse, Donald Duck, and Pluto. After the procession, we took great pleasure in popping the flowers strewn on the ground by stamping on them.

The more earthy, rank odour of weeds assailed my nostrils during walks across the veldt in the early morning fog. It was accompanied by the smell of rubber from a burning tyre that had smouldered through the night to keep a *mpoisa*, night watchman, warm. The mpoisa, wearing a balaclava and thick long brown or grey overcoat and carrying a knobkerrie (a wooden club with a knob at one end) would be followed by his dog as he strode across the veldt on his way home after the night's vigil to protect his employer's property. A short walk away was the Apies River, its banks lined with bushes, which Winston Churchill reportedly swam across to escape from the Boers.

There were no leisure amenities in Marabastad, no library, no park, no swimming pool. All we could do was attend school in the morning, and in the afternoon work in a shop or café or go to the cinema. Mariam Ismail Bagas, who taught English at my primary school, was the first person to instil a passion for reading in me. She loved teaching and would capture our interest by making stories sound so real that we were transported to another world.

Once, she asked the class to write an essay entitled "Autobiography of a penny." I imagined myself as the coin and described my life, living in someone's purse, being used for a purchase and being placed in the till of a shop, then being given to a beggar who bought some bread in exchange for me. Eventually I ended up as a collector's item. Mariam found my essay intriguing and made me read it out to the class as a good example of imaginative writing. That was followed by a second essay entitled "Autobiography of an old shoe," which described various phases in my life and how I felt. At first I was part of a fine sartorial ensemble, feeling proud and haughty. Then I entered another phase where I was part of a whole set of shoes and called upon for service only on special occasions. Eventually I was discarded and forgotten. Again, Mariam was impressed by my creativity and mentioned what she considered to be my budding talent to her fellow teachers.

I began to enjoy school and started reading voraciously, a habit that my brothers Rex and Ameer encouraged in all their siblings. But, books were difficult to come by. One day I noticed that a Kanamia pupil named Alimia Dawood had a copy of *David Copperfield*. I asked him where he had got it from and he confided that a caretaker at the library for White people had lent it to him in exchange for a few samosas made by his mother. That was, of course, illegal and I was touched that Alimia had told me his secret. I asked him if I could borrow the book when he had finished with it, in return for which I would allow him free access to the Empire cinema through the back door.

We regularly bartered books for cinema entry (both precarious activities) until one day I lost a book. The White caretaker was able to concoct a story to explain how the book had disappeared, but my arrangement with Alimia came to an end.

There are always individuals who play an influential role in people's lives, and for me and other young Ismailis in the 1950s three people stand out in this respect: our religious and moral education tutor Master Sadruddin Khimani, my cousin Mamdoo, and my brother Ameer. Each one, in his own way, helped to shape our lives.

Sadruddin Khimani gave us religion instruction in the afternoons after classes ended at our secular school. His wife Malek gave us Gujarati lessons. Master (as he was known) regarded Islam as a faith, and an ethical way of life, a metaphor for spiritual growth and intellectual search. He understood that we needed not only to know the content of the Qur'an but also to comprehend its meaning to the extent that we were capable of.

Besides Qur'anic learning, Master taught us Ismaili devotional literature, mainly the ginans, which he sang melodiously. As with the Qur'an, he also taught us the meanings of the ginans, which were a bridge for us to the importance of ethics, the virtue of engagement with life, and the ephemeral nature of life and hence the need to nurture the journey of the soul.

Another person who brought a great deal of joy into our lives was my cousin Mamdoo (Mohamedali) Hassim Keshavjee. He was a young man with lofty ideals and a zest for life. As he grew up, he was fascinated by the American dream, and extolled its virtues to all and sundry. Mamdoo loved American actors, whose speech and gait he would imitate. So we had Mamdoo's version of Bob Hope, John Wayne and other celluloid luminaries. Often, he would imitate Nat King Cole's smooth velvet voice singing "Mona Lisa."

In the 1950s Mamdoo had a small apartment on 5th street, and that was where we got to know him well. Most of his furniture could be folded up, so he was able to have a small home library without cluttering the room. He built the book shelves himself with masonite boards and vinyl tiles. He also had collected classical records and enjoyed inviting friends over to listen to his music while he served them toasted cheese sandwiches and fresh fruit juices or coffee laced with almond essence. It was at his apartment that I first heard Handel's *Messiah*.

He often held quizzes, the winners receiving useful and valuable prizes such as an electric kettle, an iron, a toaster, a book, or a long-play vinyl record of classical music, which was a luxury in those days. People paid a small fee to participate, but what we did not realize then was that the prizes were often bought by him and his wife Sugra using their own money, the quiz fees being insufficient to cover their costs. When I later asked Mamdoo why they had done that, his answer was simple: "We felt that people had no real opportunity to learn or to express themselves in a place like Marabastad, and that was one way we could share what we had with others."

Mamdoo's creative energy was endless. He disliked curry powder because of its pallid taste and the assumption that a particular mixture of spices in a set ratio would satisfy everyone's taste buds. However, there was no shop in Marabastad selling individual spices. Therefore, Mamdoo opened a little spice shop called Masala House, which sold every Indian spice individually, enabling people to create their own mixes to suit their own palates. As word spread, people came from far and wide to buy the spices. Customers who were unfamiliar with some of the spices received advice from Mamdoo on how to use them.

The third person who had a deep influence on me and other young people in Marabastad during the 1950s was my elder brother Ameer. A young firebrand, he was a precocious child and obtained a double promotion at the Pretoria Indian School in the junior section. He was popular and hard working. A quiet individual who liked reading, he was what today would be called an ambivert, a person displaying characteristics of both an introvert and an extrovert. He was a good public speaker and loved debating.

In 1957, Ameer entered the University of Witwatersrand to pursue an undergraduate course in medicine as the first step to studying genetics. While he was at Witwatersrand, African commuters, largely from Alexandra township, decided to boycott buses owned by the Public Utility and Transport Company, which wanted to increase fares by a penny—a large sum for people who were barely able to survive on their meagre income. Hundreds of thousands of Africans decided to walk the twelve miles to and from Johannesburg. On one occasion, the university students were asked to join a protest march and Ameer did so too. What he did not know until six years later was that his participation had been recorded by the police.

Ameer left university without completing his studies because he had to help run Modern Distributors, our family's nascent food industry. He took over the reins of the family business, working together with my eldest brother Rex. But, he still wanted to study part-time and applied for a course in optometry at the Union College of South Africa. To be admitted to the course, he had to be employed by a practising optician in Pretoria, but they were all Whites and none was willing to employ him.

Ameer also helped to strengthen cultural activities among the Ismailis in Marabastad. Between 1958 and the early 1960s he worked with young people to establish a library in the jamatkhana premises and started a youth union in collaboration with our cousin Murad Velshi. He encouraged debates and drama. He organized lecture evenings. Ameer also read books about Ismailis globally and sought Master Khimani's participation in the lecture evenings. Occasionally he arranged musical evenings, where my father played the harmonium.

Ameer's hitting up against a brick wall when he tried to further his education laid the basis for his later work in Canada to enable marginalized students of all communities to go for post-secondary education. Over the past twenty-five years he has helped thousands of students to gain admission and access to scholarships.

Most of our life in Marabastad was taken up with the business of making a living and surviving. The factory we had started had good potential, but it was a cottage industry and encumbered by crippling overheads. We sold a number of products, some of which, particularly the cooking oil, were top of the range. Our bottled products also included olive oil, linseed oil, cod liver oil, and Worcestershire sauce. In addition, there were liquid paraffin, benzene, and turpentine. We produced our own fountain pen inks in three colours, blue, red, and green. Later we started manufacturing beauty creams for women, particularly a copper-coloured one that suited African complexions. Our products were sold to large White wholesalers in the Pretoria area and shops in African locations like Atteridgeville, Vlakfontein, Lady Selborne, and Pretoria North. I helped in the factory whenever I could, but my main remit from 1957, shared with my sister Zarina, was to look after the café, where I was solely responsible for the purchases. I was then twelve years old. My father, in the meanwhile, started a small business dealing with hessian bags, cardboard boxes, and recycled bottles, and this augmented the family income.

It was fifty years later that I realized that he had been ahead of his time. He pioneered the recycling concept in the Pretoria area, producing bricks from ash, reusing glass wine bottles, and collecting and selling used hessian bags to farmers at a time when there was a jute shortage due to a trade boycott imposed by India on South Africa. Later, he collected the paper and cardboard packages discarded by large department stores in Pretoria, sorted and baled them, and sent them for recycling to Johannesburg. He always saw the earth's resources as finite and waste was almost sinful to him. His ideas were brilliant, but after the dissolution of the partnership with M Keshavjee and Company in June 1947 he did not have the capital to bring them to full fruition. Many of us benefitted from his thinking; for example, years later in Canada, when my brother Sam set up a highly sophisticated plastic signs business for major industries, he used recycled materials to construct most of the machinery.

The decade of the 1950s, though difficult, had some very happy moments. One of these was in May 1958, when His Highness, Prince Karim Aga Khan, within a year of his accession to the Imamat, visited South Africa as part of his visits to Ismaili communities in Asia and Africa. In South Africa, he met senior Government Ministers, members of the Ismaili community, heads of various social development institutions, and leaders of other Muslim communities. Marabastad once again was beautifully decorated for the event and people recalled the visits of His Highness' grandfather, some thirteen years earlier. We were all in a jubiliant mood to see our new Imam, whose presence in our midst filled us with a great sense of joy and happiness.

Marabastad had a rhythm of its own. People danced, they drank and picnicked, and some of them had the most beautiful singing voices. Opposite our home was the Mariammen Temple, which is now a heritage site. Near the back wall of the temple every evening, a small group of Coloureds would sit behind a cart that had been unharnessed from its horse and kept warm in the cold wintry night by a small fire, and sing till midnight. "Greenfields" was their favourite song. Their voices were hauntingly beautiful, and I looked forward each night to hearing their song. It was this human spirit that died when the ignominious Group Areas Act finally descended on the area and wrenched people away from their homes.

Chapter 14

Our Encounters With Apartheid

IN TODAY'S SOUTH AFRICA, INSTITUTIONALIZED APARTHEID is only a memory. The signs reading *Blankes* (Whites) and *Nie Blankes* (non-Whites) have disappeared. There were few such signs in Marabastad because Marabastad itself was a sign of segregation. It was a place where Whites did not live or generally visit. They came to the area only to sell goods, to encourage the townsfolk to become Christians, to heal the sick with medicine, to check that we were living according to the law with regard to sanitation. Some White teachers came during the day to teach in the Indian schools. The only apartheid sign I encountered as a child was at the post office at the far end of Boom Street, which had clearly marked separate entrances for Whites and non-Whites.

I first heard of the Group Areas Act when, at the age of six years, I accompanied my mother on her visits to her friend Amrath, a business woman who owned two properties in Marabastad and was married to Noor Madhavjee. Each time we visited her, she would say to my mother conspiratorially, "Group Areas is coming," as if imparting a cabalistic secret. I thought Group Areas was a ceremonial band, like the Muslim Brigade, and was quite excited about the forthcoming entertainment. Little did I realize then that it was a contemptible piece of legislation that was going to envelop people's properties in its awful embrace and disrupt their lives in unimaginable ways.

Sometimes life under apartheid had a funny side to it. One of my cousins, Nizoo Ismail, had such an experience when he went for a haircut at Mathews Barber. He had left it till quite late in the day, but the Coloured assistant, Barrie, agreed to cut his hair even though it was after the legal business hours. Both knew that if caught they risked arrest. In non-White areas, the police came with dogs and batons and dealt harshly even with those who committed minor infractions of the law. Barrie, a short and muscular man with a good crop of hair on his head that made him look like the singer Mario Lanza, had trimmed one side of Nizoo's head when a man ran in and warned them that the police were going around checking. Barrie hurriedly opened the back door and pushed Nizoo out into the yard. "Come back on Monday," he whispered. Poor Nizoo had to find a cap to hide his semi-tonsure when he went to a party that weekend.

There were other incidents that we were not able to laugh off so easily. One day in 1957, another cousin, Akber, his brother-in-law Tajuddin Kanji, and an employee, Ebrahim Adam, were travelling from Johannesburg when they were involved in a head-on collision with a car driven by a White man. The White man died instantly and Akber and the two passengers in his car were seriously injured. Someone phoned for an ambulance, but when it arrived the driver refused to let the injured men into the vehicle because he was only allowed to carry Whites. Luckily, a White man who was driving past recognized the car as belonging to the Keshavjees and prevailed upon the ambulance driver to take the dead man and the three injured non-Whites to the nearest hospital that would admit them. The accident also resulted in another casualty; somehow the false news reached Akber's mother in Pretoria that her only son had died in the accident and she had a severe heart attack, which ultimately led to her premature death a few months later.

I was fortunate enough not to have had a personal experience of petty apartheid until early 1959, when my maternal cousin Yusuf came to visit us from Kenya. It was Yusuf's first visit since his family left South Africa in 1951. Although I was only fourteen, I was assigned the task of taking him around Pretoria, using an itinerary charted out by my brothers. After touring various places, all the while animatedly recalling our school days, we decided to go to Bill and Wally's Café for doughnuts and malted milk, for which it was famous. We were astonished when the man at the counter said to us, "Can you please go to the non-European side, you are not supposed to be here." He did not speak unkindly, but as if he were stating a normal fact. Our ebullience dissolved in the acid of South African reality and, stung with humiliation, we walked out of that restaurant in silence.

Habib in Nairobi wanted to ensure that his children never forgot the bitter reality of apartheid and so he encouraged them to revisit South Africa to experience it again. In 1960 he sent his son Lutaf to the United States for a dry-cleaning technology course at the National Institute of Drycleaners in Bethesda, Maryland, and he had him stop over in South Africa on the way. Lutaf visited Marabastad, where, in his youth, he used to dress the stage for Tarzan films at the Empire Cinema. We took him to the cinema and he found it difficult to believe that it had been his universe once. He kept muttering to himself, "Is this the dump in which I worked?"

We drove to a drive-in food outlet called Pickin-Chicken and ordered some takeaway food, only to be told categorically, "We do not serve non-Whites here." We left in disgust and drove to the Marathon Café, run by a Greek who did serve non-Whites. We related our story to him and he was sympathetic but shrugged his shoulders helplessly. Lutaf never returned to South Africa again.

The Group Areas Act eventually led to the closure of the ABC Bakery. In the late 1950s it was the eleventh-largest baking enterprise in South Africa and the largest non-White bakery in the country. It had a permit to enter African locations each morning, but only after all the White bakers' vans had done so and the Africans had breakfasted and gone to work. In order to survive, Rajabali Velshi started sending his bread vans into the Witwatersrand area and offered all the shops there a "baker's dozen"—one free loaf for every dozen bought—as well as lower prices. That violated an unwritten agreement that the Pretoria and Witwatersrand bakeries would not sell their bread in each other's areas. Rajabali's action gave the Rand bakeries an excuse to move into the Pretoria market, which in turn led to other Pretoria bakeries entering the Rand market.

Soon there was a bread war, which lowered profits in the sector in both the areas. The Master Bakers' Association of Pretoria summoned Rajabali and requested him to stop selling in the Rand area immediately, but he refused to budge as long as there was racial discrimination against ABC Bakery. The Association then suggested that he sell the bakery but found his price too high. Finally, after months of fruitless negotiation, all the White bakeries got together and bought the bakery, which had been in business for almost four decades. Rajabali continued to "own" the land.

Since a White-owned bakery was not allowed to operate in an Indian area, the municipal authorities then dismantled the bakery building. The struggle over the bakery broke Rajabali's spirit and he made plans to leave South Africa for Kenya. It was not to be, for in June 1960, a few months after his bakery had been dismantled, he had a heart attack and died at the age of 58.

There were Indians in the area that fought the Group Areas Act. Among them, Nana Sita, a grocer instantly recognizable in his collarless white shirt and white Gandhi cap, is one of those still remembered with respect and affection. Nana Sita was born in 1898 in Matwadi, a village in Gujarat, in a family that played an active role in the Indian freedom movement. He migrated to South Africa in 1913 and stayed with JP Vyas on Vermeulen Street in Pretoria to study book-keeping from him. Soon after his arrival, Mohandas Gandhi came to Pretoria to negotiate with Smuts and stayed at Vyas's home for two months. Impressed by Gandhi's courage and principles, Nana Sita decided to emulate him and became a vegetarian, teetotaller, and nonsmoker. More importantly, he decided to resist any form of injustice steadfastly.

He played an active role in the Transvaal Indian Congress and became secretary of its Pretoria branch. All his seven children and his wife Pemi participated in the freedom struggle, and most of them consequently spent time in prison.

With the banning of the ANC in 1960 and the escalation of government repression, the ANC leaders decided to resort to armed struggle, which created a dilemma for Nana Sita, who passionately believed in nonviolence. But, in spite of the government's brutality against peaceful protesters, he continued to defy apartheid, particularly the Group Areas Act, nonviolently. In 1962, when Hercules, the section of Pretoria in which he lived, was declared a "White area" and Indians were ordered to move to Laudium eleven miles away, he refused to do so and was taken to court. He denounced the Act and reminded the court of the global significance of the day—10 December, the fourteenth anniversary of the adoption of the Universal Declaration of Human Rights at the United Nations. He told the court, "I am suffering with chronic ailments of gout and arthritis, but I do not plead in mitigation. On the contrary I plead for a severe or the highest penalty that you are allowed under the Act to impose on me."

He was sentenced to a fine of 100 rand or three months in prison and warned that if he failed to move to Laudium, the sentence would be doubled. He refused to pay the fine and went to prison. The next year, as he and his wife Pemi continued to occupy their home, he was again taken to court and sentenced to six months. The authorities charged him and his wife yet again in 1965. He appealed to the Supreme Court, challenging the validity of the Group Areas Act, and the matter dragged on for a year before his appeal was dismissed. When his trial resumed in 1967, he was sentenced again to six months` imprisonment or a fine of 200 rand and he served the term. His wife was given a suspended sentence.

On 8 April 1968, he and his wife were forcibly evicted from their home and government officials dumped their belongings on the pavement. However, they returned to their home and Nana Sita refused to comply with the order until he died in December 1969.

Unlike Nana Sita and the militants, the Indian traders in Pretoria focused their efforts on having the Group Areas Act rescinded by writing petitions to the authorities. One of them was Haji Ebrahim, whose father, MH Joosub, had arrived in South Africa in 1876 and founded MH Joosub and Sons, a firm which is still operating to this day. In 1958, in close collaboration with a small group of fellow traders, including Ahmed Dockrat, Ebrahim prepared a booklet entitled *Bitterness Towards Indians*, which described the Act as sounding the "death knell to Indian commerce" and hence threatening the very survival of the Indian community. A small group of Indians went to seek advice on the Act from the anti-apartheid fighter Joe Slovo, who was then a practising lawyer, and he told them that there was no legal recourse since the law had been passed by a majority in parliament and all the other required formalities had been followed.

One of the victims of the Group Areas Act was Ismail Mahomed, who was the first student from the Pretoria Indian Boys' High School to go for legal studies. Sometimes he and Rhemtulla met students from the school at Pema's Restaurant, where they discussed politics and the role that students could play in the struggle against apartheid. One of his cousins, Ismail Ayob, who studied with me at Gray's Inn in London, also became a human rights lawyer and later a lawyer to the Mandela family.

After graduating from Witwatersrand University with a BA Hons with distinction in Political Science and a Bachelor of Laws degree, Ismail was rejected by the Bar in Pretoria because he was not White. He was then accepted by the Johannesburg Bar, but was unable to rent chambers in the building that housed the Bar because it was situated in a White area. For twelve years, he was forced to borrow desk space from White colleagues while they were away in court, and often had to use the library when no room was available. Even after obtaining a Group Areas permit in 1969, he was barred for another five years from using the common room, by which time he had already become South Africa's first non-White senior counsel. At times he was left with no alternative but to eat his lunch sandwiches in a toilet since no other space was available to him.

A workaholic with a brilliant mind, he rose to become an authority on the Group Areas Act and one of the leading experts on administrative and constitutional law in the country. He defended many anti-apartheid activists in political trials and was widely recognized as one of the most gifted orators at the South African Bar.

Ismail's judicial career initially blossomed outside South Africa. In the 1960s, he undertook work as a senior counsel in Botswana, Lesotho, Swaziland, and Zimbabwe. Having become the first non-White in South Africa to take silk, he was appointed to the Appeal Court of Swaziland in 1979. In 1982 he was appointed an Appeal Judge in Lesotho, where he would later become president of the Appeals Court. In 1984 he was called to the English Bar and in 1991 he was appointed chairman of the Convention for a Democratic South Africa and the country's first non-White judge of the Supreme Court. That was followed by an appointment to the Appeal Court. He was also a legal advisor to the South West Africa People's Organisation, which was fighting for the independence of the territory that later became Namibia, and was a co-author of Namibia's Constitution, which abolished capital punishment. In 1992, he was appointed Namibia's chief justice.

In 1995 Ismail was made a judge of the South African Constitutional Court. In 1996 he was appointed the first chief justice of South Africa by President Mandela. As chief justice, Ismail called on the judiciary to support him in restoring the legitimacy and sovereignty of the law in the eyes of South Africa's majority population. Sadly, he died of pancreatic cancer at the age of 68, having held the post for only two years.

Ismail's decisions as a judge are still quoted and respected internationally. It was in the field of human rights law that he made his greatest mark, with judgments that were not based on seeking revenge for what had happened in the past.

Marabastad also produced another stalwart adversary of apartheid in Mrs Thayanayagee Pillay, known popularly as Thaylamay, who was a satyagrahi par excellence. Her history is intertwined with Gandhi's early struggle, in which her father Thambi Naidoo featured prominently. At the age of four, Thaylamay spent some time at Tolstoy Farm with her four brothers who had been "adopted" by Gandhi and went back with him to India in 1914.

Thaylamay was the sister of Naran Naidoo, who was vice-president of the Transvaal Indian Congress in 1946. Naran and his wife Manonmoney, known as Ama Naidoo, also played a leading role in the anti-apartheid movement. Thaylamay's mother went to jail with the women who marched with Gandhi in 1913. Thambi Naidoo's son, daughter, daughter-in-law, granddaughter, grandson, and great-grandson all participated in the freedom struggle right up to the last days of apartheid. They were interrogated, tortured, incarcerated, and exiled.

Thaylamay's husband, Peramul Pillay, and his brothers Govind, Naran, Nadesan, and Sooboo, were also involved in the freedom movement. Another brother, Krishna, was the head of the Tamil community in Pretoria and was a custodian of the Mariammem temple near which he lived. The home of the Sooboo clan was a meeting place for political activists. Yusuf Dadoo, Nelson Mandela, and Bram Fisher often used to go there and discuss defiance programmes.

Thaylamay's contribution to the freedom movement remained steady throughout her life, but perhaps her most important contribution was during the Treason Trials, which started in 1956. In the dock were 105 Africans, 21 Indians, 23 Whites and 7 Coloureds. Initially, the trial was held at the Drill Hall in Johannesburg, but in 1958 the government suddenly decided to move the venue to Pretoria, some thirty-six miles away.

That forced many of the accused to wake up very early in the morning and spend almost five hours on the road.

Aware that they did not have proper meal facilities, Thaylamay went door to door in Marabastad to collect provisions, and many Indian shopkeepers donated groceries. The food was cooked with the help of Indian women in the neighbourhood and delivered in a cream and green Dodge station wagon by Sooboo and Thaylamay's eldest son, Vissoo (Pepe).

It was a trying period for the Sooboo family, who were constantly harassed by the security police demanding to know where the money was coming from to feed the "terrorists." Despite the intimidation, Thaylamay never disclosed the names of the people in the area who donated the food.

Soon the police started harassing Thaylamay's other son, Gonaseelan (Gono) and charged him under the 90-day Detention Act. They also often picked up her youngest son Sagrin, took him to the Pretoria Central Police Station and beat him up. One of Thaylamay's daughters, Sindamonie (Sinda), and her husband Balasundram (Bobeye), were also harassed. Bobeye, following a visit to Thaylamay's nephew, Indres Naidoo, who was already under house arrest, was summoned to the security police building in Pretoria where he was stripped naked and beaten mercilessly.

In March, 1961, the trial ended with the acquittal of all the accused. As a token of appreciation and affection, Nelson Mandela ordered a sari from India in the colours of the ANC and personally presented it to Thaylamay. She was beside herself with joy, but wore the sari only once before putting it away when Mandela, Sisulu, Kathrada and others were incarcerated for life on Robben Island. It remained in her cupboard for the next twenty-eight years, until Mandela invited her and her sister-in–law Ama Naidoo to his home after his release from prison. Thaylamay lived to see the new South Africa come into being. She died a few years later, and at her funeral her body was draped in the sari that Mandela had given her.

A resident of Marabastad, Syrub Singh, was one of the first people in South Africa to succeed in challenging the Immorality Act, which prohibited interracial sexual relations. Syrub, a tall, handsome young Rajput in his twenties who dressed stylishly and looked like a film star, was an insurance agent. He had to go to a government building in town every day for matters related to his insurance work and it was there that he met a beautiful Afrikaner clerk named Charlotte Rose Bloom. He asked her whether she liked Indian curry and she answered that she loved it. Syrub could not take her to a restaurant since that was forbidden by law, so he decided that the curry meal would have to be at his family home. It was the first time that a White Afrikaner woman had visited their home and the family were charmed by her.

Syrub decided to elope with Charlotte. They travelled north to Southern Rhodesia (now Zimbabwe) in his Chevrolet, with her sitting in the back seat and him driving, ostensibly as her chauffeur. They were married in Salisbury on 29 December 1961. Three weeks later, they returned to South Africa and went to live as man and wife in an apartment in Durban. In the early hours of 26 January 1962, they were taken to a police station and charged under the Mixed Marriages Act and the Immorality Act.

Syrub and Charlotte were represented by Rowley Arenstein, who had a reputation as a fighter against apartheid and had been banned from assembling with more than a certain number of people, even at home. But, the ban did not apply to his court-related activities and he continued to defend people accused of political offences. Arenstein argued that the Mixed Marriages Act could not apply to the sovereign state of Southern Rhodesia where the wedding had taken place. Furthermore, Syrub had not been domiciled in South Africa at the time of his marriage to Charlotte. The magistrate, CP Cowan, accepted that defence and acquitted the couple. However, Syrub's problems did not end with the court ruling. He was followed everywhere by the Security Police and within a few weeks he and Charlotte left the country for good.

The couple spent the next few years in exile in Tanganyika. Syrub hardly ever received news from home and would often go to the docks to see if there was anyone from Pretoria travelling on a ship who could give him news of his family. One day, a passenger told him that his father had passed away several months earlier. Syrub left for London a decade later, where he and Charlotte eventually divorced. They have two grown-up daughters, Vasanthi and Vaneeta.

As apartheid took hold, White South African policemen became increasingly brutal against Africans. On one occasion, two policemen arrived at the entrance of the Royal Bioscope to check the passes of the cinema staff, but the door was locked. I was in the foyer and heard Zombo, the foreman, telling them from the window that the key was with the manager in downtown Pretoria a mile away. When the policemen went to check with the manager, he, unaware why they were asking about the key, told them that Zombo had it as a matter of policy. The policemen rushed back, battered down the door and mercilessly beat up Zombo, breaking two of his front teeth. Although Zombo was a big man, I saw him piteously gasping for breath as he lay on the floor, blood splattered all over his face. "*Askies baas, askies baas*," ("Forgive me, boss") he kept wailing as the police, half his age, whipped him with *sjambok*s and pummelled him. When he was barely conscious, they picked him up by his legs and hands like a carcass and catapulted him into their van.

With time, the absurdities of apartheid became more and more apparent. For example, a 1952 newspaper article publicized a proposal to change existing legislation under which a woman always took the race group of her husband. Under the proposed new bill, a White man who married a "native" or a Coloured would from then on be regarded in law as "native" or Coloured!

In 1949, apartheid confronted a wealthy Ismaili visitor to South Africa with a ludicrous situation. Tajdin, scion of the wealthy Kassam Jivraj family of Kenya, came to honeymoon in South Africa with his bride. They arrived in his own plane, piloted by a European who was an employee of their company, Jivraj Air Services. In Johannesburg, the pilot was welcomed by the hotel but Tajdin was turned away. He then came to stay with us. He told us that Kenya, too, had its own form of apartheid, with Whites not wanting to share a dining hall with non-Whites and some hotels even being closed to non-Whites.

In 1951, the African American Hollywood actor Sidney Poitier came to South Africa to make a film on the plight of Africans in the country, but he could not get accommodation in any hotel. While in the Transvaal, Poitier came to Marabastad at the invitation of Noor Habib Keshavjee and visited the home of my uncles, Allibhai Keshavjee in Pretoria and later Cassim Keshavjee in Johannesburg. In Pretoria, he appeared on stage at the Empire Cinema with Canada Lee. He was rather bashful and reserved, but Canada Lee had no inhibitions. During the interval he addressed the audience, ending his speech with the declaration "You shall be free! You shall be free!" to the roar of the packed auditorium.

The government tried to intimidate foreign artistes from performing in front of mixed audiences. Among them was the British singer Dusty Springfield, who in 1964 was arrested, confined to her hotel, and deported after performing in front of a mixed-race audience and refusing to do so before a segregated audience. When she arrived at the airport, the African porters lined up in a guard of honour and doffed their berets in salute to her.

Among the many ordinary men and women who refused to break under the daily crushing weight of apartheid, one who stood out for me personally was Joseph Siphuma, a Venda from the African location of 210 Sibasa in Northern Transvaal. On leaving primary school, he travelled the 250 miles to Pretoria, where he started to work for my family and stayed with us through thick and thin until we left the country. He was an upright and honest Christian who worked with us at home, in the café, and in the factory. He often quoted the Bible to us. "We must trust in God," he would say. Joseph worked with us as a family member and felt fully a part of our family.

One night, after the interval between film reels at the cinema, we packed the fridges, cleaned the café and decided to walk back home together. I was then a teenager. On the way, we suddenly noticed Africans scattering in panic. Joseph exhorted me to run home and then sprang through the open doorway of an Indian family home. He sped through their kitchen into the yard, over the fence, into the next person's yard and through their kitchen and out again. A *sjambok*-wielding policeman chased after him, but Joseph sprinted like a gazelle and somehow got away. I got back home safely, concerned about his wellbeing but unable to do anything for him. Before going to sleep, I went into the kitchen and saw Joseph there, thanking God for his escape and praying for an end to apartheid.

I was too young then to understand the enormous transformative potential that can lie in the shadow of human suffering. I did not realize then that Joseph's prayer may have been the bridge, or a prelude, to an eventual peaceful transformation to a better future where all races could live in peace and harmony in a nation built on forgiveness and coexistence.

While Joseph was praying for a better disposition, the peoples of Africa were restive. In some parts of the continent, among them Portuguese East Africa, Tunisia, Morocco, and Algeria, there were insurrections. It was a movement that spanned continents, with revolutionary figures such as Franz Fanon, Che Guevara, and Aimé Césaire providing the ideological underpinnings for it in Latin America and the French Caribbean. The Congo was already independent, but Belgium and the US were busy undermining democracy there in order to control that country's rich resources through a compliant government installed with their help. Africa was changing rapidly and the continent was febrile, as the chapters to come will show.

Chapter 15

Wind of Change

THE 1960S WERE TURBULENT BUT EXCITING YEARS IN AFRICA, when the modern character of the continent was being formed and when the leap towards independence in many countries changed the old imperial world, at least on the surface. British Prime Minister Harold MacMillan warned members of the South African parliament on 3 February 1960, "The wind of change is blowing over this continent. Whether we like it or not, this growth of national consciousness is a political fact." Africans in South Africa felt that wind. They read and heard how the world was changing and it fanned the hope that they, too, could win their freedom.

The reaction of the South African government was to intensify its violence against non-Whites. The Sharpeville massacre of peaceful protesters against the pass system in March 1960 was one example of its ruthless determination to maintain the dominance of Whites at any cost. The ANC and Pan Africanist Congress (which had organized the Sharpeville protest) were banned.

It was against this backdrop that, on a wintry afternoon in June 1962, just as I had finished cleaning the Empire Café after a matinee show, my brother Ameer, who by then was looking after the family members still in South Africa, arrived at the café and told me, "Get ready, you are leaving for Kenya."

"What?" I exclaimed. "You mean I have to leave South Africa, this café, Marabastad, school, my friends, and the family?"

"Yes," he answered. "I will manage this place. I think you should move from here, and Kenya is the country for you. Mamdoo Hassim is leaving by boat in the next few days. I will arrange with the Hoxies to take you and your sister Rashida to Lourenço Marques. Mamdoo is sailing to East

Africa from there. He will take you with him and deliver you to Rex [our brother] in Nairobi. Let me know what you need for the trip. I'll get you some clothes and arrange for your travel."

I was both excited and sad. The reports from our cousins in Nairobi had always evoked beautiful images—of fun, parties, mixing freely with Whites, of schools, safari parks, swimming pools, and so on. All the things we were denied in South Africa. Yet, Marabastad was home to me. I had been born there. All my friends were there. The café had become part of my life. It was the only home I knew and I loved it.

However, I did not put up any resistance. Somewhere deep in my psyche, my family's peripatetic existence, caused by the harsh environment in which we lived, was an awareness that I was not to be rooted to one place. The wind of change was not a metaphor in my life, and now it was propelling me towards new life experiences.

On the morning of 9 June 1962, we left Marabastad in two vehicles, one the shrimp truck driven by Eric Hammond, a young Coloured man, in which I sat with expectation and a sense of loss, and the other a 1954 Chevrolet sedan in which Mamdoo, his wife Sugra, their teenage daughter Anish Khatoon, and Rashida travelled with Koolsam, Mamdoo's maternal aunt. South Africa unfolded its fascinating natural features as our vehicles passed from town to town. I felt a tug of sadness. The *kloofs*, the hills, the forests, and the waterfalls that I was leaving behind were haunting.

That night we arrived in Lourenço Marques, the quintessence of continental Europe in Africa. The city was an oasis of tranquillity, with quaint little restaurants serving chicken piri piri, *Frango de guia* and jumbo prawns cooked the Portuguese way. If many Whites in South Africa were oblivious to what was happening in the rest of Africa, this part of the continent, which by then had been officially renamed the Portuguese Overseas Territory of Moçambique, seemed even less informed. Relaxed residents and carefree European tourists spent the mornings lounging under the umbrellas on pavements outside the restaurants, listening to Amelia Rodrigues singing fado songs, sipping their coffee and ordering freshly baked custard tarts. It was as if the war for freedom being waged in the jungles by Frelimo was taking place on another planet.

At the Lourenço Marques docks, the *SS Kampala* was waiting for its passenger load of 1040 souls in all three classes. Meanwhile, it was being loaded with thousands of Zambian copper ingots destined for the voracious industries of Europe. Akberali Babool, a very close friend of my father, assured the shipping agents that he was our guardian and that our parents had given permission for Rashida and I to sail on the ship without them. He also pointed out that a fellow passenger, Mamdoo Hassim, had promised our parents that he would look after us on the voyage. We were issued with economy-class tickets, and on 13 June, two days short of my seventeenth birthday, the *SS Kampala,* which was then two years younger than me, left the port and went out to sea.

To my young and inexperienced eyes, the ship was huge, almost like a little city. Whites mainly occupied the cabin class, while the economy class cabins and the 800-berth bunk class, known colloquially as the deck class, were mainly occupied by Indians. A covered promenade deck, open to the sea, was wrapped around the cabin and economy class public rooms, with a barrier dividing the two classes whilst at sea.

At around 7 p.m. we went to dinner. Our waiter was Mr Alvares, a quiet, slightly built unassuming Goan from India, who did not smile throughout the entire voyage. He was not surly, just nonchalantly but determinedly unamused. I asked him for ice cream within the first few minutes and he said none was available. I threatened to jump off the ship if I did not get any, expecting to engage in stimulating repartee with him, to which he went off to the galley and then returned looking grave and solemnly said, "No ice cream; only pudding, pudding."

We arrived at Beira twenty-four hours later and were allowed to leave the ship and walk a few hundred yards to a large hotel facing the sea, aptly called the Grand Hotel. With us were three young Englishmen in their late twenties, who decided to explore the town. The next day, one of them was sporting a bandage around his head and shipboard rumour had it that he had behaved obstreperously and had got off worst in a confrontation with the locals. While we were docked in Beira, Mamdoo got Mr Alvarez to ask the cooks to bake a cake for my birthday. It was an unexpected, wonderful treat.

On the ship radio we heard that the infamous Sabotage Bill was being given its third reading in South Africa. The Bill, which was later passed into law, defined anyone who undermined public health or safety, maintenance of law and order, or the supply of utilities or food as a saboteur. Thus, even a workers' strike for better pay or a peaceful political demonstration could be termed sabotage.

The next port of call was the capital city of Tanganyika, Dar es Salaam. As we steamed towards it, Mamdoo told us Tanganyika was "the future Switzerland of Africa" and Julius Nyerere "the Gandhi of Africa" whose commitment to the emancipation of South Africa was deep and palpable. "He is a model leader who harbours no ill-will against anybody. He does not believe in racism." Sometimes the flow of information would suddenly be interspersed with a question to his wife: "Sugra, who was that guy we met in Arusha?" And then he would give an imitation of the person to jog her memory.

As far as Mamdoo was concerned, his final destination was Tanganyika, and Arusha was the fabled Jerusalem of William Blake. It was there that he would put up a hamburger stall, to give every child in the town the opportunity to try a hamburger at least once in his or her lifetime. Eventually, he would franchise the business. He did, indeed, set up his stall, and he often gave hamburgers to children free of charge when they could not afford them.

Tanganyika had attained its independence six months earlier, on 9 December 1961, the British Union Jack being replaced by the country's new flag, the glorious colours of which—green, gold, and black—represented the land, soil, and indigenous people respectively. The new national anthem, *Mungu ibariki Afrika* (God bless Africa) was a Kiswahili translation of the ANC anthem. In the snow at the top of Africa's highest mountain, Kilimanjaro, a lieutenant of the Tanganyika Rifles had planted the national flag and a torch whose light was visible even in the border areas of neighbouring Kenya. Some Kenyans, while wishing their fellow Africans in Tanganyika well, probably also recalled being told by their history teachers that Kilimanjaro had been a part of British-ruled Kenya until Queen Victoria in 1886 presented it (and the people living around it) to her grandson, the future German Kaiser Wilhelm II, as a gift on his birthday.

Early on the morning of 17 June, there was a loud knock on my cabin door. "Wake up! Wake up! The scene is too beautiful to miss. Dar es Salaam has the world's most beautiful natural harbour," Mamdoo called out joyously to me. "You have to see it. You will never get this opportunity again." Rashida and I ran to the deck of the ship as it meandered its way like a matron into Dar es Salaam's magnificent harbour through a number of atolls.

We were met at the docks by members of the Jiwa Daya family, who were related to Sugra. Their son Nizar, in his twenties, took us in a Ford Prefect to their home, where the family served us a dish typical of the East African coast, *kukupaka*—chicken, potatoes and boiled eggs cooked with onions, tomatoes, and spices in coconut milk. It was accompanied by boiled rice. For dessert there was *madafu*—a young coconut fruit, its crown sliced off with a sharp machete. There is no other natural drink that can provide the pleasure that comes from tipping up a *madafu* and drinking the sweet and cool water within it, or of then scooping out the tender, slippery flesh with a spoon and eating it.

After lunch, Nizar took me to Ocean Road and pointed out the residence of a prominent Ismaili, Count Kassum Sunderji Samji. His son Al Noor later held ministerial positions in Nyerere's first multiracial government and in the East African Community, as well as senior positions in UNESCO and at the UN headquarters in New York. Amir Jamal, another Tanganyikan Ismaili, also had an illustrious career. His positions included, among others, Finance Minister in the post-independence Nyerere Cabinet, Tanzanian ambassador to the UN, and member of the Brandt Commission on International Development Issues and of the South Commission. We drove next to the Aga Khan School in Upanga, which had all the facilities of a first-rate educational institution and was emblematic of the Aga Khan's contribution to the educational resources of the country. I felt proud. We visited Kariakoo and Upanga, where the new Ismaili jamatkhana stood on the site where Sultan Mahomed Shah Aga Khan's Diamond Jubilee had been celebrated in 1946.

Dar es Salaam exuded a confidence born of freedom. Africans operated cranes on the docks, while in the city self-assured citizens rode bicycles along the streets. The sun was radiant, the sky a cloudless blue, the buildings, constructed by German colonizers, resplendent with the sun shining on white stucco walls. Here, an African could walk freely; no one would stop him and demand his pass.

Dar es Salaam meant Haven of Peace, and Tanganyika had given refuge to many people who were fleeing from persecution. I remembered that Syrub Singh of Marabastad had fled to Dar es Salaam so that he could live in peace with his Afrikaner wife, Charlotte Rose Bloem, and decided to call on him. Nizar took me to F Boero, the Fiat agents, where Syrub was employed. He had not heard from home for months and was very happy to see me.

In my excitement at conversing with Syrub, I forgot that the boat was to leave at 3 p.m. When I realized that the ship would be departing soon, Syrub and I jumped into Nizar's car and he drove us rapidly towards the docks. We were soon caught up in the Dar es Salaam traffic and had to slow down. Meanwhile, Mamdoo was panic-stricken, as he had no idea where I was or how to contact me. Just as the gangplank was being drawn in prior to departure, Nizar's little Ford Prefect squealed to a stop on the dock. Mamdoo got the sailors to lower the gangplank again and I could see him seething with anger as he stood at the rail, ready to explode.

Sugra calmed him down somewhat and he exchanged pleasantries with Syrub as I walked up the gangplank. Once the ship started moving, I got the full brunt of his wrath. "Did you have to go and see Syrub Singh?" he asked. "What if the ship had left without you? I have your passport with me. What would you have done?" I apologized for my thoughtlessness, but he carried on and on until Sugra once again stepped in. I went down to my cabin, in remorse. I had not realized the responsibility that Mamdoo felt for us.

Our next stop was Zanzibar, which we reached at around 7 p.m. The ship anchored a little distance from the island, since Zanzibar had no deep-water berths. The only way to reach Zanzibar town was in small motorboats. The island was experiencing political problems, its fiery nationalist, Abdulrahman Babu, having been arrested for publication of seditious material. The British Resident, Sir George Mooring, had declared a state of emergency and the ship's captain advised those going ashore to be cautious and not to stay out on the street till very late.

Mamdoo decided that it would be safer to remain on the ship. What we did not know was that one of Zanzibar's prominent citizens, Alimohamed Jessa Bhaloo, had been requested by Habibkaka to look after us while the ship was in Zanzibar waters. Bhaloo had gone to the waterfront many times, looking for us. Late that night, some South African students who had gone to the town came to us and gave us Bhaloo's card with the message that he would meet us the next morning.

The next day we found Alimohamed waiting for us in his white Mercedes Benz outside the famous Bayt al Ajaib (House of Wonders), one of six palaces constructed in 1883 for Sultan Barghash bin Said. Zanzibar was then the epicentre of East Africa and the Sultan had encouraged Indian traders to set up businesses there. The island had been exporting exotic products to major European countries long before Kenya and Uganda came under British sovereignty.

As Alimohamed drove us through the narrow winding streets of the town, I could not help wondering if the big car would be able to manoeuvre through them without getting stuck. The buildings around us had ornately carved Arab doors studded with brass cones. The shops, mainly owned by Indians, were piled with jute bags reeking of cloves, coriander, chilli powder, tamarind, and dried coconut. The women walking through narrow alleyways wore black *buibuis*, which covered them from head to toe, and the men were garbed in white robes—called *khanzus*, I found out later—topped off with white caps.

We had lunch with the Bhaloos and went to visit a nursing home set up by his mother, who was a midwife to the Sultan's family. We met Alimohamed's children, Naseem and Nurallah, with whom we had corresponded as pen pals from South Africa. His brother Husseini was deeply involved in the island's labyrinthine politics, and a year later, when the Sultan was overthrown, Husseini was imprisoned by the new administration. Alimohamed also took us to visit Aunty Fatima, Jivanbapoo's youngest daughter. Fatmafaiba's husband, Kathiara, ran a shop selling funerary paraphernalia. She received us happily, particularly because it gave her the opportunity to talk to Sugra, who was her sister's granddaughter and whom she had not seen since childhood. After giving us a tour of that paradisal island, Alimohamed deposited us back at the waterfront and we took a boat to our ship.

We docked in Mombasa's Kilindini harbour in the early hours of the next morning, and were met by Sadru Damji, of the Kassam Suleiman Damji family, who owned a car hire company and were good friends of Habibkaka. As we drove towards the town centre, we passed under a pair of giant white-painted metal tusks forming an archway over Kilindini Road. They were known as "the Gateway to Kenya."

Mombasa, which had once been part of the Sultan of Zanzibar's domain, emanated a relaxed, lazy, tropical atmosphere. The locals wore casual gear and we saw khanzu-clad Swahili Arabs vending coffee from cone-shaped brass urns kept hot over a bed of charcoal. I had seen photographs of similar coffee sellers in Arab countries. It was as if the modernity in Mombasa was only a façade covering a society in which, as in Zanzibar, time had stood still.

One of our highlights in Mombasa was a meeting with an old family friend from Marabastad. He was Winkie, a Chinese businessman who was running the New Florida Night Club, built on a choice plot of land overlooking the ocean. Winkie was a dashing gentleman with a boyish countenance. He was generous at heart. It was liberating to be at the club, watching the incoming ocean liners gliding past on the ultramarine water. We sat around the swimming pool, with the palm trees around us swaying gently in the tropical breeze. We were pleased that someone from our part of the world had done so well financially.

In the third week of June, almost two weeks after we had left South Africa and just a few days after going through the Gateway to Kenya, we took the East African Railways train to Nairobi. I have an abiding impression of the Mombasa railway station, which had red metal chairs and tables where people could sit and sip coffee. Before we left, Sugra asked me to sit down for coffee. There were many Europeans around and I felt hesitant to do so.

With trepidation I sat down beside her, but I still felt terribly uneasy. Realizing my problem, Sugra looked at me with a sardonic smile and reassured me, "You are no longer in South Africa. This is Kenya. Look, there are no signs here. Non-Whites are fully accepted! You can sit wherever you like."

Yes, I thought, I am no longer a second-class citizen. I can be myself.

Chapter 16

Uhuru na Umoja

THROUGH THE NIGHT, THE STEAM TRAIN CHUGGED AND hissed its way into the Kenyan interior, climbing laboriously from sea level to 6000 feet, passing small towns and villages speckled with flickering lanterns and kerosene lamps. The stations were deserted and there was the sense of emptiness and desolation that one usually feels when passing through stations in the middle of the night. After travelling for over fourteen hours, we arrived at Nairobi's main railway station early the next morning.

We were met at the station by Hoosen, my brother-in-law, who was one of the champions of our move to Kenya, Murad Velshi, and my sisters Guli and Mila. Mamdoo's in-laws were also there. I was amazed to be told that while Rashida and I had been at sea, Ameer had despatched my sister Khairu by plane. So by the time we arrived, a sizeable part of the family had already left South Africa to start a new life in Kenya.

Guli seated us in her blue Volkswagen Beetle and drove us through Government Road, the main street in the city, which took us to the downtown area. I found Nairobi to be a lovely modern city. The buildings were not too high and—to my delight—surrounded by jacaranda trees. At that time, Nairobi was still small, an English enclave in Africa, with parts of it occupied by the Indian community. Its Bazaar Street could have been a road from an earlier Bombay, with Indian traders and shop owners sitting in their dhotis, selling tins of ghee, bags of rice, beads, and *pangas* (machetes). It was said that the economic power of Kenya was concentrated in that street, mainly in the hands of a handful of Hindu traders—which was not true, as the commanding heights of the economy were in the hands of transnational companies, most of which were owned by

White Britons. However, the Indians were more visible.

Many White colonists were leaving Kenya because they feared chaos and retribution after independence, and Africans were jubilant over the prospect of freedom at last. Asians in the country were nervous because they were regarded as a fifth column by some indigenous people, and they were afraid that their property would be seized and trading licences annulled.

The postindependence chaos in the Congo was not reassuring. The first democratically elected prime minister of that country had been murdered within three months of taking office, after opposing the secession of Katanga province, which was rich in minerals. The secession had been supported by Belgium, the US, and Britain. Thousands of people had died since then, the most prominent of whom was UN Secretary-General Dag Hammarskjöld, who had been killed in 1961 in a mysterious plane crash over Northern Rhodesia while on his way to the Congo to negotiate a peace agreement between the warring parties. A United Nations inquiry into the crash concluded that foul play could not be ruled out and there has been evidence since then that the plane may have been shot down.

It was a trying period for the more responsible African politicians in Kenya, who needed to engender optimism among the nonindigenous segment of the population. Jomo Kenyatta, who had recently been released from prison after many years in detention, made major political speeches in which he urged Whites and Asians to stay and called on all Kenyans to forgive the past and reconcile. Speaking for hours without pause, he ended his speeches with the calls "*Harambee*!" ("Let us pull together!"), "*Uhuru na umoja*!" ("Freedom with unity!"), "*Uhuru na kazi*!" ("Freedom with work!") and "*Uhuru na Kenyatta*!" ("Freedom with Kenyatta!"), which the crowds echoed in unison.

In Nairobi, I contacted my cousins Yusuf, Sadick, and Rafique, who warmly welcomed me and took me to their beautiful family home on Welbeck Road, in what had once been a Whites-only area. The changing political situation had enabled Habibkaka to buy it the previous year. The bungalow resembled an English country home. Surrounded by a few acres of land, it was built of grey stone and had a red-tiled roof, solid hardwood floors, and large bay windows overlooking a sprawling cascading country garden with a river at the bottom. Jacaranda trees lined the driveway.

As in South Africa, Habibkaka's home was a meeting point for rising African politicians, writers, musicians, artists, refugees, and overseas guests. At the time of our arrival, the noted South African author Harry Bloom was spending a few days there. After the Sharpeville massacre of March 1960, he had been detained for forty-five days without being charged. Soon after our arrival, a South African refugee, Robinson Matseke, turned up and spent a month at Habibkaka's home. Every lunch hour saw someone new drop by. Among the visitors were the veteran Kenyan White politician Derek Erskine; Bruce Mackenzie, later to become independent Kenya's first agriculture minister; Tom Mboya, trade union leader and rising political star; the South African writer Ezekiel Mphalele, who was then director of the Chemi Chemi Cultural Centre in Kenya; Margaret Kenyatta; Shanti Pandit, a writer; and Da Gama Rose, a lawyer with an eminent firm, Shapley Barret and Marsh.

At his home as well as in his factory, Habib regarded his workers as part of his family. He often spoke to us about the compassion of Africans in spite of all their suffering. "If we genuinely show them sincerity," he said, "they will reciprocate a millionfold. Gentleness is in their nature and we are ethically bound not to betray their trust."

He particularly admired Kenyatta, whose "speeches show him to be a great statesman and elder." While Kenyatta was in the Lodwar detention camp, Habibkaka used to send him vitamin pills; on one occasion, he sent him a paraffin-powered refrigerator so that he could store his food in it. Habibkaka also admired Tom Mboya, despite his criticism of Indians in Kenya. Habibkaka's closest contact was with James Gichuru, who became independent Kenya's first finance minister and who was a friend of his son Noor, who had spent a great deal of his time in the late 1950s helping African politicians organize their political campaigns and rallies by preparing written materials for them and helping them with logistics and public relations.

Charles Njonjo, the future attorney-general, was a neighbour of Habibkaka's when he lived on Caledonian Road. A few years earlier, Gikonyo Kiano, minister for commerce and industry in the first KANU government, had been a lecturer at the then Royal College and a friend of Hoosen's, with whom he was on first-name terms. There was also a younger rising politician, educated at Makerere University in Kampala and the London School of Economics, who used to come with the older politicians. He was Mwai Kibaki, who years later became independent Kenya's third president. Habibkaka worked with him in 1964, training rising African businessmen after the country's independence, when Kibaki was assistant minister of finance. When my brother Ameer settled in Kenya, he joined Habibkaka in this endeavour.

My cousins Yusuf, Sadick, and Rafique were at three of the best schools in the country. Yusuf was in his final year at the Duke of Gloucester Boys' School, where the students were Asian. Rafique had a year earlier joined the Prince of Wales Boys' School, which used to be exclusively for Whites, and Sadick was at the newly opened Aga Khan High School in Kabete. I did not know it then, but Rafique had a rough time at his school because of bullying, especially at the hands of White boys because of his father's help to African Nationalists. It took him forty years to overcome the psychological effects of that trauma, which he relates in his book called *The Mind Has Mountains*.

I had a reunion with my cousin Lutaf, whom I had last seen in Marabastad in 1960, when he had stopped over while on his way to the US to do a dry-cleaning course at the National Institute of Drycleaners. Lutaf was highly gifted, had humanistic leanings, and was artistic and played the piano. He was very much a part of the new Kenya and lived in Muthaiga, a diplomatic enclave which until then had been an exclusively White area. He knew many of the African politicians personally and was aware of their aspirations, fears, and prejudices. He also knew many Whites in business and socially.

From him I learned how the Ismaili community was helping to shape the new nation. His Highness the Aga Khan was very highly respected and admired and had committed himself to contributing to the development of the country, and the Ismaili Imamat and social development institutions were playing an important role in fulfilling that commitment. The Platinum Jubilee Hospital in Parklands was the first multiracial hospital in Kenya, which had opened a few years earlier and was providing high-quality nursing courses for students from as far away as Zambia. The

Nation newspaper group, set up by the Aga Khan a few years earlier, was run by Africans for Africans in response to concerns expressed by some African political leaders, some years earlier, that the indigenous population did not have a voice in public fora. The Imamat's economic development institutions such as the Jubilee Insurance and Diamond Trust companies, started during Sultan Mahomed Shah Aga Khan's time, were also playing their part in building the new Kenya. Finally, the Aga Khan schools, which the present Imam had upgraded to first-class institutions, were multiracial and offered the finest-quality education in the country. "If Mohammed and Jonathan and Njoroge can take the School Certificate together and play football together, the chances are that they would get to know and understand each other far better than their parents were able to," the Aga Khan had said at its opening in December 1961. I attended the Aga Khan High School.

It was truly a school based on the educational vision of an Imam whose ancestors had given the world one of its first universities, al-Azhar, in Cairo some 1000 years earlier and who spared nothing to ensure that those who attended the Aga Khan schools excelled in everything they did. The Aga Khan took a keen personal interest in seeing the school grow, ensuring that it had the best teachers available at that time. For this, he asked the administrator of the Aga Khan Education Board in Kenya, Jimmy Verjee, a London-trained barrister, to scour the leading schools in Britain and recruit talented teachers on multiyear contracts. Jimmy visited leading public schools in England in his search and the teachers he recruited were paid handsome salaries. The headmaster of my school was Major WR Jones, who had graduated in Classics from Jesus College Oxford. He had an MA and many years of teaching experience in the UK.

I was keen to become a lawyer and Major Jones assigned Robin Grieves Cooke, who taught us English Language and English History, to counsel me on what subjects would be important to attain my career goal. Mr Cooke advised me to do Latin, concentrate on Arts subjects, and jettison those in which I was weak. Given the short time I had before my final examinations, he felt that it would be better for me to concentrate on the subjects I needed for admission to the British Inns of Court than to struggle with those in which I was not proficient.

I needed seven O-level subjects for law school and, in accordance with Mr Cooke's advice, I concentrated on History, Literature, English Language, Geography, Biology, and Accountancy. For my seventh subject, I decided to do Afrikaans as a second language, which I had to study entirely by myself since it was not taught anywhere in Nairobi.

At a time when some Asians were prevaricating whether to remain in Kenya or migrate, the Aga Khan's advice to us was to make Kenya our home. He counselled Ismailis to work for Kenya's development, to aspire to higher education, not to live ostentatiously, and above all to promote harmony through compassion and kindness. He visited the country every year and each visit represented a new developmental milestone, ranging from an economic programme or sporting facility to a new housing project or an addition to the hospital. Despite the political uncertainties, we felt a sense of security and comfort, partly because of the deep respect which Jomo Kenyatta had for the Imam.

Partying was an important aspect of my life in Nairobi. School friends frequently gave dance parties at their homes. The latest English top ten hits were in vogue. Cliff Richard and the Shadows were popular in 1962, as were the clarinettist Acker Bilk with his "Stranger on the Shore," Eden Kane with "Forget Me Not," and a host of other singers. Habibkaka's house was famous for the teetotal parties given by my cousins.

My cousin Nooroo Dada, who was also settled in Kenya through marriage, spent most of her time working for the Red Cross, which she served for the next three decades. By the time we arrived, she had set up a mobile library for the Red Cross at the Aga Khan Platinum Jubilee Hospital. She spent hours on end in the slums, ministering to the poor, homeless, and indigent. In this, she harnessed many volunteers from the Ismaili community. The International Red Cross gave her an award for her thirty-year service.

Independence Day, on 11 December 1963, was preceded by weeks of partying and various cultural events attended by foreign dignitaries who had jetted into Nairobi's Embakasi Airport from different parts of the world. The climax of the day came at midnight, when the new Kenyan flag—green, red and black—was raised amid a dazzling and spectacular fireworks display at Nairobi's Independence Stadium. The Duke of

Edinburgh handed Jomo Kenyatta the Instruments of Independence and the stadium, full to capacity with Kenyans from all walks of life, seemed to shake as the crowd roared "Uhuru!" over and over again. I watched the celebrations at home on a Voice of Kenya television broadcast. It was a truly moving scene and inspired a deep sense of pride and joy in me. In January, when the O level results were released, I found that I had received good grades. I then faced a new challenge: twenty-seven of the A-level places at the Aga Khan High School had been filled by students with first class O level passes with distinction and I was not sure that I would be among those accepted for the remaining ones. However, with some difficulty, and the assistance of my cousin Zeri Aziz, who was working in the Education Board, I managed to get accepted and the next two years were the best of my life. I became one of the main debaters in our school team and we won most of the trophies in competitions against many of the established schools in the country.

Those years in Kenya were very happy.

None of us imagined during those idyllic days that, in a little over a decade, circumstances would once again force us to migrate to other countries in search of a permanent home. A harbinger of the future came on 12 January 1964 soon after Zanzibar's independence, when the island witnessed a coup. Many Asians lost their lives, causing many others to resettle in Kenya and elsewhere.

♦

Each East African country was following its own ideological path. Tanzania had Ujamaa and African Socialism, Uganda began to move to the left with the Common Man's Charter, and Kenya adopted a capitalistic ethos with its own brand of African Socialism. Massive economic changes were being mooted and it was clear that Asians would be ejected from the three economies through restriction of work permits and trade licences.

One of the stories making the rounds among Asians in Nairobi at that time involved Chunibhai, a Gujarati jeweller whose work was so specialized and renowned that no marriage of consequence could take place without his finely crafted jewellery among the wedding presents given by the groom to his bride. Like many of his fellow craftsmen, Chunibhai decided to wait and see how stable the new country was before deciding whether to take up Kenyan citizenship. He finally decided that Kenya would be best for him, but the deadline for citizenship applications had already expired by then. One day, Damodharbhai, a Gujarati trader, told him that the wife of a leading politician wanted Chunibhai to take some of his finest wares to her home a little way out of Nairobi so that she could purchase some pieces. He suggested that such a powerful person might be able to help Chunibhai to get citizenship. Excited, the jeweller put a dazzling array of his wares together. On the appointed day, Chunibhai and his charming Gujarati wife Shantabahen drove in their dusty Peugeot station wagon to their prospective client's home. Chunibhai also had his citizenship application papers with him.

The politician's wife was unable to decide which jewellery set to buy and asked her husband to make the choice for her. He resolved her problem by saying in an outburst of extravagant affection, "My darling, you can have all five sets." Chunibhai smiled with satisfaction and was about to start negotiating the price when the politician turned to him and added, "Thank you very much for this gift to my wife, who is also serving the Kenyan nation selflessly."

A shocked Chunibhai and his benumbed wife made the long, dusty journey back to Nairobi in bewildered silence. On their arrival home, they found Damodharbhai eagerly awaiting good news. "*Citeezun malyoo?*" ("Did you get the citizenship?") he asked, and a heartbroken Chunibhai replied, "*Citeezun soo? Amaro badho dagino haailo giyo!*" ("What citizenship? All our jewellery has been taken away!")

Such stories, some of which may have been apocryphal, caused unease within the Asian community, which was already bombarded each day with disturbing newspaper reports such as those about a White being deported from the country for a racial remark or what African politicians were saying in Parliament about Indians continuing to exploit Africans.

Some Asian intellectuals had no hesitation about identifying themselves with the countries they were living in and participated in discussions about the course East Africa was taking. Among them were Professor Yash Tandon, a prominent political scientist, and Mahmoud Mamdani, both at Makerere University in Uganda; and Issa Shivji and Karim Hirji at the University of Dar es Salaam in Tanzania.

In Kenya, an Ismaili, Karim Janmohamed was inspired to study African history after attending classes by Professor Bethwell Ogot at the University of Nairobi. Ogot, a leading historian, challenged the notion that before the arrival of European colonists, there had been no history in Africa. Through his pioneering work on the history of Nilotic peoples, he demonstrated not only that precolonial East African history had been rich and dynamic, but also that oral tradition could be tapped together with other sources to reconstruct it. He told his students to ask the questions, "Who writes history? Who gets written into history? Who gets written out of history?"

Karim was part of the new postindependence generation of East African Asians who were critical of Asian attitudes towards indigenous people and advocated racial integration. This generation included Zarina Patel, Hamida Mohamedali, Mahmoud Mamdani, Bahadur Tejani, Dharam Ghai, Yash Ghai, and Shiraz Durrani. In 1973, Karim and I became part of a group of young professionals that included my sister Rashida, Zul Mawani, Firdosh Ahamed, Mirjehan Janmohamed, and Amyn Amershi, who met regularly and engaged in animated discussions about the challenges facing the Asian community as part of the changing East African social and political landscape.

♦

The Aga Khan High School was in the forefront in Kenya not only academically, but also in drama and debating. It was in debating that I made my contribution in 1965, when Shiraz Mawani and I won the Parker Oratorical Cup for Kenya and also bagged the University of Nairobi debating trophy, beating twenty-six schools across the country. Naaz Kurji and Shamin Damji were also excellent debaters. Shamin later went to Britain to read law and ended up in Canada with her husband, Akbar Lalani, a specialist on angiography. Both played a strong role in civic work in Canada and Shamin became the first East African Asian woman on the board of the United Way organization.

I took English literature, history, and geography for my A-level studies. English literature was taught at the school in a way that encouraged reflection, appreciation, imagination, and critical thinking, and it became my favourite subject and a window into life. I passed in all three subjects as well as the mandatory General Paper.

The year 1966 began with all my friends making arrangements to join universities in different countries. Some had been accepted at one of the three campuses of the University of East Africa. However, as I still held South African citizenship, I was barred from entering Tanzania and Uganda. Even if I had been admitted to study at the Kenyan campus, non-East African citizens had to pay a large capitation fee and were not entitled to a government scholarship or an educational loan.

With time on my hands, I took a teaching job at Nairobi Secondary School. The students were Africans from upcountry, some of whom had walked many miles to secure a secondary school education at a time when very few schools in the country would cater to them. There were also a smattering of Asians who had either failed to get admission elsewhere or had failed their exams at another school and were repeating a class. I taught history to the lower forms and English to O-level students.

Sometime in 1966, the Honourable Society of Gray's Inn in London accepted me as a student. I then had to find a way to pay the requisite deposit of £150, which represented six months of my salary, at a time when every penny earned by family members had to go towards the household budget. I spoke to my brother Ameer, and together we approached a close friend, Solly Hajee, a schoolteacher originally from South Africa. Solly very kindly agreed to lend me the amount for three months. A small group of Asian students at school had asked me if I would consider coaching them in the evenings for a fee, so I was able to repay Solly's loan even before the three months were up by giving them private tuition.

I was at last ready to embark on my initial law studies, and in the autumn of 1966 I started studying the first subjects—Roman law, constitutional law, and English legal history—through a distance learning course given by the world-famous Gibson and Weldon Tutors of Chancery Lane, London. I took to law as a fledgling bird takes to the air. However, Roman law and certain abstract constitutional law principles proved to be a rocky undertaking and I began to wonder whether I had made the right career choice. I did enjoy the study of English legal history immensely. Gibson and Weldon marked my homework, annotated the papers, and sent back model answers to me.

In the spring of 1967, I enrolled with the Council of Legal Education in Britain to write my first Law examination at the Kenya High Court in Nairobi. The exam papers were not as difficult as I had feared they would be. That night I went to the University of Nairobi library and pulled out a book on criminal law and was fascinated by the cases in it. The next day I went to a bookshop in the city that sold legal texts and bought a second case book on English criminal law.

By then I was teaching at a different educational institution, the Visa Oshwal Boys' School in Parklands. Again, I supplemented my income by giving extra tuition to a handful of Asian students who were to sit exams later in the year. I also gave extra tuition to a few African students for free. During this time came a seminal encounter, which, like many others in my life, presented itself unexpectedly.

In May 1967, Sylvia Hymers, a young Englishwoman who was the daughter of Habibkaka's friend from the early 50's working in Nairobi with my sister Guli at BOAC, decided to get married and asked Guli to make her a wedding dress. One day, amidst casual conversation, Guli told Sylvia about her brother who had been accepted by Gray's Inn and had just written his first set of exams at the Law Courts in Kenya. Sylvia asked why he had done the exams in Kenya instead of Britain and received the reply, "He cannot leave Kenya. He cannot get a re-entry permit." Sylvia said, "Perhaps I can speak to my father. He is an adviser in the Immigration Department and he may be able to do something."

That evening, Mr Hymers phoned Guli and, after expressing his appreciation of her help to Sylvia, added in a fruity English drawl, "Sylvia has told me about your brother. Surely something could be done. Send the young johnny down tomorrow and I will see what we can do to help him out."

The next day I called on Mr Hymers at his office and, after some discussion, he told me, "All we may be able to do for you is twenty-four months. The law cannot be stretched beyond that." I would have to finish a three-year course in twenty-four months. I calculated that, with some juggling, it could be done and gratefully accepted Mr Hymers's offer.

The £150 deposit that I had paid to Gray's Inn covered the right to use their library and all related facilities as well as all tuition at the Council of Legal Education. Now I needed a scholarship to cover the cost of living in London for two years. At that time, by chance, my brother-in-law Murad happened to mention my predicament while in conversation with a Nairobi dentist, Dr AGA Gulam, whom he knew quite well. Gulam was administrator of the Aga Khan Education Board of Kenya and sat on the scholarship committee of the Walji Hirji Trust, which had been established by Rahemtullah Walji Hirji, a pioneer Ismaili in Kenya. At Gulam's suggestion, I applied to the Trust and they replied that they were prepared to grant me £300 a year for a maximum of two years. That was £15 short of what I needed each month, but I gladly accepted the offer.

Things were falling into place, the flow was going my way. All I needed now was an air ticket to Britain. In the summer of 1967, the Dutch airline KLM decided to open a route to Kenya, and my sister Mila, who was an airline agent and their main advisor together with Murad, helped them find and set up an office in Nairobi. While KLM were waiting for their landing rights, Mila passed on a great deal of business to British United Airways, and through her contacts there she was able to get me a free one-way ticket to London.

During one of my visits to Murad at his business office, I was introduced to an African gentleman from Uganda, who was dressed immaculately in a dark lounge suit and spoke English as fluently as any English person. He was Dr Joe Luyimbazi Zake, then the attorney-general of Uganda. I was intimidated by the man's status and erudition. He was a graduate of Fort Hare in South Africa, Makerere in Uganda, the London School of Economics, Northwestern University in the US, and Gray's Inn, London. He had more academic achievements than any person I had previously come across, including my revered teachers. When I said I was going to Gray's Inn, his eyes lit up and he beamed with approval. "That's my old Inn," he said. "I was called to the Bar there. It's a great place."

I told him that I only had twenty-four months to complete my legal studies and that I was a bit apprehensive, to say the least. He laughed and said, "Young man, I come from a village where people rarely see a wheelbarrow and I had to study leases and mortgages at Gray's. Go ahead and finish it. Don't get too worried. Apply yourself and get the thing done. It's not rocket science. Anyone can do it." I was comforted by his words.

I spent the following days frantically packing and preparing for the next stage in my life, obtaining the names and addresses of contacts from people in my circle. Mariambahen, Jivanbapoo's granddaughter, was in Nairobi at that time, visiting my mother. "I'll phone my son Sam to come and pick you up," she assured me, her glasses glinting in the room light. "Don't worry, *beta* [dear], Sam will look after you. He knows London very well."

On 9 July 1967, a big group of family and friends came to Embakasi Airport to see me off. While I was excited at the prospect of flying for the first time in my life, I was also very sad to leave my family, and more particularly my friends Sadick, Diamond, and Sultan Kassamaly, with whom I had spent almost every day for the past five years in Kenya. Many other friends also came to the airport. It was a huge send-off, African style!

As I walked across the tarmac to the plane with the other passengers, a black limousine with the Ugandan flag on its bonnet drove up. An ebullient Dr Zake called to me, got out, and shook my hand. He had been part of the Ugandan delegation to an East African Community conference in Nairobi that weekend and was flying back at about the same time. "Go well, young man," he said to me, as he bade me farewell. "Pass your exams and return to us." I was proud to have been greeted by such an important personage in public.

As I climbed up the metal stairs to the door, I crossed an important, if invisible, threshold in my life. Little did I know at the time that that maiden flight of mine would be a precursor to the extensive travelling I would do in future, circling the globe a number of times over a thirty-year period while working in the secretariat of His Highness the Aga Khan serving in an international role. That was still some thirteen years and two continents away.

Chapter 17

Britain in the 1960s

THE PLANE LANDED AT LONDON'S GATWICK AIRPORT AT around 7 p.m. I took a train to Victoria station in the centre of the city and looked around for my cousin Sam Valjee, who was supposed to meet me, but could not see him. He had been waiting in another part of the massive station, accompanied by another cousin, Rashida Rhemtulla, and they turned up after a while. Sam drove us to East Putney, where their family lived.

For almost a month before my departure from Nairobi, I had been having late nights and enjoying a succession of celebratory parties, which had been followed by the long plane journey. That was beginning to have an effect on me and I was feeling unwell. But Jivanbapoo's great-grandchildren took charge of me and ensured that I was comfortable. Another cousin, Amir Noormohamed, took me to the doctor the next morning, and my problem was diagnosed as extreme fatigue.

My cousin Madat, Jivanbapoo's youngest grandson, who was then visiting London, was assigned the task of showing me around London. He took me to Gray's Inn after looking it up in a map, and said he would teach me how to use the London Underground and, most importantly, help me work out a monthly budget to optimize my meagre resources. At Gray's Inn, I was informed that I had passed the exams in all three subjects I had taken in Nairobi. That news filled me with enormous self-confidence at a time when I desperately needed reassurance.

After giving me and another cousin, Ashraf Cassim, visiting from Nairobi, a crash course on how to use the London Underground, Madat took me to a tearoom in the Temple Tube Station area, where he used a paper serviette to help me work out a budget for my monthly stipend of thirty pounds.

Compared to Nairobi, London was an impersonal place, and for several months, until I made friends at Gray's Inn, I experienced the most painful and haunting loneliness and rootlessness I had ever felt. It was a hard lesson, but a necessary one for my coming of age as an adult. I learnt to be alone and to fend for myself without the comforting safety blanket of constant concern and support from my immediate family and close friends.

My immediate objective during that long, lonely, and unbearably hot summer of 1967 was to find a place to stay, after which I would make plans to start my courses. I contacted my cousin, Dolly Aziz, who had recently bought a small townhouse in Arnos Grove in West London and was still settling down with her young family. She was the epitome of kindness and hospitality and was willing to have me stay in her house; besides, she said, a paying guest would help her to meet her mortgage payments.

A few days after my arrival, I came across Aurelio Rebello, whom I had met once in Kenya and who was now preparing for his Criminal Law exams. He suggested that I, too, should sit for the Criminal Law exam in September. "All you need to do is read thirty pages a day. We can go over them together," he said.

I had borrowed £25 from a friend in Kenya for a rainy day and I used part of it to join the Law Lending Library on Chancery Lane, from where I borrowed Kenny's *Outlines of Criminal Law, 8th Edition*. The book was weighty, metaphorically and physically, but I was determined to devour its contents and enjoy every minute of it. I calculated that, on the basis of thirty-page tranches, and with rest periods to ensure that I did not suffer a burnout, I would need about three weeks to absorb it.

After studying with intense concentration and discipline, my readings punctuated by discussions and reviews of past questions with Rebello and a Ghanaian named Kofi Acheampong, I took the Criminal Law exam in the Michaelmas term of 1967. When the results were published, I found that I had not just passed, but attained a class.

In order to work towards Part One of my Bar exams, I decided to take Law of Contract, Tort, and Real Property, which I planned to clear by the Easter term in 1968, seven months away. That was a big chunk of the course and would entitle me to do the Bar finals. I felt confident that I would pass, except in Real Property, so once again I decided to take tutorials from

Gibson and Weldon.

It was during the autumn of 1967, after my Criminal Law exams, that I made some of the most abiding friendships at the Inns. One such friend was the Ghanaian Alex Quaison Sackey, a former government minister and the first Black man in history to have been president of the UN General Assembly at its nineteenth session in 1964. Sackey had arrived in London in 1967 to study Law following the overthrow of the Nkrumah government. Many of those associated with the former president were in exile, and reading for the Bar in London. Sackey once invited me to a house-warming party in Golders Green, North London, and beamingly introduced the guests as "the former Ghanaian Cabinet, all in exile."

One evening at dinner I met Lester Bird and his brother Vere, whose father was prime minister of the Caribbean island of Antigua. Lester and I became good friends, and through him I met Barney Desai, the veteran South African freedom fighter. I later found out that Barney had been with my cousin Rhemtulla Velshi Keshavjee in Prague in the early 1950s and knew him well. He died soon after South Africa became a multiracial democratic society.

Amongst my other friends and colleagues were Brian Jubb, whose father had worked with the Kenya Broadcasting Corporation; Helena Kennedy, who was to became a Queen's Counsel, writer, and Baroness as well as head of the British Council and president of the School of African and Oriental Studies; and Nusrath Ali Shah from Pakistan, who later became a minister in the federal government. Maurice Bridges of Granada, who was later killed during a coup d'état, and Princess Elizabeth Bagaya, a member of the Buganda royal family in Uganda, were also students. She had a head start on the rest of us in eloquence as she had previously honed her skills at Girton College, Cambridge, and she was a prominent debater at the Inn.

Two of my two very close friends, Michael Ziadie and Claude Lewis, were from Jamaica. Michael Ziadie and I met one day when he arrived late for a lecture on Real Property and I agreed to share my notes with him. Michael reciprocated by inviting me to lunch. I discovered that he was very knowledgeable about Western classical music. A talented pianist, he bought tickets for every prominent concert or ballet performance in London. When he could not attend a performance, he would give his tickets to his friends.

Claude Lewis was one of the most generous persons I have ever met. Claude and I studied Contract Law together and formed a congenial nucleus of study and pleasure. A hulk of a man, more muscle than fat, and with the gait of an athlete, Claude was always immaculately dressed. He played jazz piano with joy and passion, and had a magnificent voice and would swagger into the Common Room imitating Nat King Cole singing "Walking My Baby Back Home." My closest friend with whom I studied each day was Krishna Savjani from Malawi, who, like me, was doing his Bar Part One.

I completed my Bar Part One exams by Easter 1968. I even managed to sneak in a visit to Europe so that I could get to know a little of its various countries and cultures that had played such a role in world affairs, particularly in Africa.

At Gibson and Weldon, I also got to know Ismail Ayob, a cousin of Ismail Mahomed, who would become the first chief justice of post-apartheid democratic South Africa. An incident that I shall never forget concerned one of our tutors, who was known for his dislike of non-Whites, whom he called "golliwogs." He also insulted women during lectures by involving them in hypothetical divorce case scenarios that bordered on the obscene. He once asked Ismail what he was going to do after his legal studies. "Go back to South Africa," replied Ismail. "To defend those terrorists, I suppose!" the tutor said, shooting a sharp hostile glance at my friend. "Yes, sir," said Ismail, smiling graciously. "If I have the occasion to do so." That tutor must have turned in his grave some nineteen years later, when the *International Herald Tribune* carried a front-page photograph of Ismail and South African human rights campaigner George Bizos negotiating the release of Nelson Mandela!

I sat for my Contract, Tort and Real Property exams on Easter Day 1968. On the day the results were due, some friends and I met at a newsagent's to get copies of the newspapers that published the names of those who had passed. I was astonished to see my name first in order of merit among the 627 students from throughout the world who had sat for Land Law that term. But, my name was missing from the Contract and Tort list. The obvious inference was that I had failed. Contract was my strongest subject and I just could not believe that I had failed. Aurelio Rebello advised me to go to the Council of Legal Education to double-check my status. At the Council, strangely, no one could confirm whether I had failed or passed and I sensed that something was wrong. I discussed the matter with my student advisor, James Wellwood, and he suggested that I write to the treasurer of the Inn, Sir Dingle Foot, as well as to the director of legal education, Sir Fred Pritchard. I did so and a few days later I left the country to go hitchhiking in Austria, having asked Krishna Savjani to keep an eye on developments relating to my enquiries. Little did I realize then that my case was going to make legal history and lead to a significant reform in legal education in Britain.

In his reply to me, the director of legal education wrote that, despite my past successes I should remember that I was not the best judge of my academic performance and that I should learn to accept that I could have failed. Seven other students had also failed, but none of them had questioned the results. The Benchers of my Inn heard of my case and took up the matter. Sir Dingle Foot asked for my paper to be retrieved and Professor Graveson was asked to mark it. It transpired that I had achieved a distinction and stood fourth in order of merit among the students from all four Inns of Court who had taken the exam. The director of legal education was asked to write to me, retracting what he had said in his earlier letter, with due apologies. The papers of many other students were re-marked and all of them passed. All this happened in my absence, the matter being handled by Krishna with great diligence, consummate advocacy, and proficiency.

A reporter from *The Observer* was present at Gray's Inn one night when Krishna expressed the opinion that the Council of Legal Education had been remarkably incompetent and needed to be reformed, and he wrote an article about my case. Other newspapers in Britain picked up the issue and it became a *cause célèbre*. I returned to a hero's welcome at Gray's Inn. A new body, called the Association of Gray's Inn Students, had been set up, that included my friends Bahadur Mawji Karim and Barney Desai. Additionally, a commission had been set up to review legal education in England.

In the autumn of 1968, the Gray's Inn Debating Society was due to have elections and Krishna, who due to family circumstances could not stand as president, persuaded me to stand for its vice-presidency. He was a brilliant strategist and organizer, and he mobilised all the young members of the Inn and made sure that I was voted in. I became the first non-White vice-president of the Debating Society in the 600-year history of the Inn. In the previous year, David Olateru Olagbegi of Nigeria had become the first non-White secretary. In the year following my election, Kumar Rajratnam of Ceylon became the first non-White president. At the next debating night during term, I took my place at the main table beside James Mason, the new president. All my friends came forward to congratulate me, feeling, like me, that my victory was a recognition of our presence in the mother country, England.

During my last year at Gray's, I met Matthew Thomas from Malaysia with whom I then shared a lovely bistro-style apartment in Kensington. He, Krishna, and I have remained close friends for the past forty-six years.

I took my Bar finals in the Easter Term of 1969. However, I could not receive my exam results before my Kenyan re-entry permit expired, so I would have to go back without being called to the Bar. The call is the crowning glory of every Bar student and I had to get my re-entry permit extended. I spoke to Quaison Sackey, who said he knew the Kenya high commissioner, Dr Josephat Karanja, personally and would ask him to help. He arranged for us to meet Karanja at the high commission in late June 1969. Karanja called in the member of the embassy staff who specialized in immigration matters. He examined my visa and then phoned Nairobi. When he hung up, he had alarming news for me: "This visa may not be valid; a new law has been passed." The high commissioner counselled me to return to Kenya immediately. Quaison Sackey concurred: "Don't take a chance. You can be called *in absentia*." I realized that I had no choice.

I also discussed my future with Quaison Sackey. I could not see many openings for me in Kenya, and South Africa was out of the question, as was England at that time. I wanted to join the UN system, but Sackey disagreed. "Go back to Africa," he said. "Smell the soil of Africa and remember who you are. Practise law in Kenya, get some experience. Go and help your family. There will be lots of opportunities later. You have a fine intellect, but you need the hallmark of an academic education. If you can, try and do a degree some day, but right now you need to get back and get your immigration status sorted out."

There was an autumnal feeling about my final days at Gray's Inn. I asked my Benchers to sponsor me, and Professor Graveson and ED Griffiths agreed to sign my testimonials. I submitted all my papers, and with the return of my deposit from Gray's Inn I purchased two elegant pinstripe suits from Burtons to show my family and friends at home that I was, indeed, a genuine "London Return"!

On 4 July 1969, I landed at Embakasi Airport in Nairobi, exactly within the window of time allowed to me. My family were there to receive me and I felt deeply grateful for their sacrifices for me, for their support both materially and spiritually. I was returning to a home they had created for us all in the precarious immigration situation that existed in Kenya. But there was still no certainty about the future.

Allibhai V Keshavjee garlands Prime Minister General Smuts in the presence of His Highness Sir Sultan Mahomed Shah Aga Khan and the Begum Om Habibeh, August 1945. (Photo from *Aga Khan and Africa*, courtesy of Habib V Keshavjee).

Ismail Allibhai Keshavjee in the year he participated in the Passive Resistance Campaign called by Dr Dadoo and Dr Naicker in 1946. (Photo: Van Kalker Studio, Cape Town).

H H Aga Khan Provincial Council Pretoria 1946, from *L-R*: Hassan N Keshavjee, Madhavjee Jivan Keshavjee, Ebrahim Kanjee Kassam (Khoja), Koolsam Manjee Keshavjee, Allibhai Velshi Keshavjee (President), Sakina Habib Keshavjee, Goolam M Keshavjee, Alibhai Anandjee (Khoja), Chagan Jiwa. Inset *right* Jadavjee Hajee Ramjee (Khoja), *left* Gulamhussein Sarif Janmohamed.

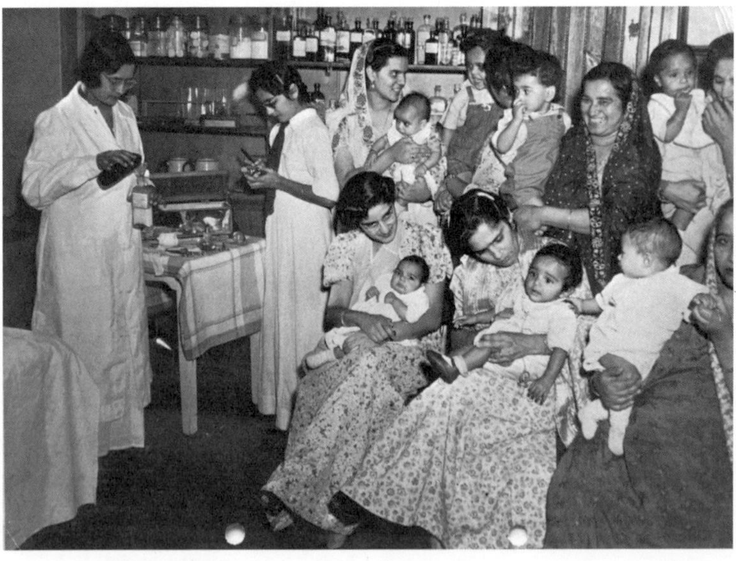

The Aga Khan Clinic Pretoria: Roshanbahen and Noorbanoo Ismail Cassim with mothers and their infants from the Ismaili community. The author is in the light dungaree, held by aunt Mrs Jena Goolam Keshavjee in black shawl. *Circa* 1947.

The Aga Khan Nursery School Pretoria, *circa* 1947. (Photo courtesy of Habib V Keshavjee).

Prince Sadruddin Aga Khan, then 15, at the Aga Khan Clinic Pretoria with volunteers from the Ismaili community, 1948.

Aga Khan Education Board Pretoria. Members with the Hon. VM Nazarali MLC, Administrator of Education from Tanganyika. Seated, *left to right*, Sherbanoofaiba, Roshanbahen, VM Nazarali, Daulat H N Keshavjee (nee Hajee). Standing *left to right*, Habib Keshavjee, Gulamaly Nathoo, Noormohamed Madhavjee. Insets (*left*) Goolam M Keshavjee, (*right*) Mohamedali Alli Velji. 1948.

Ebullient Dolly Rathebe and Dan Adnewmah in the first African feature-length film *Jim Comes to Joburgh*, directed by Donald Swanson and produced by Eric Rutherford, which had its Pretoria premiere at the Empire Cinema in Marabastad, hosted by Habib Keshavjee in 1949. (Photo courtesy of Habib V Keshavjee).

Dr Hoosen Cassim Keshavjee in his graduation sash. He was the first Ismaili medical doctor in South Africa and spent many years practicing medicine among the Africans in Alexandra township. *Circa* 1950. (Photo courtesy of Hoosen Cassim Keshavjee).

Empire Cinema with the animation of *Mighty Joe Young* set up by Marabastad's creative artist, Omarjee Suleiman, 1951. (Photo courtesy of Habib V Keshavjee).

Rhemtulla Velshi Keshavjee (extreme right, in beard) in Berlin at the World Youth Festival in 1951. Next to him are, in white shirt, Dr Percy Cohen, to his left in double breasted suit with curly hair is Pepe Ravat, and, Sonia Bunting, well known activist is on extreme left. 1951. (Photo courtesy of Dr Percy Cohen).

Jomo Kenyatta's Defence team at Habib Keshavjee's home on Christmas Eve, December 1952. Seated from *left to right*, Diwan Chaman Lall, Rani Kapila, DN Pritt, Guli Rattansi, Achroo Ram Kapila, Bundally Hassan Keshavjee at extreme right. African trade unionists standing at the back. The photo got everyone concerned into trouble. 1952. (Photo courtesy of Guli Rattansi).

Ameer Manjee Keshavjee. Engaged in debating and literary activities. 1953. (Photo: Sabi's Studio).

Mamdoo Hassim Keshavjee (1955), quizmaster to the community. (Photo: Sabi's Studio).

Dr Dolly Keshavjee, first non-White female doctor from the Pretoria area and first Ismaili woman to qualify as a doctor in South Africa, *circa* 1955. (Photo: Sabi's Studio, Pretoria).

Prince Karim Aga Khan, flanked by Ebrahim K Khoja (*left*) and Goolam M Keshavjee (*right*), in Church Square, Pretoria, after laying a wreath at the statue of President Kruger, May 1958. (Photo courtesy of *Pretoria News*).

His Highness, Prince Karim Aga Khan at the Nursery School in 1958 with Mrs Zeiller (headmistress) and Chairman of the Board, Noordeen (Blanket) Keshavjee. (Photo: Sabi's Studio).

Nooroo (Noorbanu) Hussein Dada—a Red Cross worker who spent most of her life helping the underprivileged in the slums of Nairobi. *Circa* 1960s. (Photo courtesy of Naushad Dada).

Ram Pillay (Dings), *right*, at the UN with Krishna Menon, under whose direction all existing files on discrimination in South Africa were consolidated into The Apartheid Question. *Circa* 1960. (Photo courtesy of Ram Pillay).

Joseph Siphuma from 210 Sibasa. Joseph and the author worked together for many years and became close friends. 1960.

Habib Keshavjee with Jomo Kenyatta at a political rally in Nairobi soon after Kenyatta's release from detention in 1961. (Photo courtesy of Habib V Keshavjee).

Sylvia Hymers, through whose father the author received his Kenya re-entry permit to be able to study law in England. 1967. (Photo courtesy of Guli Keshavjee).

Hassim M Keshavjee, President of the Ismaili Council of South Africa, receiving Sir Muhammad Zafrullah Khan, ex-President of the UN General Assembly, at a function in Pretoria in 1967. (Photo: Sabi's Studio).

Alex Quaison Sackey, former President of the UN General Assembly, at Rogers cable TV interview conducted by Dr Paul Weinzweig and Carole Belgiorgio of The UN Association of Ontario. The theme was the New International Economic Order. 1978 (Photo: Dr Terry Burrows).

Prince Sadruddin Aga Khan and Goolam M Keshavjee in Nairobi in the 1980s. The Prince is viewing the album of photographs of his 1948 visit to South Africa when he was accompanied by Goolam across the country. (Photo courtesy of Goolam M Keshavjee).

A jubilant Nelson Mandela on his release from prison embracing Mrs Thayanayagee Pillay, dressed in the sari he had given her some 30 years earlier for her services in feeding all the accused in the infamous Treason Trial. *Circa* 1990. (Photo courtesy of Pungie Govindasamy).

Former president Julius Nyerere of Tanzania greeting the new President Nelson Mandela of South Africa. 1994. (Photo: Zahur Ramji).

The author Mohamed Keshavjee at Carnegie Hall, New York, with cellist Yo-Yo Ma at a performance hosted by the Aga Khan Music Initiative 2001. (Photo courtesy of Aga Knah Trust for Culture).

Chinese postage stamp with Shaf Keshavjee and Jingyu Chen, to commemorate the first successful lung transplant surgery in the country, 2005. (Photo by Zahur Ramji, courtesy of Shaf Keshavjee).

Canada Reunion of South African families and friends at the Old Mill in Toronto in July 2009 with the children, grandchildren and great-grandchildren of the people who were at the opening of the Ismaili Jamatkhana some 80 years earlier in Pretoria. (Photo by Zahur Ramji).

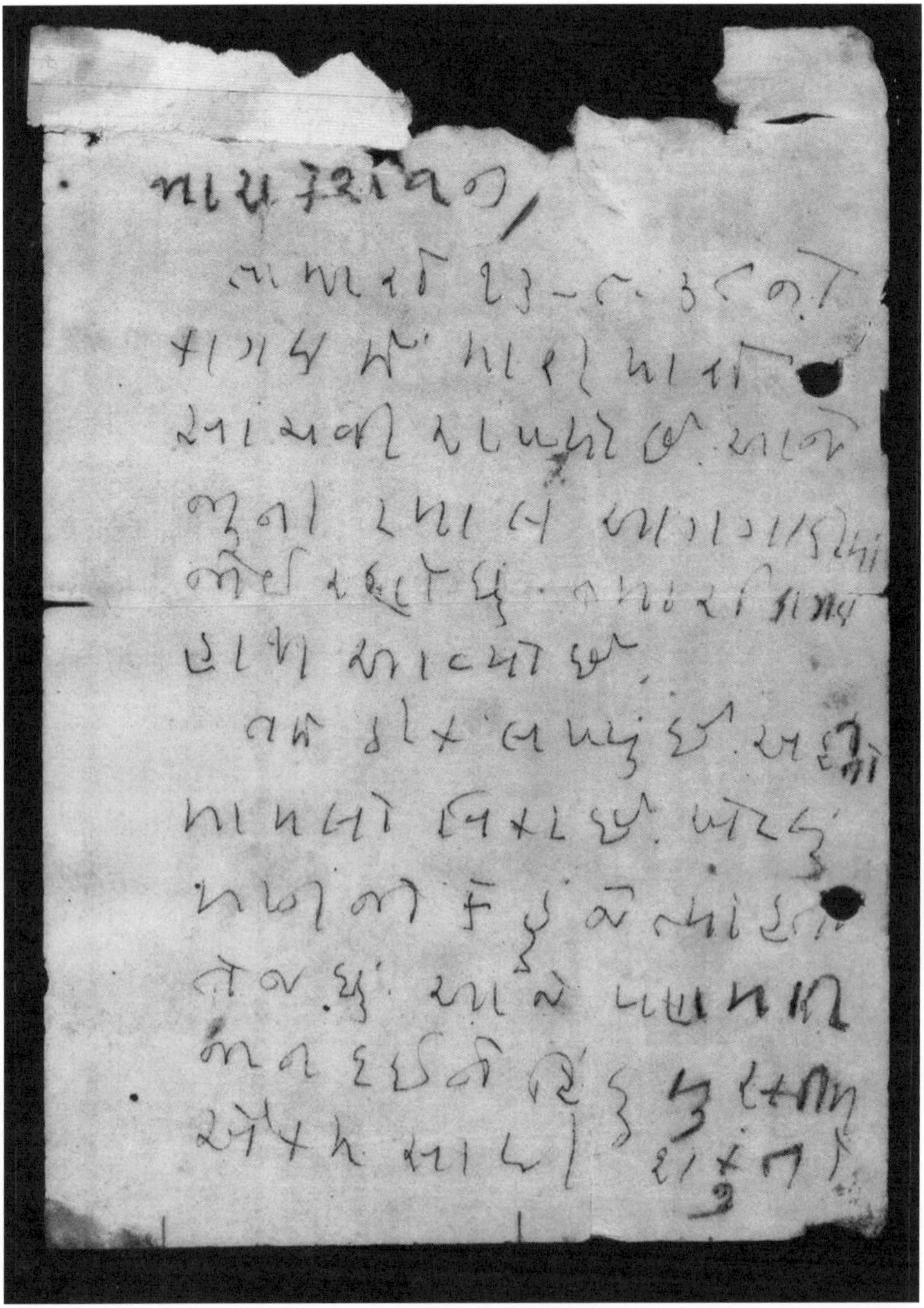

Facsimile of Gandhi's letter to Velshi Keshavjee sent from Vardha in 1939. They communicated on an ongoing basis (courtesy of Yusuf H Keshavjee).

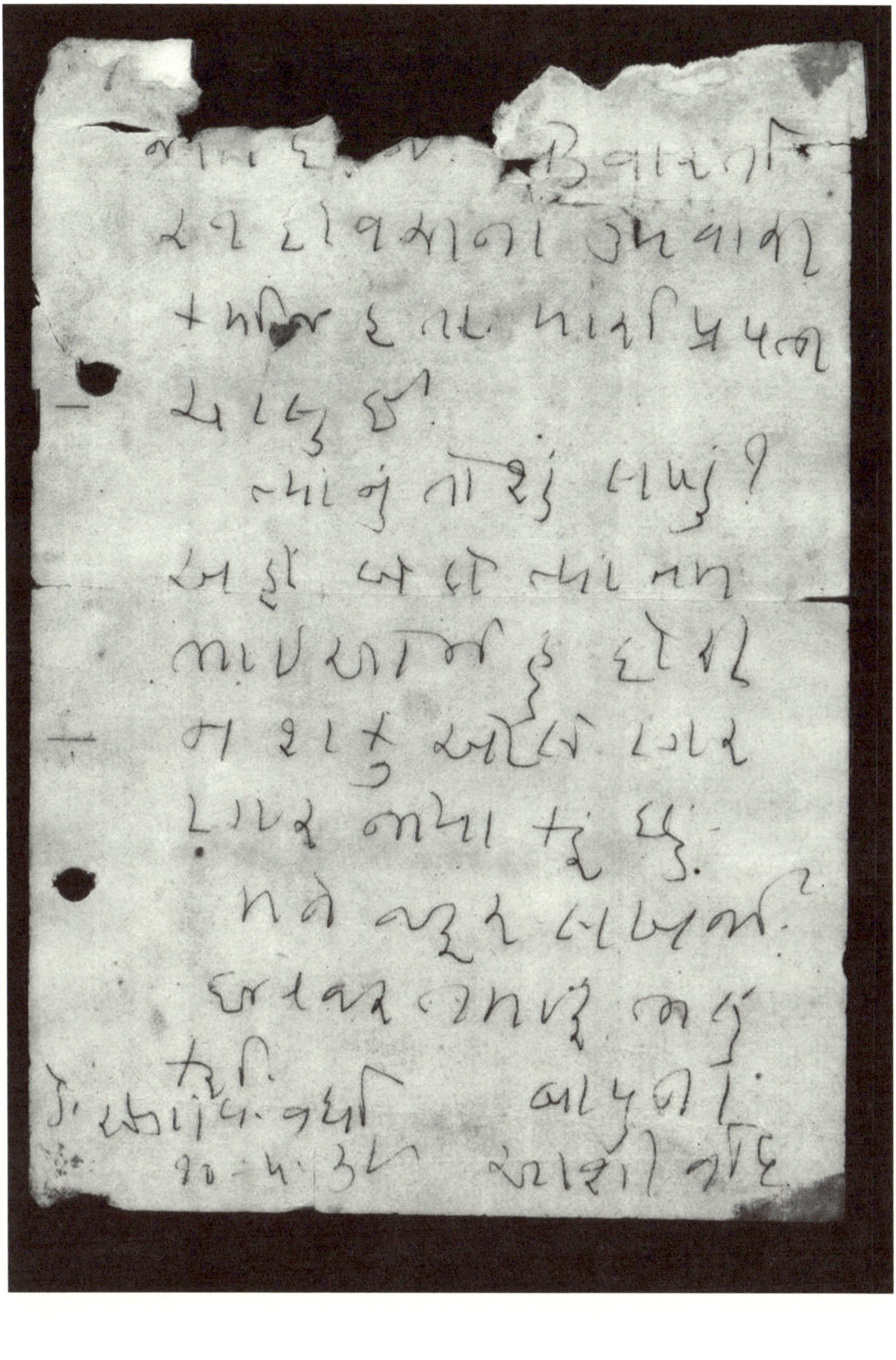

TRANSLATION OF THE LETTER FROM MAHATMA GANDHI
TO MR. V. KESHAVJEE DATED 10. 5. 39.

My Keshavjee,

I have preserved your letter of 13-8-38. Today I was going through my old correspondence in the train when I came across your letter.

You have rightly stated that the situation here is very grave.

Believe me I am the same person as I was there (in South Africa) I am prepared to achieve Hindu-Muslim unity even if I have to die.

I had fasted for 21 days for this purpose, and will continue my endeavours in that direction.

What can I write about the situation there (South Africa), as I cannot guide our bretheren from here. I am constantly keeping an eye on your situation all the time.

Definitely write to me.

May God Bless you.

Sevagav Vardha.
10-5-39.

Blessings from Bapu,

Translation of Gandhi's letter into English.

Chapter 18

Smelling the Soil of Africa

I FELT UNSETTLED IN KENYA DESPITE THE WARM CARE OF FAMily and friends that surrounded me. The government had enacted laws to shut out Asians who had failed to take up citizenship during the grace period after independence, and I was not allowed to work, even without pay. There was only one prospect for me, to do articles of clerkship, without pay, with a legal firm if I could persuade one to take me on, since that constituted educational training, not work. After a year in articles, even noncitizens could be admitted to the Bar in Kenya.

I started exploring that possibility. Within two days of my return to Nairobi, I had an appointment with Mirabeau da Gama Rose, a highly respected partner in the prominent law firm of Shapley, Barret Ennion and Marsh. Da Gama Rose had been a friend of my brother-in-law Hoosen and of my immediate family for many years. The discussion was successful, and I secured my articles.

Since my position was not a paid one, I had to look for additional work that would help me to contribute to the family finances, which was imperative because most of the family members were still attending school or unable to work since they were not Kenyan citizens. My friend, Solly Hajee, once again came to the rescue. He was lecturing at the East Africa Commercial College, which in conjunction with the Facit School of Typing was running a course for students studying for the London chartered accountancy exams or for the exams of the Chartered Institute of Secretaries. Solly offered me a position as lecturer in Commercial Law. I would give four lectures a month and be paid 100 shillings per lecture—which was one of the highest per-lecture payments in Kenya at that time. Solly paid me from his own pocket because he felt that having a qualified barrister on the faculty would lend great prestige to the course.

I enjoyed being in articles at the law firm. Our small group included Jackson Mulwa, who later became a judge of the High Court of Kenya, Farouk Adam, from a well-known business family, Horatio da Gama Rose, and Parin Rattansi, who had been called to the Bar at Lincoln's Inn. Parin had done her pupillage in Britain, and this was regarded with great respect in Kenya.

One of the interesting agreements I was asked to work on was what I called the Baboon Agreement. An overseas research institution wished to study the behaviour of baboons after transferring a troop of the primates to some land lying fallow near Embakasi Airport, and the owner of that property asked us to draw up a suitable agreement. I had to envisage what effect the imported primates would have on the existing vegetation as well as on the other animals on the land. In addition, what would be our client's liability if a voracious lion devoured a few of the baboons?

In order to practise in Kenya, I needed to sit for the national Bar exams. Fortuitously, that became unnecessary in 1969 because Kenya was on the verge of appointing its first African chief justice, Kitili Mwendwa, who had been trained at London University but was not yet enrolled as an advocate of the High Court of Kenya, which was a prerequisite for holding the highest legal position in the country. Consequently, the authorities declared a moratorium on the written Bar exams, and at the end of our articling year we had, instead, to take a verbal exam conducted by the Law Society of Kenya.

Apart from legally oriented work, a great deal of voluntary social work also came my way and I enjoyed it immensely. In 1969, the Aga Khan Education Board in Kenya set up a small careers guidance committee comprising four people, of whom I was one. Our remit was to guide students on future careers and, more critically, to help those who were on the margins to consider acquiring some skill that would enable them to pursue attractive careers later.

In 1970, after qualifying in my articles and passing the *viva voce* examination, I was inducted as an Advocate of the High Court of Kenya, together with some eighteen other lawyers. My problems did not end with my admission to the Kenyan Bar. I was occupied, but not yet gainfully.

My earnings from lectures at the East Africa Commercial College only amounted to £20 per month, so I looked for an additional job, but no legal firm was prepared to take me on because, legally, noncitizens were not allowed to be employed, or even to be self-employed.

Some people in Kenya sympathized with the plight of Asians who had migrated from South Africa, only to find themselves trapped in a diplomatic limbo, and tried to assist us. One of these was Chris Malavu, a well-connected Bugandan who was a local director of the East African branch of the British firm Lonrho as well as on the boards of several other international companies. After much difficulty, he was able to help Ameer and my father to get Kenyan citizenship. Thus, my two youngest siblings, Sadru and Khanum, both of whom were in their mid-teens and at school, and therefore my father's dependents, could become Kenyan citizens and be able to work legally.

One day, Surinder Khanna, a friend of Ameer's, told him about a Punjabi lawyer named Hardev Singh Daine, who was looking for a young energetic lawyer. Although Daine was in partnership with a Kikuyu politician from Nyeri named Henry Clement Warithii, his practice was effectively a one-man one and he desperately needed someone to help with his heavy case load. I went to see him and he offered me a salary of £100 a month, which was a lot of money in those days, particularly when compared with the maximum of £75 earned by newly qualified advocates in the city. I agreed to start immediately. I mentioned that I was not a Kenyan citizen, but he said he would try to get me a work permit.

Within a few days, I was fully in harness. My first assignment was upcountry, in Machakos, where our client was objecting to his farm animals being seized on the basis of an assets attachment order issued against his property instead of the original defendant in the case. He claimed that the animals were his and did not belong to the original defendant and therefore there was a wrongful attachment.

The proceedings were held in a half-walled tin-roofed shed on a farm, and they were presided over by a Mr Mott, a British magistrate. Mr Mott sat on a sturdy chair (while the rest of us sat on precarious benches) and studied the array of animals and witnesses that were paraded before him. This courtroom was surrounded by a motley group of spectators standing with their elbows on the half-wall as they watched.

Our client tried to convince the court that he owned the animals by touching each of them in turn, calling out its name and reciting its pedigree. The defendant took umbrage at that procedure, shouting that it was patently unfair, while the audience heaved a collective sigh of approbation or reprobation, depending on whose side they favoured. The animals ambled past the magistrate, the sheep among them bleating a ceremonious and throaty "Baah, baah" as the lively exchange between plaintiff and defendant continued, with the magistrate periodically raising his right hand to establish his authority and shouting, "Silence, silence, or I'll commit you for contempt of court!" The *opera comique* finally ended with our client getting his animals back.

Two months after I started working for him, Daine told me that the immigration authorities were reluctant to grant work permits to Asian noncitizen lawyers, particularly since an increasing number of young African lawyers were graduating from the Kenya School of Law. I fully understood his predicament and was grateful that he had stuck his neck out for me in the first place.

Once again, I was in limbo. I informed the Law Courts registrar that I would be available to do what were then known as "pauper briefs," providing a defence for any person accused of murder who could not afford a lawyer. Basically, they were pro-bono briefs for which the state paid a maximum of £10. Not long after, I was assigned a case and accepted it on the condition that the immigration authorities had no objection to my doing so. However, when I phoned the Immigration Department, I was told that even a pauper brief amounted to work. I explained the situation to the registrar's office and was told that the case would be reassigned.

The following day I received a phone call from the attorney-general's office asking me why, as a lawyer, I had refused to help an indigent who could not afford legal fees. I explained the situation to them and the official was indignant over the Immigration Department's obduracy. A few hours later, Parin Rattansi, who had become a prosecutor after being admitted to the Bar, informed me that Deputy Public Prosecutor James Karugu wanted to discuss the matter with me, after which I should make an appointment with Principal Immigration Officer Bernard Bangua to sort out the issue. When I met Karugu, an elegant London University graduate and a Middle Temple Inn barrister, he was forthright and said he was determined to protect the right to legal representation of indigent persons charged with murder.

I made an appointment with Bangua and went to see him, accompanied by my brother Ameer. Bangua, no doubt, had been briefed by Karugu, who, I gathered, was his good friend. He received us courteously in his spacious and airy office and was very sympathetic. Leafing through my South African passport, he asked me what my career plans were and I told him I wanted to start my own practice in Kenya. He asked, "Why would you not want to work for a legal office?" I responded that Kenya was suffering from serious unemployment and that if I opened my own firm, I would be able to employ two more people, which would also benefit their families. Moreover, I was confident that there was enough legal work available for a new practice. Bangua called in a senior advisor and instructed him, "Give him a section 18 (3)." I did not know what that meant, but he looked at me and said. "Kenya is your home. If you wish to open an office of your own, do so. If that does not work out and you wish to work for someone, feel equally free to do so. Please be free. You are now in your own country."

Some months later, I was saddened to hear that he had died in a car accident on one of the highways leading out of the city. I said a prayer for his soul and joined with a group of lawyers to help collect funds for his family.

The next morning, armed with my new enabling power, I went to Velco Properties in Queensway House, where Ameer and the senior partner, Sadru Ebrahim, were waiting for me. Ameer and Sadru had jointly bought Velco Properties from my brother-in-law Murad, who was planning to emigrate to Canada. They set me up in business in a typically Gujarati fashion. "Esso Africa's offices in this building are up for rental on a sub-tenancy basis," Sadru said. "There are three offices. Go and take them and we will underwrite your rent for three months." I contacted Esso's lawyers, who were in the same building, obtained a copy of the sublease, studied it that night and signed it.

Sadru and Ameer furnished my offices with a sturdy wooden desk, a high-backed chair and some other furniture from Velco, and Sadru lent me his beautiful oak bookcase. They had just concluded a major deal with some interesting spin-offs and they placed the whole deal in my inexperienced hands. "We need to form a limited company immediately," Sadru said. Then, almost as an aside, he added, "We also need a conveyance, as the company will be buying a property. And we need a loan for the property. Netherlands Bank has agreed to give us the loan; go and see the manager, Mr Niewenhuys, on our behalf." And that was not all. "Lastly, we need a lease for housing Metal Box of Kenya's staff in the property, which is a dormitory. Contact Metal Box and get the lease signed by early next week." I felt somewhat dizzy with this flurry of legal instructions descending on me like a flock of hungry birds. The only thing I knew was how to provide the legal framework for a property-holding company, so I would have to do some research in order to accomplish the rest.

That was on a Wednesday. The work had to be done by Tuesday the following week, which was after Easter Monday. I looked for a professional legal typist who would be willing to do my work even over the Easter holiday and found Ms Dempster, a Scotswoman fully steeped in the Protestant ethic, who agreed to do it. The Netherlands Bank and Metal Box of Kenya asked me to draw up the necessary documents because of the Easter holiday and brushed aside my caution about a possible conflict of interest since I was also representing Velco.

I worked hard on the Velco lease over the entire weekend. My sister Rashida helped by typing out my handwritten document, which we then handed to Ms Dempster. By Tuesday, the company, the mortgage, the conveyancing, and the lease were all ready for executing and registering. If my recollection is correct, I earned something in the region of £600 in four days, which was a handsome fee in the Kenya of the early 1970s. I could pay my office rent for the whole year in advance.

From then on, whenever Velco or its clients needed legal services, they came to me. I built up a steady flow of conveyancing and took on a staff of two people. However, though my bread-and-butter practice was assured, I did not want to abandon criminal law. For one, people in Kenya needed help; and secondly, I enjoyed criminal law. I decided to do criminal case work for a minimal fee or free of charge, if necessary. After all, I had got my major break by virtue of a murder case!

One case that I will never forget was that of a Railways Corporation employee charged with embezzlement. The defendant was a twenty-year-old man who had migrated from the countryside to the city in search of work. He was the main breadwinner in his family, helping to send his younger siblings to school. The prosecution had ample evidence of forgery, supported by a confession. I discussed a plea bargain with the attorney-general's office and they said that if my client pleaded guilty and asked the court for mitigation, the state would consider recommending a lighter sentence. I asked the court to adjourn the case to the afternoon so that I could discuss the offer with my client.

During the recess I spoke to my client's aged parents, who were deeply humiliated by their son's action. They were God-fearing subsistence farmers, eking out a bare living from their small plot of land. I also spent part of the lunch hour researching the background of the magistrate, an Englishman who had spent many years in Calcutta, notorious for the miserable poverty of many of its multitudinous residents.

After lunch, when the court reconvened, I entered a plea of guilty on behalf of my client and was given permission to speak in mitigation. I described the misery and hopelessness experienced by hundreds of thousands of desperate Africans who had migrated to cities for jobs and, as in cities like Calcutta, had ended up living on the streets without being able to meet their basic needs such as water and food, let alone provide for their impoverished families living upcountry. I admitted that my client was not in that position, but, coming from a pastoral background, he had been totally unprepared for modern urban life and had fallen victim to his own weaknesses. "Let us help him extricate himself, and by so doing, rehabilitate him in the society for which he was ill-prepared and also grant some protection to his dependent and elderly parents," I urged the magistrate.

The magistrate was evidently moved and adjourned the hearing for a week in order to ponder the sentence. However, he did intimate that if my client was prepared to give back the money he had embezzled, even in small instalments, he would consider a suspended sentence. A week later, with help from his extended family and tribe, my client was able to give back a fair amount of the embezzled money. To my delight, he was granted complete freedom. In fact, his employers even agreed to take him back and to help him to reform himself.

I was surprised when I returned to my chambers that evening to find my client's parents waiting there to discuss my fee. They were prepared to sell their meagre possessions to remunerate me and were incredulous when I told them that there would be no fee. They were simple and noble people and insisted, "Please, sir, tell us what we owe you. You saved our son from going to prison." I finally managed to convince them that they owed me nothing and asked only for their prayers and good wishes. With great reluctance they accepted that.

When I discussed that couple with my future wife, Amina Jindani, who was a specialist in tuberculosis at the Kenyatta National Hospital, she told me about an African man who had come all the way from his village in Uganda to seek treatment for drug resistant tuberculosis at her hospital. He had walked part of the trip. For some reason, it was the hospital's policy not to admit such cases, but Amina had him admitted unofficially and ensured that he was given a good meal and bed for the night. He remained in hospital for a few days before being released. He then went back to Uganda and somehow survived his illness. Months later, Amina received the following letter from Uganda, obviously written with the help of a scribe:

> Dear Dr Jindani,
>
> I returned to my village in Uganda and told all my people about my experiences in Nairobi and about the kind doctor who had taken pity on me and admitted me to the ward and saved my life. I then gathered all the people in my village and we sat in a circle, and, Doctor, we said a prayer for you. We prayed that *Mungu* should bless you, Doctor, for what you did for me.

Such honesty and simplicity of response is something that civilized society, with its complex urban modernity, has lost.

Amina remembered that Ugandan villager again some years later, after her face was badly injured in a car accident far from Nairobi. She regained consciousness several days later to find herself in an upcountry hospital. Dr Aliev, an Azerbaijani surgeon who had treated her, placed a comforting hand on her forehead and assured her that her injuries would be healed. Amina thought to herself, "This doctor from far-off Central Asia has come to work in an upcountry district as part of the Soviet Union's assistance to Kenya. He has saved my life and will reconstruct my face." It was a miracle and she felt deeply grateful for it.

The parents of the man I had defended were also very grateful. From then on, every year they sent me a bag of newly harvested potatoes with a small note written by a scribe in the village, which read, "Dear Advocate, we always think of you—may Mungu bless you. We always pray for you."

Through my legal work, I became familiar with prison conditions and was asked to serve on the two-man committee that periodically visited the prisons to check on the treatment of inmates. The other person on the committee was a doctor, Dev Ramrakha, brother of the prize-winning photographer Priya Ramrakha, who had been killed in 1968 while covering the Nigerian civil war for *Newsweek*. I felt honoured and accepted gladly. During our visits to the prisons, Dev and I found that, even though we encountered an enlightened African warden who really cared about the welfare of the prisoners, generally the purpose of the prisons seemed to be simply to punish the inmates, many of whom had committed crimes because of poverty.

Meanwhile, my brother Ameer, because of his co-ownership of Velco, was frequently asked by his ministerial friends to help Africans improve their economic situation. "Help them to get their own homes," they would exhort. Ameer was fully committed to that cause, as was Sadru Ebrahim. Ameer managed to help a number of Kenyans to purchase their own homes, and the legal documents were drawn up by me with payment in installments. The clients were scrupulously honest and none defaulted on his postdated cheques.

After some months I felt I needed a break abroad, and thanks to my cousin Madat, who had worked out my meagre budget on a serviette near the Temple tube station in London some five years earlier, I had the money to do so. Madat was running a small real-estate agency called Nairobi Homes and had retained me for some of his work. One day he told me that he had bought a building comprising eight apartments, almost all of which were ready for rental. "I want you to do all the leases," he said. "The tenants will be paying. They are all major multinationals, Coca-Cola, Burns and Blane, Union Carbide, Metal Box of Kenya, International Aeradio, Wiggins Teape, and the Royal Norwegian Embassy. I will not hand over the keys to them until you assure me that it is safe to do so." I did the work within a few days and found myself richer by five hundred pounds.

One of the airline companies for whom I had done some work gave me a free first-class ticket to Rome, London, and Copenhagen. Niels Jorgenson, a Danish professor at the University of Nairobi whom I had successfully defended against a charge of shooting an eland without a licence, offered to put me up, first at his home in Copenhagen and then with his in-laws in Aarhus in Jutland. Just before leaving, I received a cheque for 100 guineas in the post. It was from the police commissioner and was "an honorarium" for having successfully defended two policemen charged with killing a man after pursuing him to the Nairobi Dam. The prosecution had withdrawn the murder charge when it became obvious that their case was full of holes. It seemed that everything was prodding me to go to Europe, the continent of my dreams.

I asked Ameer to keep a general eye on my practice, and in the summer of 1972 I boarded an East African Airways super VC10 to Rome. There, I visited the Vatican and marvelled over the magnificent Sistine Chapel and the sculptures and paintings of Michelangelo. Then I went to Venice and spent my twenty-seventh birthday on a gondola, floating past the splendid Renaissance buildings that flank the winding canals. Next, I flew to Copenhagen and, after a week, London.

After six exhilarating weeks in Europe, I returned to Nairobi in late July 1972. On the flight back, I reflected on my situation and my legal practice. I could now earn a living through hard work. I was respected by people and, what was more, I could see a magnificent future ahead of me. Kenya was now becoming my home and I loved it. I could take on two junior lawyers and expand my practice. After that, I could return to England and do a post-graduate diploma at the Institute of Criminology, Cambridge University. I had worked it all out.

However, on 5 August 1972, events in neighbouring Uganda shook up my comfortable world and plans for the future, as thousands of Asians suffered a major change in their destiny. For most members of our family in Kenya, those events heralded an end to the African chapter of our lives.

Chapter 19

A Tsunami Named Big Daddy

IN THE EARLY 1970S, THE HILTON HOTEL IN DOWNTOWN Nairobi was one of the most popular spots among the socialites in the city. On Saturday nights my friends and I would go there after a movie and indulge in light-hearted banter over hot chocolate, with the music of the late 1960s playing in the background.

Saturday, 5 August 1972 was different. While we were in the coffee shop, someone walked in and threw the early edition of the *Sunday Nation* on the table, almost shouting, "Can you believe it? The guy has gone crazy, he is absolutely nuts!" We looked unbelievingly at the newspaper headline reporting that the Ugandan leader Idi Amin had ordered all Asians to leave the country within ninety days. He said that God had commanded him to expel them.

Uganda had become a frightening place to live in under Amin's rule. Many prominent people were being murdered because Amin perceived them as a threat. Chief Justice Benedicto Kiwanuka had been killed for standing up for the rule of law. Thousands of people were said to have been jailed without trial. Amin was a human tsunami, leaving death and havoc in his wake, and now the tsunami was targeting the Asian community.

Asians throughout East Africa were shocked by the enthusiastic support that Amin's expulsion order received from the indigenous populations in the region, whose general attitude was one of "good riddance." Despite his clownishness, Idi Amin was viewed as a hero by them. As Ugandan soldiers began a campaign of harassment, robbery, and rape against Asians, the only national leaders on the continent that spoke out against this ethnic cleansing were Julius Nyerere of Tanzania and Kenneth Kaunda of Zambia.

Trains carrying expellees to Kenya travelled nonstop to Nairobi, and the Asians were escorted straight from the train station to the airport. A Nairobi businessman, Noorali Ebrahim, heard that many refugee families were stranded without money or resources at the airport. The only clothing they had was what they wore. Noorali immediately mobilized volunteers and got Mithoobhai, owner of the Ismailia Hotel Restaurant, noted for its potato bhajias and tamarind chutney, to prepare boxes of sandwiches and cold drinks. Noorali went personally to the airport and persuaded the authorities to allow him and his team of volunteers access to the refugees. The food became a daily routine. He also helped in another way; each day, he gave me £1000 as a rolling contingency fund to pay bail for any refugee apprehended by the authorities.

Mithoobhai already had a reputation for helping people with immigration problems. He had cultivated contacts in the Immigration Department who could facilitate applications for travel documents. Some Asians joked that that there were as many passports in his restaurant as there were bhajias in his kitchen. Now Mithoobhai left his restaurant in the hands of family members and spent entire days at the airport, ministering to the needs of the refugees.

Some Asian lawyers, including myself, helped out with legal problems facing the refugees. Virinder Sikand, Pheroze Nowrojee, and some others in the legal profession convened a meeting with officials of the National Christian Council of Kenya to work out a joint strategy for helping them. John Kamau and Zarina Patel of the National Christian Council of Kenya tried to find ways to aid them and to persuade the Kenyan authorities to allow them to remain in Kenya pending resolution of their status.

Some Kenyan Asians were afraid that they, too, would become victims of such policies and began making preparations to emigrate. One Saturday morning, two young boys in their late teens came to my office and asked if I could help one of them, who had a Kenyan passport, to get a visa for Britain. The British high commission in Nairobi had refused him a tourist visa, but he had purchased a fixed ticket and would not be refunded the money if he did not travel. His friend already had landed immigrant status in Canada, where he knew someone in Saskatchewan. I leafed through his ticket and then went to the Velco Properties offices and spoke to Sadru Ebrahim, who also owned East African Sun, Sea and Safari, the travel agency that had issued the ticket. Sadru was very understanding and said, "Tell him to go to the travel agency and pick up a ticket to Canada, and to pay only the difference. I will sort out the rest." On hearing the good news, the young man was ecstatic. Years later, I heard that he and his friend had jointly started an automatic car wash business and become prosperous Canadian citizens.

In Kampala, the Asians were desperately going from embassy to embassy, pleading for visas. Amir Jetha, a pharmacist, was married to an Asian woman whose Danish husband had died in a sky-jumping accident in Nairobi some years earlier while she was pregnant. At the suggestion of a friend, he went to the Danish embassy and explained the situation to an official, who informed him that, as the adoptive father of a Danish child, he was entitled to live in Denmark. After a few years in Copenhagen, he, his wife, and his stepchild moved to Ottawa, joining his extended family there.

Ashak Nathwani, an engineer who is a maternal great-grandson of Manekfaiba, daughter of Keshavjeebapa, was waiting in a queue for the makeshift Canadian office to open its doors when he was told by a friend that Australia was also a good possibility. Since the Australian special mission opened its doors earlier than the Canadian office did, he tried there first and was immediately given a visa. Nathwani's other family members ended up in Canada, Britain, and France.

One Asian born in Uganda, who had earlier rejected major lucrative offers from prominent universities in the world, refused to leave. He was Professor Sultan MM Karim, who had done pioneering work on prostaglandins. He insisted that he owed it to Uganda to continue contributing to medical research there. Finally, after many pleas from family and friends, he was persuaded to change his mind and he flew to Singapore, where he was immediately given a post in the Department of Obstetrics and Gynaecology at the National University of Singapore.

In view of the ongoing murders of former government officials and their family members one by one, Joe Zake, who by now was a client of ours at Velco Properties, decided to leave the country. To avoid arousing suspicion among Amin's spies, he secretly dispatched his wife Margaret and their five children first and sent Ameer a message requesting him to house them in a safe place.

Kenya was not a safe refuge for fleeing Ugandans. The wife of the deposed president Obote, Miria Kalule, had escaped twice to Nairobi, only to be handed back each time to the Ugandan authorities by Kenyan security officers. Ameer arranged to accommodate Margaret and the children at Aly's Guesthouse, next to our home on Third Avenue Parklands. Agriculture Minister Jeremiah Nyagah arranged for the police to watch our home and the guesthouse day and night to ensure our safety. A few days later, my mother was making tea early one morning when she heard a knock at the front door. It was Joe Zake.

It was clear that Joe would not be safe in Kenya. A dear friend, Esmail Dawood, made various attempts to see if we could obtain a travel document for him from either the Indian or Pakistani Embassies, but this did not work out. It took Ameer about ten days to get Joe the necessary travel papers through the Kenyan authorities. Sadru Ebrahim supplied plane tickets and my brother Saadat arranged to drive the family incognito to the airport, where we had informally obtained permission to drive our guests straight to the plane. Joe was going to Britain, where Alex Lyon, a Labour MP, was making arrangements to help him get asylum until he could fly to the US where he was hoping to teach at Dartmouth College. As they left our house, Margaret clutched my sister Rashida's hand and said, "My dear Rashida, leave this place. East Africa is not for us, not for you, not for us."

The Aga Khan made extensive arrangements to secure the well-being of the community, the majority of whom had taken up Ugandan citizenship and were now declared stateless. Canada opened its doors to many such people, while Britain reluctantly accepted British passport holders. As the days passed, people managed to get out of the country with a view to going anywhere they could find a safe haven. Those who were able to go to specific countries did so. Many stayed till the end. The Ismaili institutional network also gave help to people from other communities who were facing similar difficulties

In response to an appeal by the United Nations High Commissioner for Refugees (UNHCR), Prince Sadruddin Aga Khan, five European countries—Austria, Belgium, Italy, Malta, and Spain—belatedly opened transit centres to provide temporary asylum for the last refugees. The UNHCR worked to find permanent homes for people housed in the transit centres, a process which took some years to complete.

The Canadian government, under the dynamic and far-sighted leadership of Pierre Elliot Trudeau, played a major role in rehabilitating the expellees. Most of the Ismailis who had taken up Ugandan citizenship found refuge in Canada and contributed significantly to the Canadian economy and society.

In Toronto, a church relief office was converted into a refugee centre, with volunteers ministering to the needs of the newly arrived and generally penniless refugees. After a few days of care and hospitality, they were dispatched across Canada to wherever they had relatives or friends or where a job could be found for them. Murad and Mila Velshi, my brother-in-law and sister, volunteered at the centre and opened their home to many. The refugees were willing to go anywhere and take on any work. For example, Diamond Gulamhussein, a University of Nairobi graduate in mathematics and a good friend of mine, took a job as a parking attendant.

Whatever fine public sentiments may have been expressed by those in authority and in positions of influence in Kenya, it was becoming clearer to the Asians that the East Africa of the 1970s did not want them. It was against this background towards the end of 1972 that my brothers Rex and Ameer and I had a discussion one evening, while sitting in Rex's pearl-white Volkswagen Beetle in the car park of the Intercontinental Hotel. Ameer relayed to Rex some of the anti-Asian sentiments that he had been picking up at Velco Properties. "There is no real long-term future for us in this country," he said. "At the most, we have a few years." He said we should emigrate to Canada, where we already had some family members.

That week, I was sitting at the Velco offices with a Tanzanian African lawyer, Felician Bwallo Mahatane, with whom I had done some work earlier, and I told him I was planning to leave Kenya and wanted to divest myself of my legal practice. He looked at me and smiled. "If only I could afford it, I would make an offer. But it's all academic." I put my hand in my pocket and took out my office keys. "Catch!" I said as I threw him the keys. As he caught them, I said, "It's yours. All I want from you is to be allowed to work from the office for a short while to complete the work I have in hand."

My sister Rashida left for Canada towards the end of 1972. A few weeks after her arrival, the Canadian government closed the special immigration facility that enabled people to apply for landed immigrant status from within the country. That made it more difficult for me to get immigration status, but I did not regret my decision to complete all the pending coveyancing work entrusted to me by clients before I left Kenya.

In 1973, the Labour Party came to power in Britain and I was invited by John Fraser, MP, who at different times had held the positions of Deputy Minister in the Department of Prices and Consumer Protection and in the Department of Employment, and was now deputy employment secretary in the Callaghan government, to go and work for his firm, Lewis Silkin and Partners. John had been to Kenya earlier in the year as the guest of Ameer, and Sadru and I had had the honour of accompanying him to various parts of the country. He had a strong social conscience and had gone out of his way to help Ismaili refugees in England. His firm had a large number of files on East African Asians and he wanted me to help process them while he attended to his parliamentary work.

I had undergone an immigration interview with Canadian officials in Kenya and I requested the Canadian embassy to transfer my file to London. I started working on the East African Asian files immediately after my arrival in London. It was ironic that, being a de facto refugee in search of a homeland myself, I was working with one of the leading immigration legal firms in Britain, fighting cases for others.

I spent the summer of 1973 working on the files and applying to various Canadian law schools. To my disappointment, I did not get into any of the Canadian universities that year due to an unfortunate misunderstanding in the sending of my transcripts from London. Meanwhile, my application for a Canadian visa kept moving ahead with the speed of a snail.

In the autumn of 1973, I went to Canada and managed to get interviews at the University of Toronto and Osgoode Hall Law School at York University, but was told that I could not get much academic credit for my British qualification. To practise in Ontario, I had to do an LLB at a law school recognized by the Law Society of Upper Canada. After a two-month stay with my sister Zarina, who went out of her way to make me comfortable, I flew to Kenya in December 1973. I had got a medical examination done in Toronto and I stopped over in London to deliver the report to the Canadian high commission for addition to my application file.

I arrived in Nairobi in time for Kenya's tenth independence anniversary celebrations. While I had been away, Ameer had promised his wife Sherbanoo that the two of them would travel around India before emigrating to Canada. Since I was at a loose end while waiting for my landed immigrant status and admission to a law school in Canada, Ameer offered me the position of acting managing director of Velco Properties for two months. Additionally, I had to keep an eye on his young son Salmaan and daughter Fatima.

A compeling reason for my return to Kenya was to attend to some outstanding family matters which I was able to finalize on this visit. No sooner had I done that I went to London again and sat for the Law School Admission Test, which was a requirement for Canadian law schools. I was now one step nearer to getting into Canada.

Chapter 20

A Home at Last

IN THE SPRING OF 1974 THE LABOUR PARTY WAS BACK IN POWER and John Fraser became deputy employment secretary in the Callaghan government. I was once again in the Peckham office of Lewis Silkin and Partners, working with Chris Silken, whose father, Sam, was then attorney-general.

My legal work at Lewis Silkin was more varied than during my first stint there. In addition to taking on immigration cases, I drew up wills for clients. I also attended the Central Criminal Court and the Old Bailey, which was useful for my career as a barrister. The British legal system still has a two-tiered approach, whereby a solicitor's clerk meets a client and then negotiates with a barrister's clerk for the client to be represented in court. I found it both archaic and fascinating.

John Fraser wrote on House of Commons stationery to various law schools in Canada, strongly recommending my admission. Finally, in the late summer of 1974, I received confirmation that three of the five schools in Ontario to which I had applied had accepted me as a mature student. They were Queen's, Western Ontario and Windsor. Queen's University, recognizing that I was a mature student with a Bar-at-law qualification, was willing to place me in the second year of a three-year LLB programme. On the advice of my friend Paul Damien Dole, former president of the Gray's Inn Debating Society, I sent a letter of acceptance to Queen's and went to the Canadian high commission to apply for landed immigrant status. To my horror, they said that I could only get a student visa. When the embassy gave me the visa, an official told me that I would have no chance of getting landed immigrant status after my studies, because "the country does not really need any more lawyers."

In the early autumn of 1974 I took an Air Canada flight from London to Toronto. My family were at the airport to welcome me to my new life. I did not stay long in Toronto, and by the weekend I left for the small and pretty university town of Kingston on a Greyhound bus.

In Kenya, a friend, Farida Nanji, maternal granddaughter of Ebrahim Virji of South Africa, had told me, "I have a brother in Kingston who is becoming a doctor. His name is Aziz. Do contact him if you go to Queen's University; I am sure he will be happy to help and guide you." She had given me Aziz's address and telephone number. Aziz responded warmly when I phoned him and we agreed to meet at the Hotel Dieu Hospital that evening since he was on call and would be performing surgery before then. After a wait of about fifteen minutes, I saw a young man dressed in green surgical scrubs with a cloth mask and a stethoscope around his neck walking towards me. His face seemed familiar, and then I realized that some ten years earlier, when we had both been students at the Aga Khan High School in Nairobi, I had been a prefect and had been given the task of punishing him for misbehaving during afternoon assembly. I had been doing some research on Dr Sun Yat-sen, founder of the Republic of China, and I had decided to "outsource" that task to Aziz. Fortunately, in Kingston he did not seem to remember that occasion. I later reminded him of the school incident, and from then on he frequently teased me about it.

Aziz had been studying at Makerere University when Idi Amin expelled all the Asians, and the Canadian Immigration team in Kampala had granted him a visa. He had been admitted to Queen's University where special courses had been prepared for him and a few other medical students from Uganda to enable them to comply with Canadian regulations regarding medical practice. He invited me to visit him at the medical students' residence, a large mansion in the grounds of Kingston Psychiatric Hospital, fronting Lake Ontario. The next day I met his medical friends and I became an implicit member of their fraternity, for which I will always be grateful.

I was admitted to the second year of the LLB programme on the proviso that I took two subjects without which I would not be allowed to practise in Ontario: Canadian Constitutional Law and Ontario Civil Procedure. Beyond those, I could choose whatever legal subjects I liked. I was attracted to International Law, which I took in the first semester. I also took Human Rights. All the students had to write a paper and I did mine on apartheid from a human rights perspective, which was taught by a very gentle, understanding, and empathetic professor named Jack Johnstone. My paper, entitled 'The Tyranny of Colour,' was a small study of how South Africa had violated the provisions of the Universal Declaration of Human Rights through a plethora of racist legislative enactments. Jack Johnstone made a telling comment on the paper, observing that he could not escape feeling my utter sense of indignation that permeated it even though I had been composed enough to write about the atrocities of apartheid.

To stretch out my finances, I rented a room in a house behind the graduate students' residence and minimized my spending. However, help was on the way just when I needed it. A few weeks after my arrival, I received a telegram from a former client in Kenya asking me to fly to Nairobi for a weekend to represent her in a divorce case, for which she was prepared to pay all my expenses. Since the telegram was delivered to me through the university, it did not take long for its contents to become widely known in the law school. On hearing about it, Professor George Nieuspiel of Carleton University, who taught us International Law, commented in class, "I thought my going to Caracas for a week for a major conference was unusual, but being called out to Nairobi for a weekend is something rather unprecedented." I beamed with pride.

I went to Nairobi and fought the case over the weekend. A friend told me that a new law had been passed requiring noncitizens in Kenya to register, and I felt that perhaps it would be best for me to do so in case I ever needed to return to the country. I went to the Immigration Department and registered. I returned to Canada within a week, as I did not want to miss too many classes. At Queen's I found that my reputation had grown, and I was both admired and the butt of jokes—a not unenviable position to hold in the student body!

I made many friends from various parts of the world, particularly from Trinidad. Two of the Trinidadians were Frank Meighlal, who was studying law, and Radha Faucheaux, a Trinidadian of Indian origin who was not a student but very interested in the various social activities at the

International Centre, particularly the India Association. Radha lived in a beautiful house by the lake, about ten kilometers from Kingston, to which she often invited us from the Association. She was interested in Indian cultural life and cultural activities. Both Frank and Radha were overwhelmingly warm and kind and I spent a great deal of time with them.

I also met and socialized with a contingent of Indian students, from whom I learnt about some outstanding Indians, such as the Nobel laureate Hargobind Khorana, who had done some pioneering work on the DNA molecule; Vikram Sarabhai, the Gujarati scientist who pioneered India's space programme; JRD Tata, who pioneered aviation in India; and Homi Jahangir Bhabha, who ushered India from the abacus to the computer age. I was introduced to the writings of Jagdish Bhagwati of the Delhi School of Economics by Professor Ram Rao of Pittsburgh University and the Carnegie Mellon Institute, who was then teaching at Queen's.

The India Association often screened movies from the subcontinent and the Indian students often took me to see the films of Satyajit Ray. I was introduced to Rabindranath Tagore's *Gitanjali*, the collection of poems for which he was awarded the Nobel Prize for Literature in 1913. And the pièce de resistance for me was a film of Jawaharlal Nehru's famous oration on India's independence, in which he spoke of the "tryst with destiny" and how at midnight India would awake and "redeem its pledge" to attain freedom.

My Indian friends unanimously elected me president of the India Association. I derived particular satisfaction from the election of Aziz Nanji as vice-president and Radha Faucheux as secretary. I teased my friends that it was South African Indians who had given Gandhi to India, so by voting for me they were only repaying the debt that they collectively owed us.

After lectures each day, I joined Al Noor Juma, an engineering student from Kenya, Alan Cantor from Toronto, and some of my fellow students in discussions on all sorts of topics, ranging from politics and economics to social issues and, inevitably, the role of law in our lives and the orderly pattern of societies. The discussions would go on until the late hours of the night, and we would keep awake by downing gallons of bitter black coffee.

The India Association needed a new impetus, a new life, and my friends looked to me to provide appropriate leadership. I shared an apartment with Anil Sampat, who has since become a prosperous industrialist in Mumbai, and Lalit Jain, also of Mumbai, and together with Aziz Nanji we developed a programme for the association for the coming year. In addition to screening the usual escapist Indian movies full of dance and song, which were very popular with the Kingston South Asian community, we felt that we owed Indians the opportunity to experience more than just Bollywood entertainment and decided to hold a Satyajit Ray festival. In addition, we organized cultural evenings featuring classical Kathak and Bharatnatyam dances by children from the local Indian families, followed by a raga on the vina by a young White Canadian woman who had studied the string instrument in India for some years.

The cultural evenings went down very well with the Indian community, but the Satyajit Ray festival was a failure, with very few Asians turning up. The rental fee of the Ray films was almost twice that of the ordinary popular ones, and our gate money was not enough to cover that fee. We had booked the films for a whole season and there was no way to get out of the contract. We had to find alternatives that would bring in an income to balance out the losses, and one of the India Association members, Kulbir Singh, came up with the brilliant idea of renting Mel Brooks's *Blazing Saddles*. It took only two showings on one day to make up our losses. Comedy had trumped art!

All the law students had to participate in a moot court, a mock court case that gave them practice in legal argument. I prepared my brief and presented it before Judge Delisle, a well-known personality on the Kingston Bench. It was customary for the organizer of the moot to invite all the participants for a drink at the Faculty Club and I found myself talking to Professor Ken Swan of the Law School, who had conducted the moot. Ken had done his Master's in Law at London University.

"Your presentation was excellent," he said. "Where did you study?" I told him that I was a barrister, having been called to the Bar at Gray's Inn in London. "For God's sake," he responded, "what the hell are you doing at Queen's if you are a qualified lawyer? I explained to him that Canada did not recognize my Bar-at-Law qualification as sufficient to practise in the country. "Do you intend to practise in Canada one day?" he asked. I explained my circumstances to him, which made him very angry about the inequity of Canadian immigration policies. "When I hear stories like these, I feel ashamed of being a Canadian. Come and see me tomorrow in my office and let me see whether anything can be done about this," he said.

The next day, after I had given him a fuller account of my experience, he asked me to summarize my situation on paper and send it to him. "I know someone who taught at Queen's and is now with the government. I will try and seek his views," he explained. "I can't promise anything, but let's see what can be done." In addition to apprising his friend in Ottawa of my situation, Ken also kept Dean Dan Soberman of the Law School informed about what he was trying to do. He warned me that the matter would take a long time as my immigration application had originated in Kenya and then been transferred to England.

Queen's and Kingston began to grow on me. Very often, I went to Toronto to spend a weekend with the family, who had settled in the Willowdale area. My two younger brothers Saadat and Sadru had gathered a group of friends around them and formed a disco group called The Penny Farthing. They performed at parties in hotels, clubs, boats, and even farmhouses. It was a time when Ismailis from Africa had begun to settle in Toronto and the Penny Farthing circuit helped the young people to adapt to their new country. Many got to know each other during the parties, fell in love, and got married.

I completed the second year of my LLB programme in the spring of 1975 and decided to go west to Calgary to spend the summer with my elder brother Ameer, who had been in the country for a year and had generously asked me to spend the summer with him. Whilst I was in Calgary, I contacted Professor Ryan at Queen's and began to do some work on Ismaili personal law under his long-distance guidance. I used part of my summer doing library research on personal law at the University of Calgary to provide a foundation for the subject. I also went to Vancouver to visit my cousin Sadick, and we went to Los Angeles together.

On my return to Calgary, I got a phone call from Rex in Toronto. A sad event had taken place which, like many others I had experienced, would affect the rest of my life. Noorali Dhanani, one of two Ismaili lawyers in

Toronto, had died of a heart attack at the age of 48. The firm he was working for, Elgie, Walsh and Dhanani, needed an Ismaili lawyer to replace him, to service the needs of the large Ismaili clientele that he had built up over the years. Rex suggested that I ring John Walsh and offer my services to the firm. I had already been introduced to John before by Noorali, and he remembered me. He told me that Noorali had always spoken very highly of me and asked when I would be completing my law studies. I told him that I had a year to go but did not have landed immigrant status yet. He said that he could see a possible role for me and that I should not take on any commitment without first consulting him.

Back in Kingston, Aziz Nanji managed to secure a small apartment for us. There were three occupants at 325 University Avenue: Aziz, Candy the cat—an *éminence grise* who deigned to live with us within the confines of our tiny apartment—and I. We made the place a veritable social and intellectual watering hole for all sorts of people. Our university friends came to enjoy our sumptuous Indian meals.

The last quarter of 1975 was mainly taken up with examinations and finalization of papers. Most importantly, Ken was in regular contact with his friend in Ottawa who, I had been told, was himself a former refugee and had been made homeless twice. Through the friend, Ken was made aware of changes in the Canadian immigration procedures.

To get landed immigrant status in Canada, I would have to be offered a job with a profile that no Canadian lawyer could fit. The job that John Walsh had in mind would be ideal from this viewpoint. Elgie, Walsh and Dhanani needed a lawyer who was from East Africa, knew the laws of Kenya, understood the family law issues of Ismaili Muslims, spoke Gujarati, had a background in Canadian law and was prepared to work as a legal clerk. John Walsh told the Immigration and Manpower officials in Toronto that he had interviewed thirty-eight people in Canada and had found me to be the only eligible candidate for the position.

In the spring of 1976, I passed my LLB exams and was rated in the top 10% of the graduating class at Queen's that year. Later, Dean Soberman informed me that Ken Swan had kept him fully informed about his negotiations in Ottawa and that I had the official backing of Queen's Law School.

On Ken's advice, I decided to apply for landed immigrant status from Boston and then wait there for the outcome of my application. It was the most convenient place, as my cousin Rafique was doing a PhD in Social Anthropology at Harvard. He was planning to go to Iran to do his field work, but would still be around for a few weeks and was prepared to put me up at his residence in Cambridge. I was given a visa by the US consulate in Toronto and bought a ticket from Tourama Travels, run by my sister Mila and her husband Murad.

At Harvard, Rafique and two of his friends, Mohamed Abualy and Liaquat Ahmed from Kenya, constituted a nucleus around which people of all disciplines, orientations, cultures, nationalities, and traditions mingled. Rafique and Mohamed would often put up those people at their homes, or, if they could not do so, persuade friends to take them in. Sometimes they would lend them furniture. Often, they would lend them other people's furniture. They were wheeler dealers of friendship and hospitality.

Through Rafique's student network, I found quite a few people ready to help me when I needed to get my medicals done for the Canadian consulate. Rafique had asked Anne Sweetser, a student anthropologist, to take me to a doctor and help me process my medicals. Laurie Mcknight, who later married Mohamed Abualy, generously took care of me. I waited in Boston for almost six weeks while my papers were being processed. Then came a phone call from Ken Swan informing me that I had been granted landed immigrant status and that I would be given a visa to re-enter Canada. I received the visa the next day from the Canadian consulate in Boston. Rafique had left for Iran with Liaquat Ahmed, so Mohamed Abualy arranged for me to get a lift with his friend Dick Boehm, from Harvard, who was driving to Toronto. We entered Canada at Philipsburg, where I was given a pink landed immigrant certificate after filling in a form. On the form, I had to state what my assets were and what I would be bringing into the country. I opened my wallet and counted my cash. All I had to my name was the princely sum of US $90. Outside the immigration post, I saw the Canadian flag fluttering against a deep-blue summer sky. I was overcome by emotion and clutched the flagpole and held it tightly for a few seconds. That flag symbolized a new life for me. It was the first time in my life that I could call a country my home.

The Toronto that I returned to in July 1976 was another world. For Ismailis, mid-July is a time of festivities to celebrate the accession of His Highness the Aga Khan to the office of Imam on 11 July 1957. I had an additional reason to be happy, because of my job at Elgie, Walsh and Dhanani. My first client would be the firm's receptionist, Ruby, who was divorcing her husband. The divorce papers had been filed and the hearing was scheduled for the following week. When I met Ruby, she looked at me with the same warmth as I had looked at the Canadian flag in Philipsburg and exclaimed, "I have been waiting for your arrival. John says that you will be handling my divorce case. I desperately need your help. I need to get on with my life." I reassured her and told her that I was looking forward to acting on her behalf.

I was young, eager, and ready to work hard, and Ruby's divorce was an opportunity to make an impact in my new job. The fact that she was working in the practice made my work easier because she knew exactly what was needed and did all the paperwork. I represented her in the Supreme Court of Ontario on the appointed day and she received her divorce. John had a slew of divorce applications pending and had decided that I should handle them. I became adept at family law.

Even though he was not always in the office, John took on a great deal of civil litigation work as well as big personal injury cases. Often, I did the interim motions, either for an adjournment or for filing extra papers. In due course I became interested in immigration law, which was a growing area of legal process and litigation.

I still had to complete my articles for one year as well as the Bar admission course and exams, so I was not yet a full-fledged lawyer. Ironically, my birth in South Africa had become an asset, since the Ontario Law Society Act stipulated that only Canadian citizens and British subjects could be admitted to the Bar in the province, and South Africans were still considered to be British subjects

As 1976 jogged on, I became increasingly involved in Toronto life. I moved in with my parents and four unmarried siblings, who had migrated to Canada in 1973 when I was still with Silkins, and lived in a charming apartment in Willowdale. They were generous, patient, and kind. In my leisure time, I nurtured my love of music, especially classical compositions, by attending, together with a close friend, Sabzaly Nazaraly, the many concerts that the city hosted through the year. Toronto also afforded the opportunity to savour operas and ballet. Occasionally, the Bolshoi Ballet would visit the city. Alexander Gudonov gave his last performance in Toronto at the O'Keefe Centre before defecting to the West. The city, with its art galleries, lively newspapers, restaurants, and general multiethnic ambience, was marvellously cosmopolitan.

I bought a pinstriped suit with a waistcoat, as well as a pocket watch on a chain, so that I could look the part of a lawyer, and then decided to purchase a small car. That required a bank loan and brought me face to face with a problem that I had never faced before: I found that people who had not borrowed money in Canada, and therefore did not have a credit history, were not trusted by the banks. No financial institution wanted to risk lending me a paltry $1000 to buy a second-hand Volkswagen Beetle even though I had a good job with a decent salary. I found myself in a frustrating catch-22 situation as my applications to the banks, along with a proud proclamation that I was totally debt-free and therefore in a position to repay the loan were rejected *because* I was debt free!

I spoke about my problem to my friend Diamond Gulamhussain, who had been employed by a leading Canadian bank on the basis of a recommendation I had written for him on my Kenyan legal firm letterhead some four years earlier. Diamond did some discreet checking and then advised me to apply to a particular bank for a larger sum of money than I needed and to tell them that I intended to buy a brand new Volvo car. I did as he advised, and the loan materialized.

For some reason, Elgie, Walsh attracted more than its fair share of foreigners, particularly of Portuguese origin. Even though John did not speak a word of Portuguese, he became the *advogado* of our Portuguese clients. He had a good sense of humour but occasionally had to repress it. In one case, a partnership between two Portuguese businessmen ended in an exchange of blows, leading to one charging the other with assault, who then asked us to defend him in court. John called a Polish immigrant to testify on our client's behalf. On the stand, the witness told the court that he knew enough English and did not need a translator, but within the first few minutes of his testimony it was evident that he did not have a vocabulary exceeding thirty words. He launched into a charade, showing how one person had hit the other. "Boom! Boom!" he shouted in a heavy baritone, punching himself on the chin and the chest. He then collapsed to the floor and began to roll on the ground. I went into a fit of hysteria and had to leave the courtroom. John, however, managed to keep a straight face and told the court gravely, "I wish he had listened to me. I knew his English was not good."

As part of my civic work, I provided my services on a pro bono basis to Ismaili community institutions. I also gave honorary legal advice to the Foundation for International Training, which carried out development work in the Third World, and helped Canadian University Service Overseas to interview volunteers who were being sent to do development work in Africa, Asia and Latin America. It was during one such session that my sister Mila introduced me to Terry Burrows, a tall, well-built young Canadian doctor specializing in stress therapy, who was involved with the United Nations Association (UNA) of Ontario which was then headed by Dr Paul Weinzweig. Terry, Paul and I decided to ramp up our efforts to help people in the Third World. Each of us represented one of the three Abrahamic faiths, which helped to create a remarkable synergy between us.

Other kindred souls working with the UNA joined us in due course. One couple, Clare and John Ward, sold UNICEF cards to help the underprivileged. Others, among them Helen Tucker, attended every international conference in the world to support the work of the UNA. Dr Norman Alcock, a member of the Canadian Peace Research Institute, was also involved. They all wanted to contribute something to Canada's international vision. Together with many other volunteers, we brought the work of the United Nations to the attention of the public. Occasionally, we used space at the City Hall for different ethnic groups to celebrate their cultures with dancing, artistic performances, and cuisine. The major theme that ran through all those events was the idea of pluralism and hospitality—the participants had found a new home in Canada and they wanted to share their world with their fellow citizens.

Our greatest contribution, I feel, was through the generation of TV programmes. Rogers Cable TV of Ontario generously made their studios available to us to make films about the UN's work. The Canadian International Development Agency gave us a small grant, and with careful management Paul used it to keep the United Nations Association office in Toronto open. He allocated the task of TV production to Terry, myself and a small group of board members. I recall working on a script on UNESCO's activities and doing some research on its origins. The film started with this quotation from Archibald MacLeish: "Since wars begin in the minds of men, it is in the minds of men that the defences of peace need to be established." Wise words, and like most wise words, easy to admire but difficult to put into practice.

Occasionally, an important UN official would pass through Toronto and Paul would make sure he gave us an interview for our TV programme. The highlight of my work with the UNA was a visit by my friend Alex Quaison Sackey, who had been appointed Ghana's ambassador to Washington. Speaking on the "New International Economic Order," he gave a brilliant lecture on the North-South dialogue. Alex and Dr Norman Alcock also shared the podium at a colloquium on North-South relations at a college in Toronto, with Sackey pointing out the dangers of the widening gap between the countries of the North and the South.

In 1977, just before my Bar admission course, Amina Jindani and I decided to get married. Amina's family were from Zanzibar and she had qualified as a medical doctor in England, where she had been sent to school at the age of fourteen. She was already gaining a reputation as a specialist in epidemiological research on tuberculosis in Africa and was working with two world-renowned figures in the field, Dr Denny Mitchison and Dr Wallace Fox, under the aegis of the British Medical Research Council. Amina was exceptional not only in her profession, but also in her background; having been sent to a Church of England private school at a young age, she was equally at home in the Muslim and Western worlds. Always a diligent student, she had bagged the prize for both Divinity and Latin at her school, which must have been a first for an Asian Muslim girl at that time.

Amina's work in Africa had opened her eyes to many issues, most prominent of which was the need for greater social justice for the poor and oppressed majority in underdeveloped countries. She had seen poverty and illness on the ground and it had fuelled her sense of purpose as a doctor. Working among the impoverished in slums and villages, she had collaborated in research which developed new combinations of medical drugs that reduced the time taken to control or cure tuberculosis from eighteen months to six months. That was an important breakthrough and was published in *The Lancet*. In 2013 she demonstrated in a clinical trial that there was potential for reducing the curative time even further, to four months, through once-weekly treatment with a combination of two drugs. She was invited to speak on that finding at the March 2013 Conference on Retroviruses and Opportunistic Infections, which is a very prestigious conference in that field.

Both of us have been, and continue to be, exercised by the plight of minorities in many countries, both in the underdeveloped world and in Western societies. The migratory trajectory of our respective family histories, which saw members of our families move from India to Africa and then on to the West, in conjunction with millions of other Asians and now also indigenous people from the continent of Africa, has clearly affected us. When she lived in Kenya, Amina was often disturbed by the level of apathy she witnessed among the well-heeled classes in the Nairobi social circuit. They appeared to ignore the precariousness of their political future. We found common cause in this sense of frustration at the mindlessness of the well-off and the poverty of the majority who were left to suffer in their townships and villages. We went our different ways after our first meeting in Nairobi in 1972, but destiny brought us together again later. In the summer of 1977, we were married in Toronto in one of the most understated wedding ceremonies in history. We both wore denims, and our entire wedding cost a mere $25.

The reason for our modest wedding was that we were saving up for a trip to India. Amina had met a Canadian, Dr William Storrar, while he was doing some work in Nairobi for the Aga Khan Health Services and, during their discussions, had been inspired to offer her services to the Aga Khan Foundation as a volunteer to review the tuberculosis situation among the poor in Bombay. She was going to pay all her expenses herself and I was going to accompany her. We both still believe that it was money well spent. Not only did I get to see India and its problems at first hand, but I also got to know Gujarat and travelled to my ancestral home. The visit helped me to understand who I was and where my ancestors had come from. The trip changed me. I became more aware of the world at large and began to feel the urge to work internationally, beyond the confines of a legal office in downtown Toronto.

My work was exciting, but I constantly pondered the sheer waste of time and energy spent in an adversarial legal system. It was a ravenous and sometimes debilitating system for all the parties involved. On one occasion, a mechanic's lien for only $325 was placed on a building and led to protracted litigation involving three legal firms at a cost of over $25,000. The lawyers kept on claiming that their course of action was "a matter of principle." Of course there were also times when the civil procedure rules could be used constructively to reach an optimum outcome.

In the autumn of 1977, a few months after my marriage, I took the gruelling Bar admission examinations and passed them. I was called to the Ontario Bar by Chief Justice Holland of the Ontario Supreme Court at the O'Keefe Centre. It was the third Bar I had joined. John was delighted that I had become a full-fledged barrister and solicitor of the Supreme Court of Ontario and began to give me more important cases to handle.

Meanwhile, Amina had joined the National Cancer Institute of Canada and was also an assistant professor of medicine at the University of Toronto. Her work was blossoming and she enjoyed it. However, she, too, had doubts about the direction her life was taking in Toronto. She needed a greater sense of purpose than being a successful medical practitioner in a rich country; she wanted to be of help to people in the poorer areas of the world. To build on her qualifications and experience, she decided to embark on her MD through London University. She used all the knowledge she had accumulated in East Africa while doing research for her MD thesis under the supervision of Dr Denny Mitchison. Meanwhile, she continued to work in cancer research with the National Cancer Institute of Canada based in Toronto.

In the spring of 1979, John asked me to join Elgie and Walsh as a partner. Around the same time, I was asked by the secretariat of His Highness the Aga Khan whether I would consider working at his office in Paris, in the recently established Information Department. I flew to France, where I was told about the vision of the Aga Khan and the tremendous work being done in the developing world, and especially in the field of Islamic cultural renaissance, through the new institutions he was setting up. Amina and I decided to move to Europe by the end of 1979 and I gave my notice to John, assuring him that I would spend the rest of the year finishing the pending work. John was sorry to lose me, but he understood the importance of the work being done by the Aga Khan internationally and wished me well in my new life.

Towards the beginning of December 1979, on a cold wintry morning in Toronto, a woman entered our office with a little blonde girl and asked for Peter Derry, an associate in our firm. The secretary told her that he was not in. "Can anyone else help me?" she asked desperately. "I have a custody motion today. My husband is threatening to abduct my daughter and take her away to the Maritime Provinces and I may never see her again. Please, can someone help me?" The secretary referred her to me. The woman had a legal aid certificate with Peter Derry's name on it as her lawyer and I told her we could ask the judge if he would accept another lawyer to represent her. Taking the wind-chill factor into account, the temperature was minus 40 degrees Celsius as the three of us walked to the court, where the judge allowed me to represent her. After hearing the motion, he gave her interim legal custody of the girl.

About three weeks later, as I was closing all my files, I received an envelope with my name and address scrawled on it in childish handwriting. I opened it and drew out a card with a small passport-sized photo of that blonde girl in the top right-hand corner. On the card I read: "Thank you Mr Keshavjee. Mummy tells me that I am with her because of your help." It was a moving end to my work in Toronto and I cherish it to this day. That was what I had studied law for and I remain grateful for the fact that in all of the countries where I have worked, I have had the opportunity to contribute towards improving someone's lot in life, even though it may have been only a small contribution.

After New Year's Day, I flew to New York for training at a public relations company and spent the next fortnight in an intensive programme that included visits to the UN Security Council, the *New York Times*, Reuters, and other news organizations. Nick King, press officer to George Boland, the US ambassador to the UN, as well as press officer to George Bush senior, taught me to write press releases.

A totally new chapter was beginning in my life. For the next quarter-century, the world would become my habitat and the aeroplane my office, as I became part of the team that manages the work spearheaded by the Aga Khan through the Aga Khan Development Network.

This memoir focuses largely on my family and my life in Africa and our move to the Western world. It does not intend to address the vast range of work to which I had the good fortune of being exposed to as part of a team that was involved in the work of the Ismaili Imamat and the AKDN.

In 2010, after spending some thirty years at the Aga Khan's Secreatariat, I decided to retire from my full-time employment and Amina and I went to live in the United Kingdom. I came to see then how much I had grown, and how much I had learned from this experience and from my relationship with the community that constitutes a frontierless international brotherhood of which I was but a tiny speck. It is largely to them and to what I learnt from His Highness that I attribute the richness of the many years I spent on this work. I feel that it has made me a much better person than I would have been had I continued to practice law in an adversarial arena.

Chapter 21

Whither the Rainbow Nation?

TIMES OF OUR TRANSFORMATION ARE ETCHED INTO OUR MEMories. For example, I can remember where I was when my parents died and I can just about recall the feeling of numbness, the immediate reaction of the mind closing off from such terrible events. Then there are public events, such as the first time that a man walked on the moon. Or when President Kennedy was assassinated in Dallas. One such defining day for me, and I believe for many millions of people across the world, was Tuesday, 11 February 1990. My wife Amina and I were at the home of friends in Gouvieux near Chantilly, in France, having been invited to watch the live coverage of the release of the world's longest-serving prisoner of conscience, Nelson Rolihlahla Mandela, on their large TV screen. We all wanted to share our joy over an event that marked an important juncture in the history of South Africa, as well as in the wider story of racial oppression that still demeans societies across the world.

With South Africa isolated internationally and a rising wave of resistance to apartheid across much of the world, it had become clear that there had to be a transition to a multiparty, nonracist democracy, and that Mandela, the indefatigable fighter for independence and human dignity, was the only person who could bring it about. The White South African government had issued a statement that Mandela would be released on 7 December 1988, after having spent 10,000 days in gaol. However, that did not happen until some time later.

Suddenly, the gates of Victor Verster Prison near Paarl, to which Mandela had been moved were flung open and an elderly man, his tall figure stooped a little, walked out with authoritative and confident steps. Mandela was no longer the young, feisty boxer with full beard and chubby face of the 1950s; what the world saw was a man in his seventies, whose face was marked by age, suffering, and deprivation. Yet he was not a broken man. I wept copiously as that remarkable man waved and walked towards the media cameras. I had expected him to look angry, but he looked calm. He was flanked by his wife (whom he later divorced) Winnie Madikizela and other family members, and he smiled gracefully as he walked towards a waiting car. Time and the travails of prison seemed to have seasoned him, transforming him into a wise statesman.

There was no doubt that when the elections took place to usher in an era of democracy, they would be won by the ANC, and a gargantuan task lay ahead for its leaders. How on earth would they restructure a society defined by a White racist culture, which had oppressed its native Black population with brutal arrogance for the past 350 years? How would they manage the expectations of both Black and White South Africans? How would they deal with an intransigent Afrikaner minority, whose sullen anger lay just below the surface of their consciousness of the changes that were occurring? In short, how would each side extricate the other, as Alan Paton put it, "from the fear of bondage and the bondage of fear"? Many of the principal players were already elderly, looking time-wearied. Could they muster the necessary determination and courage?

The apartheid government had been supported by most Western countries. As I watched Mandela stride out of prison, carrying with him the hopes of millions, I thought, Would those countries allow the ANC to construct an economy in which the chief priority was improvement of the lives of the majority of the population?

♦

In 1992, I went back to South Africa, which I had left in 1962 but still regarded as home. As the plane circled over Johannesburg, I was listening to the grandeur of Beethoven's 7th Symphony on the classical music channel, and it acted as a counterpoint to the stark Africa below. I looked out of the window and saw enormous mine dumps and huge shanty towns surrounding the city. They were a sharp contrast to the turquoise and ultramarine swimming pools of the White suburbs. From the air, the city was a microcosm of how South Africa was still patterned like a patchwork quilt of areas where race coincided with class and the lighter your skin, the more affluent you were.

From the outside, Jan Smuts Airport looked more or less the same as I remembered it from the 1960s. On the shuttle bus from the plane to the terminal building, I became aware of the informality among the passengers as they chatted animatedly, their English spiced with Afrikaner words pronounced with a typical rustic accent, their conversations tinged with a tone of humour. In the immigration hall, in contrast to the past, there were a few non-Whites manning the counters and there were no signs guiding Whites and non-Whites to separate counters. People walked about with a sense of tentative confidence. For me, this was a new South Africa.

Karim Rawjee, a cousin who was a partner and CEO of Hoxies, one of South Africa's largest seafood companies, was waiting for me and drove me to Killarney, a suburb of Johannesburg that was part of fashionable South Africa, where Bahadur and Malek Premji, newly settled Ismailis from Kinshasa in the Democratic Republic of the Congo, lived in a penthouse apartment. They had prepared a sumptuous lunch in my honour. The apartment was spacious, beautifully done up, with its own roof garden, and for a moment I wondered whether I was in South Africa. The only link that I could find to the past was Rosie, their Bantu domestic servant, who was treated like a member of the family. Rosie lived in the apartment.

I spoke to the Premjis about their being the second wave of Ismaili immigrants into South Africa, a hundred years after Jivanbapoo's arrival, and regaled them with stories of the early settlement. After lunch, I was able to have a discussion with Rosie in the kitchen. I mentioned African leaders of the past and she was astounded that I knew of Dr Xuma and Dr Tsele. We also talked about the 1957 bus boycott. When she spoke of the past, it was not with bitterness, but with a sense of calm reminiscence and hope. For both of us, this was a new South Africa. It was one that I had not experienced and one to which she was just beginning to be exposed.

In the afternoon, my hosts and I went to the Asiatic Bazaar of Marabastad in Pretoria, which I found now had a busy informal sector, with African stall-keepers selling their goods on the pavement in front of shops originally built, and still owned, by Indian retailers. The Royal Bioscope had been razed to the ground. The Coloured location was one big empty space. Boom Street was the only road that was almost like I remembered it. Rah's, my favourite restaurant, was still there. However, there was one major change in the area: a terminal had been set up for privately owned public transport and it was buzzing with activity as packed minibuses arrived, disgorged their passengers, crammed in a new load of people, and departed. There were a few rundown buildings in the Bazaar and others had been demolished, leaving only the scars of their foundations in the ground. They were a keen reminder of what apartheid had tried to do to the spirits of non-Whites.

We drove down Boom Street, where EB Sabis was running the same barber shop, with the same single green-backed chair inside. It was a historical relic. He was still an enthusiastic photographer. The Empire Bioscope had been converted into a retail shopping mall.

To the north of Barber Street, the formerly empty veldt stretching out to Magaliesburg Mountain was covered with buildings that housed the big wholesalers from Prinsloo Street—HS Ebrahim, MH Joosub and others. The main Indian residential area and commercial establishments were in Laudium. Some Indian shops were also to be found in Pretoria town or in the northern part of Marabastad. The architecture in Laudium was eclectic, the houses, of varying size and opulence, were built close to each other, but the neighbourhood was wealthy. There was a first-rate school, largely financed by the generous and philanthropic Dockrat family, and a graceful mosque and other places of worship. It is said that Laudium contained the highest concentration of Mercedes Benzes in the world, but few were visible to me. However, I did see many BMWs. Perhaps, fashion had a role to play in the type of car to be found in the district at various times!

On the site of my previous school, the Pretoria Indian Boys' School, I was shocked to find a petrol station and a major highway running past it (which is now called the Es'kia Mphahlele highway after the famous writer). Despite my early dislike for the school, I felt a sense of loss.

We then went to the site of the former M Keshavjee family house, which we had called simply "274," and which we located by virtue of the jacaranda tree that had been planted in front of it in 1940 by my uncle

Goolambapoo. The whole area was a derelict parking space for informal-sector taxis. We dared not get out of the car for fear of being mugged.

I wanted to find out what South Africans, particularly those of Indian origin, thought about the new political order. To my surprise, the Indians appeared to be less aware of the dynamics of change, unlike those in East Africa.

There were, of course, some exceptions, typified by Sattar Motani, who had worked with the ANC, who told me, "It had to come. The Africans have suffered for far too long." Ahmedji Dockrat, another contributor to the freedom struggle, had the most sympathetic and fair-minded understanding of the situation. He recalled Walter Sisulu, whom he had known since his university days, telling him, "You know, Ahmedji, we told our people that we are together with the Indians. We suffered together, our struggle was together. But they fail to understand. They say, 'It can't be. Look at them, they have BMWs, they are doctors and lawyers, etc. What are we? We are still deprived and left to rot in the townships.'" Both Ahmedji and Sattar said that the Indian community needed to be more proactive in politics and be seen to be contributing to the social betterment of the indigenous Africans.

Whilst I was in South Africa, I met my dear friend and benefactor, the writer Ezekiel Mphahlele, now known as Es'kia Mphahlele. He lived in one of the suburbs of Johannesburg, having returned to South Africa under an amnesty to lecture at the University of Witwatersrand. He was conscious of the urgent need for social transformation, quoting the freedom fighter Hilda Bernstein's observation that Africans were being told, "[Now that you are free,] you should be able to swim the Atlantic." How could the government work miracles with their hands tied behind their backs? The formal end of apartheid had not brought about the enormous changes expected by most Africans in their lives. They remained poor and therefore oppressed. A massive restructuring of the economy was necessary.

I wanted to meet Joseph, our former domestic employee, and ask him what he thought about the new South Africa. He was employed by the Reserve Bank of South Africa on Prinsloo Street and I telephoned him to arrange a meeting. Later, I met him on the street outside his place of employment, we clasped each other with spontaneous warmth, feeling a deep mutual connection. Three decades had passed, but he was still the same kind soul I had known as a young boy. Joseph was not keen to discuss politics and he sidestepped my questions. The passersby probably wondered what the two of us—an urbane-looking Asian and an African dressed in overalls—were up to as we talked in hushed tones. At the end of our discussion, Joseph looked at me earnestly and said, "God is kind. God has looked after us so well. We have to thank the Lord." I hugged him and wished him well.

I travelled to Cape Town for the first time in my life. The famous Table Mountain was a wonderful sight for me, not only for its beauty but also for its historical resonances. I also visited Port Elizabeth for the first time. When I returned to Pretoria, Shayin Rawjee, a niece, took me to visit her son Sameer's school, the Loreto Convent, where I saw a young African boy and a blonde little girl on a slide in the playground, the boy with his arms around the girl's waist as they glided down. They laughed with innocent joy as they jumped off the slide and ran back hand-in-hand, for another go. It was a moving sight. I spoke to the teacher, a White former Southern Rhodesian, who told me, "This is the only hope for the future in South Africa. I know what price we have paid in Southern Rhodesia." It was then that I felt that a change was really occurring in the country. The process of truly burying the past would take time, but there was hope.

Whilst I was in Pretoria, I had the opportunity of meeting Ismail Ayob, my dear friend from Gray's Inn days, who was a lawyer to the Mandela family. I went to his office high up in one of the many steel-and-glass skyscrapers in Johannesburg's commercial centre, rising towards the sky, symbolizing the metropolitan wealth of the modern world. Looking out from his office, I could have been in New York or Hong Kong or any other large modern metropolis.

Whilst Ismail and I were talking, I noticed a framed portrait of Mandela on the wall. It appeared to be a watercolour. He told me that an American magazine had wanted a picture of Mandela while he had been in prison and a portrait had been painted on the basis of a palaeontologist's impression. It had been sent to Ismail for verification. After publishing the article, the magazine had sent him the picture as a mark of appreciation. I suggested that he get Mandela to autograph it, since it would have a historic value one day.

In December 2002, my wife Amina and I spent the Christmas holidays in Durban. At a personal level, the visit had a certain poignancy since my grandfather Manjee Keshavjee had landed at Durban as a migrant in 1901. He had worked in a restaurant, washing dishes to earn a little money before moving inland to the Transvaal. I wanted to visit the city to see the docks and where the Indians had lived and worked.

At our hotel, I noticed that the doorman and waitresses were Indian, which suggested that Indians were placed on the same level as Africans when it came to menial jobs in Durban. After depositing our bags in our room and freshening up, Amina and I started exploring the city.

Whites still dominated Durban economically and culturally even though Zulus and other Blacks comprised the majority of the population. The main architectural style was (and still is) Victorian. Indians still held managerial positions in business and some professions, such as teaching and medicine, and some buildings were similar to those in Bombay. On the pavements, we came across a multitude of street stalls, mainly owned by Africans.

South Africans of all races seem to suffer from a collective amnesia with regard to the country's recent past. For the élite, history seems to have been sacrificed on the altar of rampant globalization, and collective memories are being dumped in the furious drive to become rich and consume the products of capitalism. Of course, South Africa is not alone in suffering from this phenomenon. One sees it in Nigeria, Russia, Brazil, and India – the rich get richer and the poor have yet to present a robust challenge to the powers that continue to oppress them.

How many Indian or African youths of today know—or even care—that Monty Naicker was an Indian political leader in Natal? Mandela was once amazed when he met a young Indian boy named Naicker to discover that he had never even heard of his namesake, the anti-apartheid fighter. How many African teenagers are familiar with the role played in the freedom struggle by Anton Lembede or even Chief Luthuli? I am not even sure how many White youths would be aware of the positive as well as negative roles played in South African history by General Smuts and Dr Verwoerd. Perhaps if Mandela had not become a political prisoner of international repute, and had not presided over the democratic transformation of South Africa, his contribution to the struggle against apartheid, too, might not have survived for long in the historical fog that surrounds the rank and file of South Africa's youth.

The little that I saw of White youths is also revealing. Generally, they are polite towards the other races, perhaps even over-polite. I got the distinct feeling that young Whites want to make up for twenty-one generations of injustice, that there is a feeling of hopeful goodwill among them. Some of the Whites who used to enjoy a privileged life purely on the basis of their skin rather than ability have been reduced today to the pathetic status of "poor Whites." I was amazed and, I must admit slightly saddened, to see many of them sitting on the pavements of Durban, begging for money. They are lost people in a land that they have lost.

During discussions with friends and acquaintances in Natal, I found that working-class Indians see themselves as part of the larger Black majority. They, too, have suffered from the ravages of apartheid and are still struggling to earn a decent living. They work cheek by jowl with the Africans. Many live in very poor and deprived areas where vigilantes and gangsters, some of their own race, operate. Even indigenous Africans from tough neighbourhoods are afraid to enter some of these areas. Being excluded from affirmative action on the basis that they are not "Black" makes no real sense to the Asian workers. But, they are not cowed. To quote a young Indian man, they will "donder [hit] anyone that fools around with them." Inevitably, they will challenge the government over the lack of jobs and social services.

Then there are those Indians who selflessly joined hands with the Africans and gave of their time, skills, resources, and in many cases lives to the struggle for freedom. They contradict the stereotype that claims that "Indians always sit on the fence and never want to contribute." Can such an accusation be levelled against people such as Ismail Meer, who spent thirty-eight years of his life under detention orders because of his political activities and yet contributed handsomely to the struggle? Or Ahmed Kathrada, who spent twenty-six years in the Robben Island prison?

Many such people have done an initial stint in the government and are now engaged in various civic activities. Initially there was an element of euphoria, idealism, and recognition of their contribution to the struggle, but it is now beginning to be forgotten. Mandela never failed to recognize their contribution, but even the details of his own struggles are beginning to dim among many young people.

There is another group of Indians who were part of the struggle but have adapted successfully to the new South Africa. They do not seem bitter, but are "realistic," which in itself is an ambiguous moral position. Whilst recognizing the need to change gears and help the Black population, they lament that not many Indians today share their "realism."

Finally, there is a group of Indian yuppies who love the new South Africa. They have been to university, live in suburbia, drive BMWs, and are members of élite golf and tennis clubs. They enjoy their new-found wealth, spending it on expensive consumer goods and jaunts to the beautiful hotels and wildlife parks and lodges of South Africa, and to chic destinations abroad. For them, South Africa is heaven on earth. Point out to them that South Africa has one of the highest crime rates in the world, and they respond that there is crime even in New York. Things will get better over time, they assure you.

The majority of Indians in South Africa have decided to stay in the country, unlike some of their White fellow citizens, who left for countries where they felt better accepted. The Indians do not exhibit the anxieties of a minority population that fears the fall of the axe, as in East Africa in the 1970s. Given this, some form of accommodation will have to be worked out if real interracial harmony is to be achieved.

Could Indians be expelled from South Africa as they were in Uganda? The answer, I feel, is Yes, notwithstanding the Indians' own estimation of their indispensability. In Uganda, too, the Indians were critical to the economy. Enterprises such as those of the Madhwanis at one time produced about seventy consumer goods that were used by the average Ugandan, from margarine and sugar to cardboard boxes and glass. Yet, the economic importance of the Indians did not protect them.

What can Indians do to avoid an escalation of racial acrimony in South Africa? To start off with, they need to ensure that South Africa becomes, and remains, a true democracy with all the sacrifices of privilege that that entails. A truly democratic South Africa would be the best guarantee against the erosion of their human rights. For this, they need to vote, with ethical purpose, for a government that is truly committed to national wealth and improvement. Good governance would also be a strong hedge against erosion of the rule of law.

In addition, Indians should work to develop a strong and more broad-based African middle class by helping the indigenous population to prosper in the distributive trade whilst they themselves diversify into other areas of the economy. They would thus not be regarded as the immediate ceiling and strangle point for rising African entrepreneurs.

The Indians in South Africa also need to be more proactive in making known both their historic and contemporary contributions to the freedom struggle. Few South Africans know that the Passive Resistance Campaign of 1946 and the Defiance Campaign of 1951-52 were entirely financed by the Indians. How many are aware of India's championing of the South African Indian cause at the UN? Or of the Indian government's contribution to the ANC's election victory and its financing of Shell House in Johannesburg, which was the headquarters of the ANC? Such reminders will help to forestall possible use of negative racial stereotypes for cheap political gain. At the wider level, they will also help to show that Indians in the diaspora are not merely stepchildren of a bygone colonial empire, but a significant and productive minority in a pluralistic world.

Finally, Indians should continue to take part in politics. They have contributed to the raising of political consciousness in many African countries and have played an important role in the evolution of some modern African nation states. They should embrace the new South Africa, which is their home, and help the indigenous Africans to reap the fruits of majority democracy, the tree of which was planted and nourished jointly by all the races.

There is discontentment among the Whites too. Some three million Afrikaners feel that they have suffered in silence for too long. They are fed up with being collectively demonized as nasty racists with a shameful history and resent being told that Whites who "whinge about crime" are free to leave the country. After all, it is their country as well, where their ancestors have lived and toiled for a few hundred years. The Constitution offers no special deal for political minorities and many Afrikaners now feel betrayed. Many fear that they are losing their language. Afrikaans, once one of the two official languages (along with English) is now just one of eleven languages that supposedly enjoy equal constitutional protection.

Even some Whites who supported the anti-apartheid struggle have become disillusioned with postindependence South Africa. This was dramatically brought to international attention on 29 November 1998 when the London *Sunday Times* published a heart-rending explanation by Anne Paton, widow of acclaimed South African writer and anti-apartheid activist Alan Paton, for why she had decided to leave South Africa after living there for thirty-five years. She described a series of brazen robberies and attempted robberies, even while she was in her house. This had happened to some of her friends as well. An elderly woman had been raped and killed. Another had been shot dead.

"I love this country with a passion, but I cannot live here anymore," Mrs Paton wrote. She quoted a Black character from her husband's novel, *Cry, the Beloved Country*, which was written during the heyday of apartheid: "I have one great fear in my heart, that one day when they are turned to loving they will find we are turned to hating." She ended her letter with the fear that by the time Blacks "turn to loving," they might find that Whites "are turned to hating."

Of course, crime has been halved in South Africa since 1998, but the country still has one of the highest rates of crime in the world, particularly of rape and murder, and the victims are of all races.

Nelson Mandela, whom I consider to have been one of the greatest apostles of freedom that the twentieth century has produced, whose role was pivotal in the dismantling of apartheid, died in the early hours of 5 December 2013 at the age of 95. I was in London, where I had made my home after thirty-one years in France, and once again I was sitting in front of a television, watching as tributes poured in from across the world. As I watched the coverage, I said to myself, "This is exactly what he would have wanted to see, a rainbow shining outside his home—young, old, rich, poor, Black, White, Jewish, Christian, Muslim, and Hindu holding hands and singing the ANC anthem." His greatest legacy was that he united a nation across the colour divide. As the last apartheid president, FW de Klerk, put it, ". . . he was a unifier, and that he successfully broke the bridge between the conflict of the past and the peace of today."

Mandela's struggle was characterized by two major principles: reconciliation and forgiveness, two of the vital assets required today if we want genuine peace in our conflict-ridden world. For Mandela, forgiveness was not merely political expediency. He believed in it, lived it, and practised it. As he wrote in his autobiography, *Long Walk to Freedom*, "As I walked out of the door toward the gate that would lead to my freedom, I knew if I didn't leave my bitterness behind, I'd still be in prison." Yet, at the same time, he also realized that "to be free is not merely to cast off one's chains, but to live in a way that respects and enhances the freedom of others."

Mandela stood out in a world where many leaders seem to have abandoned ethical values and principles, a world where the moral ozone layer that protects society is fast depleting. He was a true democrat, not a power-hungry leader out to enrich himself. One of his lasting contributions to the culture of democracy in South Africa was his stepping down after only one term in office, an almost unique occurrence in postcolonial Africa.

It is difficult to understand how a person who had been incarcerated for twenty-seven years, most of them spent in a cell three feet wide by ten feet long, and who had been subjected to so much humiliation, could emerge from prison and forgive those who had hurt him. What was the nature of the transformation that must have taken place in him, which had given him such moral strength and vision? There could be no doubt that he was a great soul. It is no wonder that so many books and thousands of articles have been written about him.

Mandela was no saint, and he never pretended to be one. He admitted to his failings and was probably not surprised by the criticisms levelled at him. There are critics who feel that he did not bargain hard enough with the apartheid regime, many Africans in the country are still languishing in poverty because during the negotiations for full democracy he accepted conditions that severely restricted the new government's ability to secure their economic well-being. Others accuse him of having done nothing for the millions of people who contracted HIV/AIDS, or of having done too little, too late. Some say that he relinquished power too soon at a time when the country still needed him at the helm. There is criticism in the area of foreign affairs as well, particularly over his failure to speak out publicly against the excesses in Zimbabwe. Mandela, like any other human being, had many blemishes, but he did not let them become obstacles. "Do not judge me by my successes," he is reported as saying. "Judge me by how many times I fell down and got back up again."

When we judge him on this basis, we see that Mandela was a courageous man who confronted some of the greatest odds any modern leader has had to face, yet he did not give up but instead surmounted them. Of course he could not win all his battles. Some of the forces he faced were too strong; in other situations, he had the moral stature but not the enforcing capability, or was not in a position to say anything by virtue of his position. For him, courage was not the absence of fear, but the triumph over it. That was what inspired hope in people who got to know him or heard of him. Even his erstwhile foes, who branded him a terrorist, came to realize that he fought relentlessly to uphold his democratic and humanitarian principles. And he lived by them.

Mandela played an important role in making sports in South Africa what they are meant to be – a bridge between cultures and peoples. His encouragement to the Springboks in 1995 and his donning the captain's shirt in a packed stadium were dramatic acts of a conciliatory populist in a country where rugby had been associated for years with White and Afrikaner hegemony. Then there was also Mandela the consummate negotiator, master of what today is called transformative mediation. Conflict creates a negative spiral in the so-called offender as well as the so-called victim. Like Gandhi and Martin Luther King Jr, Mandela was able to transform the negative spiral of conflictual hatred, demonization, and anger into a positive spiral of humanization, love, and recognition. In doing that, he was living the concept of *ubuntu*. According to Archbishop Desmond Tutu in *No Future Without Forgiveness*, ubuntu stands for the principle that I am me because of you. I humanize myself through humanizing you and degrade myself if I continue to demonize you through the negative feelings that conflict inevitably engenders in me.

In prison, Mandela learnt Afrikaans and set out to understand the White prison warders, discussing their problems, politics, and fears with them. He impressed them with his dignity and won their respect. After the ANC's election victory, he invited three of his former jailers to his inauguration ceremony, publicly referring to them as "guests." Once in office, he continued to show that extraordinary magnanimity by inviting the former prosecutor at the Rivonia Trial to lunch, visiting the widow of Hendrik Verwoerd, the high priest of apartheid, and appointing one of his former prison governors as the country's ambassador to Austria.

Ahmed Kathrada, Mandela's close friend and fellow prisoner, recalled in his memoirs that the Security Police and warders warned the freedom fighters at the Rivonia trial that they would be hanged unless "we gave them useful information about ourselves, our colleagues and about our organization and its activities." Mandela was adamant that they should not give in. He said the trial was a political one and they should not apologize for their activities or plead for mercy. If they were sentenced to death, they should not appeal.

At Robben Island, the prisoners were treated differently on the basis of their race. As an Indian, Kathrada was allowed to wear trousers and socks, while Mandela, although very much his senior in age, had to wear shorts and was denied socks. In the mornings, both Kathrada and Mandela were given porridge, soup and coffee, but Mandela's coffee had less sugar in it. For lunch, Kathrada was given rice with maize while Mandela had boiled maize on the cob. For supper, Kathrada got a quarter of a loaf of bread while Mandela was given porridge.

Kathrada considered the difference in treatment degrading and humiliating and wanted to refuse the limited "privileges" given to him, but Mandela dissuaded him from doing so, because, "politically it would be wrong for us to give up what we have got. Our struggle should be for equality on a higher level, instead of playing into the hands of our gaolers."

There is yet another aspect of Mandela that endeared him to the world—the human being with a human soul. He was a compassionate man who could reach out and touch the heart of the most humble human beings and bring them joy. Kathrada relates the story of a young Afrikaner girl in the Transvaal named Michelle Brits, who was dying of leukaemia after the change of government and had expressed a wish to visit Robben Island. Thanks to an NGO called Reach for a Dream, she was able to do so and a photograph was taken of her there with Kathrada. Then Kathrada was told that the visit to the notorious prison was but half of the child's dying wish; the other half was to meet President Mandela. Kathrada told Mandela about the girl and asked him if she could visit him, either at his home or his office. "His response was pure and vintage Mandela":

> The President of South Africa, a universally respected statesman with one of the busiest schedules on earth, flew to Mpumalanga town of Secunda by helicopter, bearing gifts for a sick child. It seemed the entire population of the town turned out to welcome him, and pray for Michelle's recovery. The emotional meeting between Madiba and Michelle was shown on national television, and as she clasped her little arms around his neck and kissed him, the eyes of millions must have filled with tears, just as mine did.
>
> Michelle was an Afrikaner child, born and raised in a right-wing environment, but her dying wish was to meet the first Black President of South Africa, and to see his prison. By her simple and spontaneous gesture of affection, she brought home, more powerfully than all the complex documents and carefully crafted speeches that are the lifeblood of the politicians, that our children are the future.

Mandela, to quote Walter Sisulu, his one-time mentor, believed in "ordinary respect" and this is what he fought for all his life. This was the antithesis of apartheid, which according to John Carlin exemplified "extraordinary contempt."

It is now up to Mandela's successors to continue his work. The South Africa of today is a much better country. No one is barred from voting in the elections or participating in society because of his race. There is freedom of movement for everyone. The economic inequalities among South Africans have been reduced to some extent and a minority elite have become rich. However, rigid racial inequality has been replaced by inequality based on class, with restricted opportunities to move upwards, and much still remains to be done. Like in many other countries there are concerns over issues of corruption and nepotism. Unemployment continues to be high and the government is taking steps to significantly improve the lives of the majority of the population. It is not an easy task. The challenges are enormous and by their very nature and complexity are likely to take time to resolve. No doubt, the majority of South Africans today are geared to the challenge and are working hard towards fostering a more pluralistic and nonracial society. But this will take time!

Chapter 22

India and the Diaspora Rediscovered

ENORMOUS CHANGES HAVE TAKEN PLACE ALL OVER THE world since I first decided to write this memoir. The US, Europe, and Japan are no longer the best-performing economies on our planet. China has become an economic colossus and leads the world in many fields. India, likewise, has become a major global player. More than a billion people worldwide are now communicating through digital social media, and this number is increasing every day, and globalization and electronic advances have made the world a much smaller place. To paraphrase Marshall McLuhan, we are living in a global village.

In my childhood, places such as Durban, Dar es Salaam and Nairobi were referred to as mini-Bombays; today this appellation—though with the current name of the city, Mumbai—can be applied to parts of many other cities. London, for example, has its own Indian areas where the English White population feels itself to be a minority. This new multiculturalism presents both challenges and opportunities.

Outside the Tooting Broadway underground station, situated in a South London area that is now heavily Asian, stands the statue of Edward VII, king of Britain during the first decade of the twentieth century. The statue of the king, dressed in regal robes and high riding boots and holding a sceptre, was once the public expression of imperial grandeur but is now ignored by the locals as they pass by. Little could the king have guessed, when Britain seemed to be at the apogee of its power although in fact it was beginning to decline, that this meagre section of his capital would become a busy London suburb teeming with Asians from East Africa, Central Africa, Sri Lanka, India, Pakistan, and the Caribbean, and also with people of other ethnicities from the West Indies, Africa,

Afghanistan, and—more recently—Eastern Europe.

In the main street, Asian shopkeepers sell saris, shoes, halal meat, jewellery, video cassettes, paan, and produce normally found in an Indian bazaar in Africa or Asia. The pavements overflow with boxes of fresh mangoes, okra, karela, and a variety of other fruits and vegetables which are normally impossible to obtain. During the Eid festival, the pavements are dotted with girls getting their hands henna-ed in the most intricate patterns. Up the road is the Anand paan shop, which is reputed to be frequented by Bollywood celebrities during their trips to London, as evidenced by a large number of photographs on the wall.

One does not get singled out by one particular identity anymore.

India, too, has been transformed considerably since Jivanbapoo and Haji Cassam left their ancestral homes in Kathiawar in the 1890s. It is no longer perceived as an impoverished backwater of the world and has won international stature on account of its growing economic power and intellectual achievements in the modern knowledge-based society. The image of overseas Indians is no longer defined solely by the picture of an emaciated Bihari child on an Oxfam poster, or by a heap of dead bodies of Indians piled up in a corner after an African coup, with the Indian and Pakistani ambassadors looking on helplessly.

I do not mean to paint a triumphalist and hubristic picture of the new India. There may be 60 million people whose lifestyle may surpass that of the citizens of the West, but they are a minority in the vast population of the country. The great majority of Indians are desperately poor. Indian society is permeated with inequality economically and socially and a lot needs to be done.

Nevertheless, for the first time in centuries, India has the opportunity to rise from its slumber and become a powerful international country with the promise of providing a decent life for the majority of its citizens. But it must modernize its infrastructure and the traditions that hold it back. It needs to create the sort of opportunities at home that its migrants enjoy abroad. Overseas Indians have given all Indians a standing, and one feels a sense of esteem when one sees eminent professionals, scientists, engineers, and artists are of Indian origin. One does not feel ashamed of being an Indian, and consequently one feels more predisposed to learn about

India and to embrace one's past with a degree of comfort and confidence.

My first visit to Argentina, to speak at the Fourth International Conference of the World Mediation Forum in May 2003, was a revelation in this context. Not far from my hotel in Buenos Aires, I entered a leather goods boutique in a fashionable shopping area and was greeted with effusive warmth by Eduardo, a migrant from—of all places—Tashkent, who owned the shop. What on earth was he doing in a place like Buenos Aires, I asked, and how had he got there? I realized as soon as I had put the query to him that it rang with unwitting irony. "My mother was from this part of the world," he replied, "but I was born in Central Asia." When I told him my name was Mohamed, he responded with *Alhamdulillah* (praise be to the Almighty). On learning of my Indian origins, he spontaneously started singing the signature song from the 1950s Indian film *Awaara*—which had had its world premiere in Moscow. I realized that here was another individual who, to quote the British actor Peter Ustinov, "was as 'ethnically filthy' as myself and perhaps as proud to be so, as I am."

A foray into the pedestrians-only streets brought me face to face with an older woman whose hair reminded me of Ginger Rogers. She beckoned to me to enter her leather goods shop. When I complied, she smiled and asked me where I was from. "Africa," I replied. "But you are not black," she said. "My people were from India," I explained. "India!" she exclaimed. "How wonderful! I love India! I love the Indian people! My favourite hero is Zubin Mehta. I attended his performance here in Buenos Aires. He autographed my programme. What a charming man. For me, he is the greatest conductor in the world today." "Yes," I said, "he belongs to the same genre of great musicians as your own Daniel Barenboim and Martha Argerich." It pleased her that I knew of them. They no longer lived in Argentina, but in some deep sense they still belonged to her country.

It was a unique and exhilarating experience to find my image as an Indian being associated with someone who was respected instead of being part of a somewhat despised and neglected minority. In Africa in the past, even some Indian migrants had returned from visits to India with disdain for their country of origin. "We would not be able to survive there. The place is dirty and people have to work like ants to survive. There is so much corruption. The struggle to survive is relentless and the Indians are too crafty for us," one was told. They came back shocked at the enormous gap between the tiny minority of rich people and the hundreds of millions of poor in the mother country. But India is changing and continues to change.

These days when I drive through Marine Drive in Mumbai, with its impressive mansions and smart commercial establishments, and see a well-off Indian confident of his identity—whether it is a clerk or office worker on a small motorcycle, with a pretty girlfriend riding pillion, or a more affluent businessman sitting in an expensive Mercedes Benz like a new rajah, with his elbow protruding through the window—I see a new India reaching out to take its rightful place in the community of nations. It strengthens my pride in being an Indian, albeit an Indian once-removed because of the migratory history of my family.

My experiences in South Africa, Kenya and Britain were not the sort to encourage confidence in who I am, and who I am is a complex amalgam of identities taking in all those countries but ultimately based on my Indian origins. The education system in which I was brought up, though largely humanistic, was profoundly Eurocentric in that it was based upon Western, and more particularly Anglo-Saxon, models and values. The Western world was *the* world, and the rest was barbarian territory, a bit like Tacitus' Germania. It was a place to civilize or shun. I only discovered Tagore's poetry in Canada, and Nehru's prose—particularly his inspiring independence speech—spurred me on to find out more about the fascinating Indian civilization.

Yes, my imagination was fed on Shakespeare, whose endlessly marvellous poetic insights and beauty of language deeply influenced me. The Bard is as much a part of my identity as the grand Lutyens buildings are an integral part of Delhi, a city made great by its multiple identities. I enormously enjoy the visionary poetry of Blake, which draws and fascinates me in the same way that Sufi poetry does. I have read Yeats, Jane Austen, Coleridge, and Keats and I feel I would be the poorer had I never been exposed to the richness of Western literature. But, I am also enriched as a person by reading the great works of literature from the East, poets like Tagore and Rumi, Iqbal and Ghalib, and Hafiz, whose verses any taxi driver in Tehran or child in the mountains of Tajikistan can recite by heart. I continue to be replenished by Eastern artists, writers, musicians and sages. They have helped me to understand and take pride in the Indian part of my identity.

Over the last three decades I have visited India many times and have come to love the country. During some of these visits, I have had the opportunity to see other aspects of the country. I have met some outstanding poets, writers, artists, businessmen and businesswomen, judges, and journalists, and India has come to grow on me. No longer do I feel a sense of alienation when I arrive in Mumbai. I love being driven around the city, and when I see its statuary, the history that I did not know before becomes real and assumes a special significance for me. On Marine Drive, near Chopati beach, I see the statue of Rabindranath Tagore and recall the moving verses of *Gitanjali*. I take pride in the fact that he won the Nobel Prize for Literature as early as 1913. It was Tagore who gave Gandhi the title of Mahatma. He was also the composer of the national anthems of two countries in the region.

Elsewhere in Mumbai, I see the statue of Dadabhai Naoroji and think of his contribution to the UK parliament and his contacts with Gandhi in the early days of the South African struggle, I see the statue of Dr Bhimrao Ambedkar, the remarkable social reformer, and recall his contribution to the welfare of the Dalits. He was one of the drafters of the Indian Constitution. At the Maharashtra Legislature building I see the statue of Mahatma Gandhi, loincloth wrapped around his hips and staff in hand and reflect on his contribution not only to South Africa but also to the world. I proudly tell Indians that Gandhi was one of the greatest Indians that ever lived and that he was also a South African.

I enjoy the liveliness of the city, the different cultures that converge there and its frozen-in-time London ambience, which is particularly visible in the law courts and cricket clubs. Some of the old buildings are straight out of nineteenth-century Victorian England. Above all, I feel a sense of identity as I sit outside the Sukh Sagar restaurant near Chopati beach and imbibe a large glass of fresh mango juice or strawberry juice with chunks of fruit in it. I feel equally at ease when I chat with a Gujarati cobbler on the pavement as the traffic rushes by, as I am in the Jehangir Art Gallery looking at paintings by modern Indian artists. There are facets of India that now speak to me with a new voice. But I appreciate that my experience remains largely limited as Mumbai does not represent life in the vastness of India which is largely rural, but rapidly changing.

My construction of reality has also changed. I have different lenses of perception. I am no longer a refugee in search of a homeland and no longer view India as a dump. The depiction of India is not now provided to me ready-made by racist regimes, but one that I have come to understand after years of wrestling with my own identity. I now deeply experience the greatness of the civilization that India has always been, but one that was denied to me as I grew up in Africa in the twentieth century. It is this India that I love so much, an India that makes me feel a part of it.

Hundreds of millions of people in India are still mired in poverty, but Mumbai exudes a sense of vibrancy and life and I often ponder my connection with the country. Keshavjee Ramji, the person whose name I and a large number of his other descendants bear from across some twenty-three countries, lies buried with his wife Mithima in a village cemetery not more than an hour's flight from this major metropolis. Our DNA lies deep in India's soil and it forms an integral part of who I am.

Chapter 23

Meeting Destiny Head-on

THE NINETEENTH AND TWENTIETH CENTURIES WERE marked by periods of homelessness for millions of people globally as they fled from oppression, economic difficulties, mass killings, and famine. My ancestors, too, were forced to migrate and left their imprint wherever they went. This chapter highlights some of the significant diasporic footprints left by my family and other migrants of Indian origin.

Our journeys began in Chotila, India, where Keshavjeebapa and his wife Mithima lie buried in the village cemetery. Today, over a thousand of us in a score of countries are part of the family to which he gave birth, either through direct descent or marriage. Some of our diasporic history can be seen in the burial sites of our elders.

My grandfather, Manjee Keshavjee and his wife Noorbai Jamal, who successfully built their lives and the lives of their family in South Africa, a country then steeped in racism, are buried in the Rebecca Street cemetery in Pretoria West. Death transcends all divisions and, ironically, among the other graves in that large complex is that of a former deputy prime minister in the Smuts government, Jan Hoffmeyr. Noorbai's parents were interred in Lamu, Kenya, where her father, Tarbhai Jamal, arrived from the village of Tithwa in India with his family. My parents, Bapoo and Ba, lived out their last years in Canada and were laid to rest in the Garden of Peace cemetery in Calgary. My eldest brother Rex, who was one of the architects of our move from South Africa to Kenya, is also buried there.

Many from our extended family are of biracial heritage, their mothers or fathers belonging to a wide range of peoples that includes the indigenous people of Malagasy, Cherokee Indians, Anglo-Saxons, Ukrainians, Serbs, Argentineans, Danes, Irish Celts, Filipinos, Croatians, and Poles.

In some marriages, the partners come from different faiths. Some of the family were born in Brazil and Argentina, others in Switzerland, France, Britain, Portugal, Cyprus, and Denmark. Over the last four decades, many of the new generation were born in Canada, the US, and Australia. Some, like one small branch of Jivanbapoo's direct descendants, never left Pretoria.

Perhaps our history is embodied in the way one of us, Ashak Nathwani, ended up in Australia after the dictator Idi Amin expelled all Asians from Uganda. Ashak, a cousin from Manekfaiba's line, as mentioned earlier, was standing in the queue outside the Ugandan Immigration Office in Kampala, waiting for verification of his Ugandan citizenship, when he was told by a female official that his citizenship was not valid. She peremptorily took his Ugandan passport, snipped off the four corners, stamped "CANCELLED" on it, and handed it back to him. He had been rendered stateless within minutes. He ended up in Australia, purely on the basis that the Australian visa office opened half an hour earlier than the Canadian one. When I think of Ashak's experience, I recall Imam Hussein's words: "Man journeys in darkness. His destiny journeys toward him." Many members of our family have met destiny head-on as it journeyed towards them when it seemed that all was dark, and through hard work and good fortune they overcame the obstacles that faced them.

Today, some seventy years later, the larger family throughout the world has produced a number of doctors in various specialties—among them my nephew Shaf (grandson of Sherbanoofaiba in this narrative) who, as surgeon-in-chief at the University Health Network, has made Canada the world hub of thoracic surgery and lung transplantation by building up a team comprising some of the outstanding surgeons in the world. Shauki, Jivanbapoo's great grandson, is the only one who went into psychiatry. Another nephew, Salmaan, ended up as Director of Harvard Medical School's Centre for Global Health Delivery in Dubai, which opened in October 2015.

Not all the members of our large family have gone into the more traditional fields of endeavour where a good income is the norm. Some have gone into the humanities, politics, and journalism. My sister Mila and her husband Murad were the ones who entered politics, Murad eventually becoming a Member of the Ontario Legislature. Their son Ali, after stints at Toronto's report on Business TV, and CNN, is now an anchor at Al Jazeera.

Gulnar, granddaughter of Sacoorbhai, who was married to Naran Keshavjee's eldest daughter Poori, and also a granddaughter of Allibhai Keshavjee, has become an artist of note in Portugal. Serena, granddaughter of Cassim Keshavjee is an art historian teaching at the University of Manitoba where she holds a tenured position. Ameera Nimjee is the granddaughter of Roshan (Roshanbahen in this narrative) and Cassamaly Nimjee, who lived on the same street as us in Pretoria's Asiatic Bazaar, is a concert-level pianist and has performed with the Toronto Symphony Orchestra. Her brother Shahid, a vaso neurosurgeon, is doing pioneering work in the USA on brain aneurysms.

But we are still Gujaratis, and the old axiom still holds good: "Scratch a Gujarati and his blood will ooze out with commerce." M Keshavjee and Company, started in South Africa by my grandfather around 1912, was wound up in the 1970s due to the Group Areas Act. Manjee Keshavjee's grandson Murad, my cousin, migrated to Toronto and started a business, called Tropical Treets, which supplies more than fifty exotic flavours of ice cream and fruit drinks to some 500 supermarkets in the Greater Toronto area.

White Rose Drycleaners, started by Habib Keshavjee in 1952 during the Mau Mau insurrection, is still thriving in Kenya. My cousin Yusuf, who runs it, has also set up an internationally acclaimed social enterprise called Honey Care Africa (HCA), which manufactures hives and trains bee-keepers. To date, the company has helped over 12,000 small-scale beekeepers (over 45% of them women) across Kenya, Tanzania, Southern Sudan and Malawi to raise their income.

Enterprise has had a different dimension for the Lalji family, maternal descendants of Manekfaiba through her daughter Hirbai who was married to Lalji Mangalji. The family emigrated to Canada in the 1970s at the time of the Ugandan Asian expulsions and is headed by brothers Shiraz, Aminmohamed, and Mansoor Lalji. Their successes in the past forty years have firmly established them as one of Canada's foremost real estate families. The Laljis have endowed the Centre for the Comparative Study of

Muslim Societies and Cultures, Simon Fraser University, and they have endowed jointly with the Swift family, The Centre for Social Innovation and Impact Investing at the Sauder School of Business, University of British Columbia.

Another enterprise owned by someone with a strong sense of ethics and philanthropy is the one developed and run by Pyarali Nanji, also a descendant of Manekfaiba, under the name Belle-Pak Packaging. Pyarali was almost penniless when he arrived in Canada from Uganda in the 1970s. He and his wife Gulshan are benefactors to many of eastern Canada's foremost hospitals, including St Mary's Hospital in Montreal, Sunnybrook Hospital in Toronto and North York General Hospital in Toronto. At Sunnybrook, they contributed the Pyarali and Gulshan Nanji Ambulatory Centre.

In Mozambique and South Africa, the Rawjee Babool family, known as the Hoxies, have been very much involved in business and community service. The Sarif Janmohamed family in the Cape area of South Africa has produced a prize-winning novelist and filmmaker, Shamim Sarif. Her debut novel *The World Unseen*, set amongst the Indian community in South Africa, won the Pendelton May First Novel Award and was later adapted into a film starring Lisa Ray and Sheetal Sheth. The film had its debut at the Toronto International Film Festival before going on to garner twenty-three international awards, including eleven SAFTAs (South African Film Awards). Another film, *The House of Tomorrow*, shot on location in Israel and Palestine, had festival debuts in New York and Sarasota in 2012 and won an award in France in 2015.

In Lausanne, Switzerland, resides the novelist and scholar of comparative religion and sociology, Shafique G Keshavjee, whose book *The King, the Wise Man and the Fool* highlights the fundamental ideas of the five major religions, Judaism, Christianity, Islam, Hinduism, and Buddhism, as well as atheism, showing their similarities and differences. A founder of the Arzillier House of Dialogue, Shafique has contributed to the promotion of peace between churches, religions and spiritualities.

Knowledge transference has also been important in the family. Saida Rasul, maternal granddaughter of Ebrahim and Sakina Kanjee Kassam, a dentist and a volunteer, has been focusing on improving the dental health of the less fortunate, not only in BC, but also in other countries, largely through the Aga Khan University, where she is based with her husband, Firoz Rasul, President of the University.

But enough of resumés and blowing the family trumpet. Our experiences as a family and a community are not unusual. They are typical of many South Africans, both in the diaspora as well as within the country. The story of Ram Pillay, known among his friends as Dings because he was born on Dingaan's Day, is also representative of many South Africans of non-White origin who found themselves scattered around the world during the fifty-year apartheid period.

Dings' parents, Subramaniam Pillay and Luxmi Naidoo, marched with Gandhi in the early part of the twentieth century and he was baptized in the freedom struggle. He grew up in the Doornforntein area of Johannesburg in the 1940s and early 1950s. As a young man he worked as a volunteer with Dr Yusuf Dadoo, Maulvi Kachalia and Roy Naidoo, well-known figures in the freedom struggle. Unwilling to put up with racial indignities, he became a target for White boys and on one occasion was beaten unconscious and had to receive eight stitches. He had a penchant for photography and earned an income from that. However, Dings' ambition was to study radiography and one day he saw a newspaper advertisement for a radiographer's assistant and applied for the position. To his surprise, he was called for an interview by a Jewish doctor, Ernest Faerber, one of the foremost specialists in the field, who had placed the advertisement. Because non-Whites were not allowed in the profession, Faerber could only employ Dings clandestinely. He also gave Dings' sister a job and paid them the same salaries that he would have to Whites. After a while, he secretly took Dings to the gold mines and allowed him to take X-rays of the miners. Sometimes he sneaked him into an operating theatre to take X-rays of White patients unconscious under general anaesthesia.

In 1957, Dings saw a newspaper advertisement by the New York Institute of Photography offering an opportunity to study photography in the US. With the help of Faerber and a fellow Indian student, Nanoo Desai, who also applied for the course, Dings managed to raise enough funds to get to New York. They decided to go via London, where they met Ramesh Bhandari, Krishna Menon's secretary, who provided them with a student visa to travel through Europe while they were waiting for the school term to start in New York. On their return from the tour, Krishna Menon, who was then defence minister in the Indian government, happened to be in London and agreed to a meeting with them. Dings showed him a letter that Gandhi had written to his father and Menon realized that he was speaking to a person whose parents were in the thick of the anti-racism struggle in South Africa. He provided them with a letter of introduction to Arthur Lall, who was head of the Indian Mission to the UN. In New York, the subject of possible jobs came up and Lall explained to them that since they were not Indian citizens the only way he could give them jobs was by creating two lowly positions as messengers. Dings and Nanoo accepted the offer. Dings was soon elevated to the registry department where he was responsible for the custody of sensitive documents. While working as a messenger, he started taking an evening course in radiography at the Manhattan Dental and Assistance School. The Indian Mission assigned him the task of looking after Indian dignitaries visiting the UN, starting with Rajagopalachari when he came to address the UN on nuclear disarmament. Later, Dings was delegated to accompany Prime Minister Jawaharlal Nehru as his personal photographer when he was on a state visit to the US. Dings was also assigned to Krishna Menon when he came to the UN each year between September and December. One of the tasks given to him by Menon was to work with an Indian diplomat, AK Mitra, on consolidating all the existing racial issues against South Africa into one document, called The Apartheid Question.

Dings qualified as a radiographer and secured a job at the Mount Sinai Hospital in New York, and finally moved to Canada.

Some of the people who remained in South Africa were tempered in the fire of the struggle against racism but also managed to excel professionally. A prominent example of such a person is former UN High Commissioner for Human Rights (2008-14) Navanethem Pillay, who even today firmly defends the rights of people who are being abused. Navanethem Pillay was the first woman to open her own law practice in Natal and provided legal defence for political activists detained by the government. In 1973 she fought and won the right for political prisoners to have access to legal counsel.

Born in Clairewood, an Indian area of Natal, she graduated from the University of Natal with a BA in 1963 and an LLB in 1965. She did her articles with Narainsamy Thumbi Naicker, a banned member of the African National Congress who was placed under house arrest in 1967. She received her Master's in Law from Harvard University in 1982, followed by a doctorate in Juridical Science in 1988. In 1965, she joined the International Criminal Tribunal for Rwanda, and in 1999 she was elected as its Judge President and served two four-year terms. She was appointed the United Nations High Commissioner for Human Rights in 2008 and held the position till 2014.

The family of Cassam Noormohamed, the person with whom Jivanbapoo first arrived in South Africa in 1894, struggled on. In 1953 Cassam's grandson Osman Gani and grandson-in-law, Osman Mohamed, started the earlier-mentioned Kit Kat restaurant in Marabastad. The restaurant burnt down and they rebuilt it, but then had problems with the landlord. In 1973, Cassam's two great-grandsons, Abdul Kader and Abdul Razzak, converted the premises into a self-service supermarket. In 1989 they opened a hyperstore in Pretoria town and in 1999 a megastore in Pretoria West.

Another South African who has distinguished himself in the diaspora is Deva Pillay, a grandson of Subramaniam and Luxmi Naidoo, the couple who marched with Gandhi in South Africa. He is a respected judge in the UK and a bencher of the Middle Temple Inn.

In this book, I have focused largely on Marabastad, where I was born. My life in South Africa revolved around what happened in that neighbourhood. I may have unwittingly given the impression that all the great anti-apartheid movements took place in my little location. That, of course, is not true. South Africans of all races in many other parts of the country played an important role in the freedom struggle. Among those of Indian origin, the Naidoos of Doornfontein, Johannesburg, played a major role for many years. The Dadoos, Kachalias, Kathradas, Asvats, Chibas, Timols, Mintys, Moolas, Pahads, and Saloojees also gave their lives to the struggle. In Natal, there were the Naidoos, Pillays, Meers, Singhs,

Rustomjis, Kajees, Naickers, Nairs, Coovadias, Thamba Pillays and others. In the Cape there were the Gools, Desais, and many others

I have often asked myself why Jivanbapoo had to go to South Africa. Of all places on earth, could he not have found somewhere else to go? I now have a better idea of the struggle he faced in India and the challenges that he confronted in Africa, as well as of the courage it took for him to do what he did. I now also realize that this was a destiny that was preordained for him and his progeny and that it was his struggle that changed our lives for the better. For this I will be eternally grateful to him.

Many of the people featured in this narrative are no longer alive today. My dear and good friend, mentor and colleague, Dr Alex Quaison Sackey, died sometime in the 1980s. I have always remembered his kind advice to me, exhorting a university education. Barney Desai died after Nelson Mandela was released, while South Africa was preparing for its first multiparty government, in the lead-up to which he played an active part in the negotiations. Claude Lewis, the pianist, my very dear friend of Gray's Inn days, died of leukaemia in the mid 1980s in London. He was the most generous of people I have ever encountered. Michael Ziadi, who looked after my legal work when he practised as a solicitor, also passed away in London in the 1990s.

Other friends thrived. Krishna Savjani became the honorary consul-general of Britain in Malawi and a prominent mining lawyer. He was one of the members of a commission of inquiry that probed the political assassinations of four former members of the Banda government in May 1983. Krishna always aspired to be the best in his field, and his forensic advocacy, coupled with a sharp intellect, predisposed him to be a member of the commission. I can say without hesitation that our days at the Inns of Court were some of the happiest in our lives. We were a trio with Matthew Thomas, who went back to Malaysia and worked as an insurance lawyer in Kuala Lumpur.

Dame Helena Kennedy, who was a good friend of ours at Gray's Inn, became a Member of the House of Lords and a leading human rights lawyer.

Many others went to different parts of the world. Lester Bird became Prime Minister of Antigua. Nusrath Ali Shah for a short while became a minister in the Federal Government of Pakistan. Bruce Pitt, whose family hailed from Trinidad, inherited his father's peerage and practised law in London for many years. Paul Damien Dole, a past president of the Gray's Inn Debating Society, married a Canadian diplomat and lived in Tanzania, India, and Portugal, where his wife served as Canadian ambassador at various times. Ismail Ayob thrives as a corporate lawyer in Johannesburg and I often hear of him through mutual friends.

My wife Amina and I have come to live in the United Kingdom, where she remains a committed researcher in the field of tuberculosis treatment. We have come across many friends, some of them Whites from South Africa. We have found them warm and helpful. I see in them the kindness and warmth that characterized people such as the Afrikaner Bram Fischer, who gave his life for freedom, Father Trevor Huddleston, who worked in Sophiatown, Helen Liebermann, who worked against all dangers in the slums of Langa, and Dr Chris Barnard, who made it his mission to save lives across the colour divide in the interest of a shared humanity. I have realized how ideology robs people of their basic humanity and how people are good when society allows them to be human.

All of Keshavjeebapa's grandchildren, and many of his great-grandchildren, have died. Most died in the countries where they resettled. Following South Africa's transformation to multiparty democracy in 1994, I have visited the cemetery in Rebecca Street in Pretoria West a number of times to offer prayers for my ancestors and others. As I walked through the pathways, I saw rows upon rows of gravestones, silent sentinels reminding me of our common destiny. I spotted the names of people who, at one time or another, lived in the city where I was born.

The Indian section brought back memories. I read the names of Makhuloo Hoopan and Essop Moosa and Judge Ismaili Mohamed. As I entered the Ismaili section, I saw the graves of my ancestors, towered over by the imposing Union Buildings on Meintjieskop Hill which overlooks it, garlanded by a blaze of jacarandas that give the city a beautiful purple hue in spring. I saw the gravestone of my uncle Ismail Manjee Keshavjee, who was the oral historian of the family and who inspired me to study my family's history. I saw the large gravestones of Jivanbapoo, Manjee Keshavjee, and Velshi Keshavjee; and of Naran Keshavjee, Kanjee Kassam Panchaan, his wife Mongi Nanji Amarsi, Sherbanoofaiba, Ladoobai Varin, Alli Velji, and many others. In the midst of all these graves, one stands out, that of Mrs Abdullah Hasham Gangji of Zanzibar, who died in South Africa after travelling there for medical treatment in the late 1940s. I felt sad that my ancestors never lived to see the day when the first African president Nelson Rolihlahla Mandela, was installed as head of state of a multiracial South Africa.

Graveyards are fascinating places if we give them time to revive our memories. Not only do they hold and honour our dead ancestors, families, and friends, but also they are a permanent reminder of the ephemeral nature of all human life. The transience of all life is beautifully expressed in the Holy Qur'an: "Nothing in this world will remain except the glorious face of God – full of Majesty, Bounty, and Honour."

Yes, we mourn our loved ones, but our mourning takes on another level of understanding when we realize that we, too, are on this journey towards oblivion, that we weep not only for those who have left us, but also for ourselves and for those generations that will follow and who will in turn mourn us. On looking around, I was reminded of what Homer wrote:

> As is the generation of leaves,
> so is the generation of humanity.
> The wind scatters the leaves on
> the ground, but the live timber
> burgeons with leaves again in
> the season of spring returning.
> So one generation of men will
> grow while another dies.

I am grateful that, unlike my ancestors, I have been able to tell my story. For, as the Czech writer Milan Kundera so eloquently reminds us, "the struggle of man against power is the struggle of memory against forgetting."

I have written this memoir of my life, which is inextricably connected and contained by the lives of others, by the lives of my family and forebears, by the lives of fellow citizens of South Africa, by the ever-present shadow of India, the country of our origin, by the new lives being formed by the diaspora of Indians making their way across the world, in several continents. This memoir is about my life but it is also about theirs. By writing it, I hope to attain a sense of the heaven of freedom that Tagore wrote of in his poem "Where the Mind is Without Fear," not only for me, but for the country of my birth and indeed for all of us.

Notes

CHAPTER 5, p. 51

* Among these families were Kanjee Kassam Panchaan and his son Ebrahim (known as EK Khoja) who set up KK Khoja and Company, which in the 1920s became a leading enterprise and later pioneered the commercial manufacture and mass distribution of *achaar* (mango pickle) in the South African market. Then there was Habib Kanjee (known as HK Khoja, which was also the name under which he traded) who established his shop in Marabastad after 1930. Some, like the Hajee Ramjee family from Ranavav in India, went to Northern Transvaal and established themselves in Louis Trichardt, trading as HR Khoja in the case of the elder brother Jadavjee Hajee; Khoja's Cash Store in the case of Gulamhussein Hajee (who was also known as GH Khoja); and Elim Stores in the case of the middle brother, Cassam Hajee Khoja. In Elloff and Delmas, there were Habib Valjee Hirji and his brother Gulamhussein, who used the name HV Khoja and GV Khoja for their shops, Khoja's Cash Store and Khoja's Modern Store, respectively. Mohamedali Alli Velji, Jivanbapoo's maternal grandson, used the name MA Khoja and traded as Amay's Cash Store. In the Johannesburgh area, Ebrahim Virji Vally and Rhemtullah Kanji Vally used the name EV Khoja and RK Khoja, respectively. Their brother Mohamedali was a sworn translator of the Supreme Court in Johannesburg and was known under the name MK Khoja. In Pretoria West, Alibhai Anandjee, who developed a huge wholesale and retail business, traded as AA Khoja and Company. His nephew Cassamaly Nimjee used the name CN Khoja. Kanjee Nanji Amarsi Hooda and his brother Saboor Nanji Amarsi Hooda, while using the name Nanji, set up Khoja's Corner and Columbia Tea Room, respectively. In the Lady Selborne area, Noormohamed Jadavjee Hajee traded as Basie's Store but used the name Noormohamed Khoja.

CHAPTER 7, p. 75

* That intrepid party consisted of Mrs Thambi Naidoo, Mrs N Pillay, Mrs K Murugasa Pillay, Mrs Perumal Naidoo, Mrs PK Naidoo, Mrs K Chinnaswami Pillay, Mrs NS Pillay, Mrs RA Mụdalingam, Mrs Bhavani Dayal, Mrs Minachi Pillay and Miss Baikum Murugasa Pillay.

Works Cited in the Text

CHAPTER 3

Gandhi, M K. *Satyagraha in South Africa*. Ahmedabad: Navajivan Publishing House, 1928. (Translated by Valji Govindji Desai).

Ginwala, F. *Indian South Africans*. London: Minority Rights Group (volume 34), 1977.

Meer, F. *Higher Than Hope: The Authorized Biography of Nelson Mandela*. London: Hamish Hamilton, 1990.

CHAPTER 4

Gandhi, M K. *Satyagraha in South Africa*. Ahmedabad: Navajivan Publishing House, 1928. (Translated by Valji Govindji Desai).

CHAPTER 6

Gandhi, M K. *Satyagraha in South Africa*. Ahmedabad: Navajivan Publishing House, 1928. (Translated by Valji Govindji Desai).

CHAPTER 7

Gandhi, M K. *Satyagraha in South Africa*. Ahmedabad: Navajivan Publishing House, 1928. (Translated by Valji Govindji Desai).

CHAPTER 10

Paton, A. *Cry, the Beloved Country*. New York: Charles Scribner's sons, 1948.

CHAPTER 12

Anderson, D. *Histories of the Hanged*. London: Weidenfeld and Nicholson, 2005.

Kathrada, A M. *Memoirs*. Cape Town: Zebra Press, 2004.

Meer, I. *A Fortunate Man*. Cape Town: Zebra Press, 2002.

CHAPTER 22

Carlin, J. *Knowing Mandela*. London: Harper Collins, 2013.

Bibliography

Abraham, P. *Tell Freedom*. London: Faber and Faber, 1954.

Anderson, D. *Histories of the Hanged*. London: Weidenfeld and Nicholson, 2005.

Attwood, W. *The Reds and the Blacks, a Personal Adventure*. New York: Harper and Row, 1967.

Basil Williams, A F. *Botha, Smuts and South Africa*. New York: Colliers Books, 1962.

Bernstein, H. *The Rift*. London: Jonathan Cape, 1994.

Bhatia, P. *Indian Ordeal in Africa*. New Delhi: Vikas, 1972.

Callinicos, L. *A Place in the City: The Rand on the Eve of Apartheid (A Peoples History of South Africa)*. Braamfontein: Ravan Press and Maskew Miller Longman, 1993.

Callinicos, L. *Oliver Tambo: Beyond the Engeli Mountains*. Claremont: David Phillips, 2004.

Calpin, G H. *Indians in South Africa*. Pietermaritzburg: Shuter and Shooter, 1949.

Calpin, G H. *A I Kajee—His Work for the South African Indian Community*. Durban: Iqbal Study Group, undated (c. 1940s).

Carlin, J. *Knowing Mandela*. London: Harper Collins, 2013.

Desai, B and C Marney. *The Killing of the Imam: South African Tyranny Defied by Courage and Faith*. London: Quartet Press, 1978.

Field, S. *Lost Communities, Living Memories: Remembering Forced Removals in Cape Town*. Claremont: David Phillip, 2001.

Fischer, L. *The life of Mahatma Gandhi*. London: Granada Publishing, 1982.

Friedman, T. *The World Is Flat: The Globalized World in the Twenty-first Century*. London: Penguin, 2006.

Gandhi, M K. *Satyagraha in South Africa*. Ahmedabad: Navajivan Publishing House, 1928. (Translated by Valji Govindji Desai).

Gandhi, M K. *The Collected Works, Vol 11 (Diary)*. Ahamedabad: Navajivan Trust, 1964.

Ginwala, F. *Indian South Africans*. London: Minority Rights Group Report No. 34, 1977.

Goonam, Dr. *Coolie Doctor*. Durban: Madiba Publishers for the Institute of Black Research, 1991.

Huddleston, T. *Naught for Your Comfort*. London: Collins, 1956.

Itzkin, E. *Gandhi's Johannesburg*. Johannesburg: Witwatersrand UP in association with Museum Africa, 2000.

Johnson, R V. *South Africa: The First Man, the Last Nation*. Jeppestown: Jonathan Ball Publishers, 2004.

Joosub, M H. *A South African Adventure*. (Family brochure, self published), 1983.

Joosub, H E. *Bitterness Towards Indians*. Pretoria: Pretoria Commercial Association, 1958.

Joseph, Helen. *If This Be Treason*. London: Andre Deutsch, 1963.

Joshi, P S. *Struggle for Equality*. Bombay: Hind Kitab Ltd, 1951.

Joshi, P S. *The Tyranny of Colour—A Study of the Indian Problem in South Africa*. Durban: E P and Commercial Printing Company, 1946.

Joyce, P. *The Making of a Nation: South Africa's Road to Freedom*. Cape town: Zebra Press, 1994.

Kathrada, A M. *Memoirs*. Cape Town: Zebra Press, 2004.

Kathrada, A M. *Letters from Robben Island: A Selection of Ahmed Kathrada's Prison Correspondence, 1964-1989*. Michigan: Michigan State UP, 1995.

Keshavjee, H. *The Aga Khan and Africa: His Leadership and Inspiration*. Durban: Mercantile Printing Works, undated (c. 1948).

Khandpur, S. *A Vision of India: Gujarat*. Mumbai: Navneet Publications, 2001.

Khandpur, S. *A Vision of India: Profiles of Excellence*. Mumbai: Navneet Publications, 2002.

Lapiere, D. *A Rainbow in the Night: The Tumultuous Birth of South Africa*. Cambridge, Mass: De Capo Press, 2008.

Lapping, B. *Apartheid: a History*. London: Paladin Grafton Books, 1986.

Lelyveld, J. *Move Your Shadow: South Africa, Black and White*. New York: Penguin, 1985.

Listowell, J. *Amin*. London: IUP Books, 1973.

Makeba, M and J Hall. *Makeba: My Story*. London: Bloomsbury, 1988.

Mallaby, S. *After Apartheid: The Future of South Africa*. New York: Times Books, 1992.

Mamdani, M. *From Citizen to Refugee*. London: Francis Pinter, 1973.

Mandela, N. *Long Walk to Freedom: The Autobiography of Nelson Mandela*. London: Little Brown, 1994.

Mandela, N. *No Easy Walk to Freedom*. London: Heinemann, 1965.

Mathabane, M. *Kaffir Boy: Growing Out of Apartheid*. London: Bodley Head, 1986.

Mayat, Z. *A Treasure Trove of Memories: A Reflection of the Experiences of the People of Potchefstroom*. Durban: Institute of Black Research/Madiba Publishers in association with the Women's Cultural Group, 1996.

Meer, F. *Portrait of Indian South Africans*. Durban: Avon House, 1969.

Meer, I. *A Fortunate Man*. Cape Town: Zebra Press, 2002.

Meer, F. *Higher Than Hope: The Authorized Biography of Nelson Mandela*. London: Hamish Hamilton, 1990.

Meredith, M. *The State of Africa: A History of the Continent Since Independence*. London: Simon and Schuster, 2005.

Mitchison, N. *A Life for Africa: A Story of Bram Fischer*. London: Merlin Press, 1973.

Mphahlele, E. *The African Image*. New York: Frederick A Praeger, 1966.

Mphahlele, E. *Down Second Avenue*. London: Faber and Faber, 1971.

Murray-Brown, J. *Kenyatta*. New York: E P Dutton, 1973.

Naidoo, M. *Stories from the Asiatic Bazaar*. Durban, 1990.

Naidoo, J. *Coolie Location*. London: S A Writers Association and Taurus, 1990.

Paton, A. *Cry, the Beloved Country*. New York: Charles Scribner's Sons, 1948.

Pandit, S. *Asians in East and Central Africa*. Nairobi: Panco Publications, 1963.

Pritt, D N. *The Autobiography of D N Pritt, Volume 3: The Defence Accuses*. London: Lawrence and Wishart, 1966.

Quaison-Sackey, A. *Africa Unbound: Reflections of an African Statesman*. New York: Frederick A Praeger, 1963.

Russel, A. *After Mandela: The Battle for the Soul of South Africa*. London: Windmill Books, 2010.

Ross, R. *A Concise History of South Africa*. Cambridge: Cambridge UP, 2008.

Reddy, E S. *Yusuf Dadoo: His Speeches, Articles and Correspondences*. Durban: Madiba Publishers in association with Institutre of Black Research,1991.

Sampson, A. *The Treason Cage*. London: Heinemann, 1958.

Samspson, A. *Mandela: The Authorized Biography*. London: Harper Collins, 1999.

Sparks, A. *The Mind of South Africa*. London: Mandarin Paperback, 1990.

Stengel, R. *Mandela's Way: Lessons on Life, Love, and Courage*. London: Virgin books, 2010.

Tutu, D. *The Rainbow People of God*. London: Doubleday, 1994.

Tutu, D. *No Future Without Forgiveness*. London: Rider, 1999.

Van der Waal, G M. (editor) *Marabastad: Fountain of Life*. Pretoria: Pretoria Inner City Partnership, 1972.

FILMS

Come Back, Africa. dir. Lionel Rogosin. 1960.

Cry Freedom. dir. Richard Attenborough. 1987.

Cry, the Beloved Country. dir. Darrell Roodt. 1995.

A Dry White Season. dir. Euzhan Palcy. 1989.

End of the Dialogue. dir. Antonia Cacchia, Simon Louvish, Nana Molete. 1974.

Gandhi. dir. Richard Attenborough. 1982.

Invictus. dir. Clint Eastwood. 2009.

The Kitchen Toto. dir. Harry Hook. 1988.

The Last King of Scotland. dir. Kevin Macdonald. 2006.

The Making of the Mahatma. dir. Shyam Benegal. 1996.

Something of Value. dir. Richard Brooks. 1957.

A World Apart. dir. Chris Menges. 1988.